Paul Hattaway, a native New Zealander, has served the church in Asia for most of his life. He is an expert on the Chinese church, and the author of *The Heavenly Man*; *An Asian Harvest*; *Operation China*; The China Chronicles series (ongoing) and many other books. He and his wife Joy are the founders of Asia Harvest (www.asiaharvest.org), which supports thousands of indigenous missionaries and has provided millions of Bibles to spiritually hungry Christians throughout Asia.

Also by Paul Hattaway:

The Heavenly Man

Back to Jerusalem

An Asian Harvest

Operation China

China's Book of Martyrs

Living Water

The China Chronicles 1: Shandong

The China Chronicles 2: Guizhou

The China Chronicles 3: Zhejiang

The China Chronicles 4: Tibet

The China Chronicles 5: Henan

The China Chronicles 6: Xinjiang

The China Chronicles 7: Shaanxi

The China Chronicles 8: Hainan

FUJIAN

The Blessed Province

Paul Hattaway

© 2025 Paul Hattaway

Published 2025 by Langham Global Library
An imprint of Langham Publishing
www.langhampublishing.org

Langham Publishing and its imprints are a ministry of Langham Partnership

Langham Partnership
PO Box 296, Carlisle, Cumbria, CA3 9WZ, UK
www.langham.org

ISBNs:
978-1-78641-132-7 Print
978-1-78641-156-3 ePub
978-1-78641-157-0 PDF

Paul Hattaway has asserted his right under the Copyright, Designs and Patents Act, 1988 to be identified as the Author of this work.

All rights reserved. No part of this publication may be reproduced, stored in a retrieval system or transmitted, in any form or by any means, electronic, mechanical, photocopying, recording or otherwise, without the prior written permission of the publisher or the Copyright Licensing Agency.

Requests to reuse content from Langham Publishing are processed through PLSclear. Please visit www.plsclear.com to complete your request.

Scriptures taken from the Holy Bible, New International Version®, NIV®. Copyright © 1973, 1978, 1984, 2011 by Biblica, Inc.™ Used by permission of Zondervan.

British Library Cataloguing-in-Publication Data
A catalogue record for this book is available from the British Library

ISBN: 978-1-78641-132-7

Cover & Book Design: projectluz.com

Langham Partnership actively supports theological dialogue and an author's right to publish but does not necessarily endorse the views and opinions set forth here or in works referenced within this publication, nor can we guarantee technical and grammatical correctness. Langham Partnership does not accept any responsibility or liability to persons or property as a consequence of the reading, use or interpretation of its published content.

Fujian

福 建

"Established Blessing"

Map of China showing Fujian

Fujian

Pronounced:	"Fu-jehn"	
Old Spelling:	Fuh-kien, Fukien	
Population:	34,398,913 (2000)	
	36,894,217 (2010)	
	41,540,086 (2020)	
Area:	46,900 sq. miles (121,400 sq. km)	
Population Density:	886 people per sq. mile (342 per sq. km)	
Highest Elevation:	Mt. Huanggang – 7,080 feet (2,158 meters)	
Capital City:	Fuzhou	2,824,414
Largest Cities (2010):	Xiamen	3,119,110
	Jinjiang	1,172,827
	Quanzhou	1,154,731
	Putian	1,107,199
	Nan'an	718,516
Administrative	Prefectures	9
Divisions:	Counties	85
	Towns	1,107

			Percent
Major Ethnic Groups	Han Chinese	33,514,147	98.3%
(2000):	She	708,651	1.1%
	Hui	109,880	0.3%
	Tujia	29,046	0.1%
	Miao	22,065	0.1%

Fujian

Note for this Volume – A Tangle of Names!

Although over 98 percent of people in Fujian are proudly Han Chinese, the province is home to an array of more than a dozen diverse Chinese languages and dialects that bear little resemblance to the national language, Mandarin. Being a great sea-faring people, millions of Fujian natives have spread out across other parts of China and ultimately throughout Asia, where today they boast large communities in Taiwan, Singapore, Malaysia, Myanmar, Thailand, Vietnam, Indonesia, the Philippines and elsewhere.

As Fujian people arrived in other nations, immigration officers would ask their names. As the officers were often Englishmen who could not speak Chinese, and as no standard system of Romanization was used at the time, they often guessed by writing down the sound they heard. As a result, some baffling anomalies emerged.

Surprisingly, it is difficult to find any comprehensive list of Fujian name variations online or in print, and the Chinese we consulted seem confused by the subject themselves. For the sake of this volume, we would like to submit the following partial list, which will hopefully provide a measure of clarity both for English readers and for the Chinese themselves, who often appear baffled by how their own names have been transcribed throughout Asia.

> The popular Chinese family name 黄 is rendered "Huang" in Mandarin; "Wong" in the Cantonese language of south China; and "Ooi," "Uy," "Oei," "Wee," and "Ng" in the various Chinese vernaculars of Fujian.
>
> Wang (王) is rendered "Ong," "Bong," "Heng," or "Vang" in Fujian depending on the region's dialect.
>
> Wu (吴) is "Ng" in Cantonese, but "Goh" or "Ngoh" in the Hokkien and Teochew languages of Fujian.

Fujian

Chen (陈) is "Tan" in Teochew.

The Xu (许) family name has been spelled many different ways in Fujian and among Chinese diaspora communities, including "Koh," "Kho," "Khor," "Khoo," and "Hee."

Yang (杨) is often transcribed as "Yeo" or "Yeoh."

Zhang (张) is rendered "Teo" or "Teoh" in Fujian and Southeast Asia.

Zhao (赵) is also rendered "Teo."

Zhou (周) is "Chew" or "Chiu" in the Chinese vernaculars of Fujian Province.

In this book, the Mandarin *Pinyin* version of a name is used (if known), with the common local Fujian spelling in parenthesis.

Contents

Foreword	xi
Reactions from Christians in China	xii
The China Chronicles *Overview and Publisher's Note*	xv
Introduction	1
A Linguistic Babble	13
Nestorians in Fujian	22
Early Catholics in Fujian	26
1830s and 1840s	39
1850s	47
1860s	56
John Wolfe — "The Fujian Moses"	67
1870s	76
1880s	89
1890s	96
The Gutian Massacre	103
1900s — The Putian Revival	115
Amy Oxley-Wilkinson	127
1910s and 1920s	139
Margaret Barber	145
Leland Wang	155

Contents

1930s	160
John Sung — "China's John the Baptist"	166
John Sung — "China's Greatest Evangelist"	184
Watchman Nee — The Early Years	206
Watchman Nee — The Latter Years	220
1940s to 1960s	235
1970s	241
1980s	253
The Local Church Today	264
1990s	276
2000s	289
2010s and 2020s	300
The Future of the Church in Fujian	311

Appendix

Table 1. Evangelical Christians in Fujian (1842–2024)	314
Map of All Christians in Fujian	316
Table 2. All Christians in Fujian	317
Table 3. People Groups in Fujian	320
Researching Christians in China	321
Map of China's Christians	323
Notes	324
Selected Bibliography	342
About Asia Harvest	348

Foreword

Over many years and generations, the followers of Jesus in China have set their hearts to be the witnesses of Christ to the nation. Many have paid a great price for their ministry, and the brutal persecutions they have endured for the faith have often been unimaginable.

The Bible commands all believers to "Go into all the world and preach the gospel to all creation" (Mark 16:15). Many foreign missionaries responded to this command in the past, traveling to China to proclaim the Word of God. They blessed the land with their message of new life in Christ and suffered greatly when the darkness clashed with God's light. Their faithful service, despite great hardship was a beautiful example for Chinese believers to emulate as they served God.

China today still urgently needs more laborers to take the gospel throughout the land. God is looking for people who will stand up and declare, "Lord, here am I. Please send me!"

The day of our Lord is near. May your hearts be encouraged by the testimonies of what the Lord Jesus Christ has done in China, to the praise of His glorious Name!

May the Lord raise up more testimonies that would glorify His name in our generation, the next generation, and forevermore!

Lord, You are the victorious King. Blessed are those who follow You to the end!

A humble servant of Christ,
Moses Xie *(1918–2011)*[*]

---

[*] The late Moses Xie wrote this foreword for The China Chronicles prior to his death in 2011. He was a highly respected Chinese house church leader who spent 23 years of his life in prison for the Name of Jesus Christ.

Reactions from Christians in China

The book you have in your hands is part of The China Chronicles, which the author is writing primarily to bless and encourage the persecuted church in China. Each book in the series is being translated into Chinese, and thousands of copies are being distributed free of charge throughout China's house church networks.

The Communist authorities in China have blocked the publication of most Christian books, especially those that deal with revival and persecution. Consequently, these books have been like living water to the thirsty Chinese believers, who eagerly desire to read about the mighty acts God has performed in their nation. Here are just a few reactions from house church Christians:

> *"We never had a good understanding of how the Lord established His kingdom in our midst, but thanks to these precious books, now we know how God has achieved great and amazing works through His servants in each province. We continue to pray that more life-giving books will flow to us!"*
>
> Brother Yang, Chongqing

> *"I am an authentic Tibetan who recently got a copy of The China Chronicles: Tibet. I clearly see that Jesus loves us Tibetans. It made me cry. Through reading the book I understood that the gods we believe in are false, that we should cherish and honor the people who loved us enough to come and preach the gospel to us, and that*

Reactions from Christians in China

the love of God links us to our past and will continue to shine upon our future. This makes me very happy. If I have more books, I will surely pass them on to others."

Tashi, Tibet

"We believe the revival fires of the Holy Spirit will again be lit in our generation, and the mighty power of the Lord will sweep millions of our countrymen and women into the family of God. These are really amazing books. Please send more!"

Brother Jiang, Hubei Province

"It is vitally important for the children of God to understand the history of the church in parts of China. After all, history is His Story. These are precious books, offering us in-depth accounts of the history of the body of Christ. We eagerly await each book in the series, as they will give us a more comprehensive understanding of God's glorious work in China."

Brother Zhai, Beijing

"My husband and I read your book together, and we shared many thoughts and tears as we discovered testimonies we had never heard before. Our spiritual lives have been deeply enriched and encouraged. We hope to receive new books in the series as soon as they are available."

Sister Xu, Shanghai

Reactions from Christians in China

"We live in Wuhan and read your book while our city was going through its unprecedented trial. As we read how the Lord established and empowered His church, we realized that He has always been in control of the past, the present, and He will continue to be in control in the future. Thank you for sharing these priceless nuggets of gold with us!"

Brother Cai, Hubei Province

"I shared your book with my fellow brothers and sisters in our Bible study group. We all loved it. Such living and relevant Christian history is nowhere to be found in our country, and we treasure it. We beg you to send more of these books."

Brother Zhou, Zhejiang Province

"I gave your book to my son, who is a college student. He studies history, but he said that none of the textbooks in his school teach anything like this. It's eye-opening and refreshing to our souls."

Sister Ping, Jiangxi Province

"As the sovereignty of our Lord Jesus Christ was revealed to us through all the incidents in history, we grew acutely aware that He is in complete control, and we have nothing to fear. As a result, we now have more confidence and faith in Him, knowing that He cares for us and the Spirit of God is at work behind the scenes, weaving together a beautiful narrative as His salvation spreads throughout our nation."

Brother Gong, Sichuan Province

The China Chronicles
Overview and Publisher's Note

Many people are aware of the extraordinary explosion of Christianity throughout China in recent decades, with the church now numbering in excess of 50 million members. Few, however, know how this miracle has occurred. The China Chronicles is an ambitious project to document the advance of Christianity in each province of China from the time the gospel was first introduced to the present day.

The genesis for this project came at a meeting I attended in the year 2000, where leaders of the Chinese house church movements expressed the need for their members to understand how God established His kingdom throughout China. As a result, it is planned that these books will be translated into Chinese and distributed widely among the church in China and overseas. Millions of Chinese Christians know little of their spiritual heritage, and my prayer is that multitudes would be strengthened, edified, and challenged by these books to carry the torch of the Holy Spirit to their generation.

I consider it a great honor to write these books, especially as I have been entrusted—through hundreds of hours of interviews conducted throughout China—with many precious testimonies that have never previously been shared publicly.

Another reason for compiling The China Chronicles is to have a record of God's mighty acts in China. As a new believer in the 1980s, I read many reports from the Soviet Union, where despite many Christians experiencing brutal persecution, the kingdom of God was growing rapidly as multitudes of people met Jesus

Christ. By the time the Soviet empire collapsed in the early 1990s, no one had systematically recorded the deeds of the Holy Spirit during the Communist era. Tragically, the body of Christ has largely forgotten the miracles God performed in those decades behind the Iron Curtain, and we are the poorer for it.

Consequently, I am determined to preserve a record of God's work in China, so that future generations can learn about the glorious events that have transformed tens of millions of lives there.

In the back of each volume appears a detailed statistical analysis estimating the number of Christians living within each province of China. This is the first comprehensive survey of the number of believers in China in nearly a century—covering every one of its more than 2,800 cities, districts, and counties. Such a huge undertaking would be impossible without the cooperation and assistance of numerous ministries and individuals.

I appreciate mission organizations such as the International Mission Board, Overseas Missionary Fellowship, Revival Chinese Ministries International, and many others that graciously allowed me to access their archives, libraries, photographs, collections, and personal records. I am indebted to the many believers whose generosity exemplified Jesus' command: "Freely you have received; freely give" (Matt. 10:8).

Many Chinese believers, too numerous to list, have lovingly assisted in this endeavor. For example, I fondly recall the elderly house church evangelist Elder Fu, who required two young men to assist him up the stairs to my hotel room because he was eager to be interviewed for this series. Although he had spent many years in prison for the gospel, this saint desperately wanted to testify of God's great works so that believers around the world could be inspired and encouraged to live a more consecrated life.

Finally, it would be remiss not to thank the Lord Jesus Christ. As you read these books, my prayer is that He will emerge from the pages not merely as a historical figure but as Someone ever present, who longs to seek and to save the lost by displaying His power and transformative grace.

Today, the church in China is one of the strongest in the world, both spiritually and numerically. Yet little more than a century ago, China was considered one of the most difficult mission fields. The great Welsh missionary Griffith John once wrote,

> The good news is moving but very slowly. The people are as hard as steel. They are eaten up both soul and body by the world, and do not seem to feel that there can be reality in anything beyond sense. To them our doctrine is foolishness, our talk jargon. We discuss and beat them in argument. We reason them into silence and shame; but the whole effort falls upon them like showers upon a sandy desert.[1]

How things have changed! When it is all said and done, no person in China will be able to take credit for the amazing revival that has occurred since the 1970s. It will be clear that this great accomplishment is the handiwork of none other than the Lord Jesus Christ. We will stand in awe and declare: "The LORD has done this, and it is marvelous in our eyes. The LORD has done it this very day; let us rejoice today and be glad" (Ps. 118:23–24).

Paul Hattaway

The China Chronicles Overview and Publisher's Note

Publisher's Note: In The China Chronicles we have avoided specific information—such as individuals' names or details—that could directly lead to the identification of house church workers. The exception to this rule is when a leader has already become so well-known around the world that there is little point concealing that person's identity in these books. This same principle applies to the use of photographs.

In this series, the term "Evangelical" is used to describe all Christians in China who are not Catholic or Orthodox Christians. While many writers still use the term "Protestant" to describe such Christians, renowned researcher Patrick Johnstone, who authored multiple editions of *Operation World*, has rightly pointed out that the term "Protestant" has been largely rendered obsolete today, especially in a country like China where no one in the Evangelical community is protesting Catholic rule, as they did during the Reformation in Europe 500 years ago when the term was founded.

Several different systems for writing the sounds of Chinese characters in English have been used over the years, the main ones being the Wade-Giles system, introduced in 1912, and Pinyin, literally "spelling sounds," which has been the accepted form in China since 1979. In The China Chronicles, all names of people and places are given in their Pinyin form. This means that the places previously spelled Chung-king, Shantung, and Tientsin are now respectively Chongqing, Shandong, and Tianjin; Mao Tse-tung becomes Mao Zedong, and so on. The only times we have retained the old spelling of names is when they are part of the title of a published book or article listed in the notes or bibliography.

Introduction

*A unique Hakka "Round House" at Tulou
Walled Village in southwest Fujian.*
Keng Po Leung

Fujian Province, which is situated along the southeast China coast, is one of the most interesting and complex parts of the country. It has always held a dear spot in my heart, as it was in the city of Xiamen more than 30 years ago that I first got to know my future wife, Joy, during a Bible courier trip in the early 1990s.

Many Chinese consider Fujian an "out-of-the-way" province, tucked into a corner of the country and hemmed in by the ocean on one side and mountains on the others. The region is traditionally said to be "eight parts mountain, one part water, and one part farmland."

Introduction

A missionary in the early twentieth century described the landscape of Fujian in these words: "Its rugged coastline, studded with a thousand splintered islands . . . is exceedingly mountainous, with fertile valleys lying between the hills, broadening out every here and there into alluvial plains, sown thick with towns and villages."[1]

Fujian is bordered by Zhejiang Province to the north, Jiangxi to the west, and Guangdong to the south, while the eastern boundary is formed by the Taiwan Strait. Taiwan sits just 110 miles (180 km) off the coast and is clearly visible on a fine day. Indeed, Fujian includes a complex array of more than 2,200 islands, most of which are inhabited, and some of which are claimed by both Taiwan and China.

With an area of 46,900 miles, Fujian is comparable in size to Pennsylvania or Mississippi, but it contains 3 and 13 times more people, respectively, than each of those two American states. By another measure, Fujian is slightly smaller than England in area, and its population of 41 million is fewer than England's 55 million.

Most of Fujian is lush and subject to heavy rainfall, and with much of the province sitting at the same latitude as southern Florida, high temperatures and stifling humidity can soar in the summer, especially in coastal areas.

The Taiwan Strait has witnessed many devastating typhoons, with July to September the most common time of the year for storms to strike. Winter temperatures in Fujian can be chilly in the mountains, but typically the province enjoys a warm, tropical climate.

Today, Fujian boasts the highest forest coverage of any province in China. Sixty-three percent of the land is still forested and contains an abundance of wildlife. Tigers were found in large numbers in the province until they were hunted to extinction in the 1970s.

Introduction

Han Influence

Archaeological evidence shows that people lived in Fujian long before the Christian era, with the first cohesive government in the province established by the Minyue kingdom between 334 and 110 BC. The Minyue lasted until the rulers of the Han Dynasty (206 BC–AD 220) sent massive forces by land and sea from four directions to crush the Minyue. Before their defeat, most of the subjects of the kingdom were non-Han ethnic minority tribes collectively known as the Baiyue. Scholars say the customs of the Baiyue were similar to those still practiced by some of the indigenous tribes of Taiwan.

The first waves of large-scale Han migration to Fujian occurred in the early fourth century AD, when civil war in the north forced thousands of noble families to flee south to the province. Four clans (the Huang, Lin, Chen, and Zheng) were prominent among the early immigrants, and these four remain the prominent family names among the people of Fujian today.

It wasn't until the Tang Dynasty (AD 618–907) that the people of Fujian were fully incorporated into the Han Chinese sphere, with one source saying, "The aboriginal male population was practically exterminated, the women becoming the wives of the invading Tangs."[2]

Although most Han in Fujian today would vehemently deny their ancestors were ever tribal people, the widespread displacement and societal upheaval as Han culture was imposed may help explain why the province is home to such a bewildering array of languages and customs, which change from one district to the next. Differences can even be observed among people living on the opposite banks of a river or in adjacent mountain valleys.

The provincial capital Fuzhou (which literally means "wealthy town"), was founded in the sixth century AD and grew rapidly to become a commercial port specializing in the export of tea and other products. Further south, the city of Xiamen (which was previously known by its local name Amoy) was not founded until the mid-1300s but has grown to become the most populated city in Fujian today.

Marco Polo in Fujian

Marco Polo and his uncle, Maffeo, passed through Fujian in 1292, near the end of their epic thirteenth century journey through the Orient. Marco's descriptions of the people and terrain of the region are fascinating. After entering north Fujian through the rugged Wuyi Mountains, the Polos made their way toward the capital city of Fuzhou.

Though first they passed through a dangerous stretch of territory that was inhabited by cannibals, which many scholars think were members of an unknown mountain tribe, perhaps the ancestors of today's She minority group. The Venetian explorer wrote,

> The people in this part of the country are addicted to eating human flesh, esteeming it more delicate than any other. . . . When they advance to combat, they throw loose their hair about their ears, and they paint their faces a bright blue color. . . . They are a most savage race of men, inasmuch that when they slay their enemies in battle, they are anxious to drink their blood, and afterwards they devour their flesh.[3]

After safely crossing the mountains, the Polos arrived at Fuzhou, which Marco described as

> the seat of great trade and great manufactures. The people are idolaters and subject to the Great Khan. And a large garrison is maintained there by that prince to keep the kingdom in peace and subjection. For the city is one that is apt to revolt on very slight provocation. There flows through the middle of this city a great river, which is about a mile in width, and many ships are built at

Introduction

the city which are launched upon this river. Enormous quantities of sugar are made there, and there is a great traffic in pearls and precious stones. For many ships of India come to these parts, bringing merchants who traffic about the Isles of the Indies.[4]

Marco Polo continued south to the impressive coastal city of Zaitun (now Quanzhou), which at the time was one of the greatest trading ports in the world. He noted the city was home to many merchants from India, the Middle East, and other parts of the maritime world. Quanzhou was also the base of a major Chinese naval fleet which a short time earlier had failed both in 1274 and 1281 to invade Japan.

China's Great Seafaring Province

Because of its proximity to the ocean and its abundance of rivers, the people of Fujian have always been skilled fishermen, but by

Fishermen at sunset off the coast of Fujian.
IMB

the fourteenth century they had learned to duplicate the shipbuilding skills of foreign visitors, and large ships were being launched. Trade and migration from Fujian began to spread out over a wide area—up and down the Chinese coast and then as far as Japan and Southeast Asia.

The greatest of the Chinese adventurers was Admiral Zheng He, a Muslim from southwest China who came to prominence under Emperor Yongle of the Ming Dynasty. After the emperor constructed a fleet of massive ships at least twice the size of any seen before, Zheng sailed throughout the known world from the naval base in Quanzhou collecting animals, food samples, and other cultural items that thrilled noblemen back in China.

Some scholars claim that Zheng's fleets sailed as far as the coasts of North and South America (71 years before Christopher Columbus "discovered" America in 1492), Europe, and Australia and New Zealand; and records exist that exotic animals such as giraffes were captured in Africa and brought back to parade before the emperor. In recent years, Zheng's journeys have been chronicled in a series of best-selling books by author Gavin Menzies, including *1421: The Year China Discovered the World*.[5]

The same deep-water ports that enabled the Chinese to launch ocean-going vessels also enabled foreign forces to invade Fujian, and a succession of Japanese pirate ships attacked towns along the coast for many years. As a result,

> The population was pulled back from the sea in order to deny the attackers their spoils. The withdrawal brought an end to Min Bei prosperity. The Ming decision in 1433 to ban maritime trade completed the disaster and left Fuzhou without the means of communication and transportation it required to play any major role in national life.[6]

Over the next several generations, multitudes of Fujian people began to migrate across the seas, but their adventures were not

Introduction

A sketch of a giraffe that was presented to the Yongle emperor in 1414, brought back on a ship commanded by Admiral Zheng after explorations along the East African coast. When people began saying the animal was a mythical Qilin, the emperor was unhappy as Chinese legend held that the beast only appeared before the imminent passing of an illustrious ruler. The emperor died in 1424.

without some harsh lessons and setbacks. Historian Jonathan Fenby remarked,

> In 1567 the emperor had lifted the ban on foreign trade and even allowed the people of Fujian Province to go to sea—the result was a new wave of Chinese communities throughout Southeast Asia. A Spanish colony set up in Manila in 1570 acted as a magnet for migrants from China. But, when the newcomers were searched for weapons, they prepared to defend themselves. In 1603 a massacre resulted, in which 15,000–20,000 Chinese were killed.[7]

Introduction

After a pause, the exodus of people from Fujian soon recovered and grew to such a level that the Qing government attempted to stop the outflow. One source noted,

> Ports like Xiamen were steppingstones for droves of Chinese people heading for Taiwan, Singapore, the Philippines, Malaysia, and Indonesia. In 1718 the Manchus attempted to halt Chinese emigration with an imperial edict recalling all subjects who were in foreign lands. Finding this ineffectual, in 1728 the court issued another proclamation declaring that anyone who did not return to China would be banished, and those captured would be executed.[8]

An even greater outflow of people left Fujian in the nineteenth century, as a shortage of arable land and increased economic hardships prompted thousands of families to abandon their homeland and start new lives in Southeast Asia.

The Fujian Economy

Rice, sweet potatoes, wheat, and barley constitute the province's main crops. However, due to the scarcity of arable land, Fujian is not a major agricultural producer. Seafood is an important resource along the coast, with numerous aquatic farms providing tons of shellfish to the Chinese and overseas markets.

Because of its geographic proximity to Taiwan, since the 1940s Fujian has been considered the frontline in any potential war between China and Taiwan. As a result, it has received less investment from the Chinese government and has developed at a slower rate than much of the rest of China until the 1980s. Since then, as China opened its markets to the world, Fujian has received billions of dollars of investment, often from the descendants of people who had left Fujian for Southeast Asia generations earlier.

Introduction

Today, although the region ranks 23rd in size and 17th in population among China's provinces, its per capital GDP ranks sixth highest—with only the three mega-cities of Beijing, Shanghai, and Tianjin, and the nearby provinces of Jiangsu and Zhejiang boasting greater economic output.

Rampant Superstition

Among all the provinces of China, Fujian must be considered one of the more religious, despite seven decades of attacks on "superstition" by the Communist authorities. Official concerns about Fujian's religious fervor date to ancient times when the central government described the province's "devil worship" as totally unacceptable and outside Confucian norms.

The deeds of tribal people on both sides of the Taiwan Strait were especially abhorrent to the Chinese rulers of the day. For

Statues of the goddess Mazu at a temple on Meizhou Island, Fujian.
Image Professionals

example, the Paiwan tribe (who today are found in both Fujian and southern Taiwan) were feared as fierce headhunters. When they returned from their forays,

> The women would gather together in front of the courtyard to welcome their heroes and would sing songs of triumph. The heads of their enemies were then hung on stone pillars in front of which were displayed wine and offerings. The sacrificial rite started, and the soul of the dead was duly consoled by the sorcerer. A tuft of hair was removed from the skull and solemnly put in a basket which was used for divination.[9]

In the early 1830s, the first Evangelical missionary to visit Fujian, Karl Gutzlaff, remarked on the spiritual fervor of the people he met there:

> The Amoy [Xiamen] people, though otherwise very reasonable men, have always shown themselves to be bigoted heathen. Whether at home or abroad, they have everywhere built splendid temples, chiefly in honor of Mazu, the "queen of heaven," to whose intercession they attribute the increase of their wealth. They rival Rome in the adoration of images and are most devout after a profitable voyage or an escape from a storm.[10]

Little has changed among the people of Fujian to the present day. Statues of the goddess Mazu, a deity that has been worshipped for centuries as a protector of fishermen, are still found dotted all along the coast. Fujian is frequently hit by powerful typhoons, and millions of people trust Mazu to protect them.

The array of deities revered by the people of Fujian are often mixed together. Syncretism is frequently observed in Catholic areas, with statues of Jesus, Mary, and the saints placed alongside statues of Buddha, Guanyin, Mazu, or a host of Daoist gods and goddesses. All of this is overlaid with a strong belief in ancestor worship, which keeps people trapped in fear, unwilling to risk offending their ancestors by changing their traditional beliefs.

Introduction

The traditional religious practices of people in Fujian appear to be solidified by the powerful clan system that remains in place throughout the province. Family lineages remain closely bound together, with each clan having its own set of favorite deities and protective spirits.

Christianity in Fujian

The church in Fujian Province has had a long and varied history since Nestorian Christians first introduced the gospel more than a millennia ago.

Although Catholicism first took root in the 1300s, five centuries passed before the first Evangelicals entered Fujian. Slowly but surely, the gospel took hold after initially having to overcome fierce opposition, as the close-knit clans fought to preserve the status quo.

Each book in *The China Chronicles* has a different emphasis, depending on how and when Christianity took hold and flourished in the province. In Fujian, the gospel faced enormous challenges before it gained a foothold in the nineteenth century, and as a result, this book devotes more space to the fascinating earlier stages of the missionary enterprise in Fujian than books on some of the other provinces in *The China Chronicles* series, which have broader sections on the revivals that have affected them over the past 50 years.

By the twentieth century, Fujian had become the breeding ground for some of the most successful and controversial figures in Chinese church history. Watchman Nee was a native of the province, as was revivalist John Sung, who was dubbed "China's greatest evangelist" by the hundreds of thousands of people saved under his ministry in the 1920s and 1930s. This book includes two chapters on each of these enigmatic characters.

Introduction

From the 1980s to today, Fujian has not experienced as many dramatic accounts of revival as other parts of China, where the house churches yield massive influence. The churches in Fujian tend to be comparatively more established and conservative, reflecting the establishment of Western denominations in Fujian during the missionary era.

Today, Fujian is home to approximately 5.8 million Christians of all descriptions, with roughly two-thirds belonging to Evangelical and one-third to Catholic churches. Fujian's overall Christian community comprises 14.7 percent of the population—the fifth highest among all of China's provinces.

Despite the encouraging number of Christians and the courageous lives of many godly Fujian men and women over the years, the province is also a hotbed of various cults and sects. The church in Fujian has been hampered by doctrinal issues and a lack of Bibles in recent decades, while the complex linguistic makeup of the province has also created barriers to the smooth spread of the gospel.

Finally, millions of Christians today in countries like Singapore, Malaysia, Indonesia, Thailand, and the Philippines have their ancestral roots in Fujian, but many have never heard how the gospel first took hold there and spread throughout the province, transforming multitudes of lives. May the scattered Fujian believers learn of the wonderful work God has performed in their homeland, and of the sacrifice many foreign and Chinese Christians made that helped the kingdom of God advance.

A Linguistic Babble

Christians from the tiny Gaoshan minority group, who number just 2,000 people in China.

Any introduction to life in Fujian would be incomplete without an explanation of the linguistic diversity found there, as language has played a major role in shaping the province into what it is today.

Although over 98 percent of Fujian's population identify as Han Chinese, among those 33 million Han people is found a bewildering variety of tongues, without parallel among the Han anywhere else in Mainland China. An ancient Chinese proverb, commenting on the linguistic babble in Fujian, says, "Every three *li* [about one mile] the dialect is different."

A Linguistic Babble

Over the centuries, differences in language between communities north and south of the Min River contributed to tensions among the different people groups of Fujian, with one scholar noting:

> Rivalry has long existed between the Min Bei [Northern Min] and Min Nan [Southern Min] peoples. Economic factors, such as competition for trade, has been involved, but so too have political factors. The position of Fuzhou as provincial capital has been resented by the Min Nan peoples, and the south has tried to retain as much local autonomy as possible. In overseas Chinese communities in Southeast Asia, the Min Nan and Min Bei peoples have carefully preserved their separate identities, as have smaller communities like those that speak Putian.[1]

According to one scholar, the centuries of slow progress it took to bring Fujian into the Han Chinese fold "may well have helped stabilize old dialectical forms in the various valleys and other regions of that mountainous province, forming the basis for the complex linguistic mosaic that Fujian still displays."[2]

By the tenth century, more than a dozen language groups had formed in Fujian and had established separate identities. Over time, each group developed their own distinctive characteristics, cuisine, customs, and even traditional forms of opera.

Early missionaries who arrived in Fujian were often thrown into a state of total confusion as they realized that the task of communicating their message was far more complicated than they had expected. When Joseph Walker—who was diligently studying Chinese at the time—travelled inland from Fuzhou in 1878, he remarked,

> What a babel of brogues and dialects there is among those wild mountains! A native can hardly pass the limits of his own village before his speech will betray him. The tones are the most unstable element. . . . They shoot up to the sky, then plunge into the bowels

of the earth. They stiffen straight out, they double up and twist about; they sing, cry, whine, groan, scold, plead; here, are musically plaintive; there, are gruff and overbearing.³

A prospective Bible translator summarized the challenges he faced in trying to share the Word of God with the people of central and northern Fujian in vernaculars they *could* understand:

> The extent of territory over which any particular dialect pertains is a comparatively small one, usually about as large as one or two English counties, and consequently, a fresh colloquial version is needed whenever work is commenced in a new district. Thus, we have in Fujian besides [two classical Chinese versions of the Bible], a complete version of the Bible in the Fuzhou dialect, both in the Chinese and Roman character, which is used for about 50 miles round Fuzhou City, as well as incomplete versions in the Putian, Jianning, and Jianyang dialects.⁴

By the 1920s, when the gospel had spread and foreign and Chinese evangelists traveled throughout the province more extensively, many believers grew frustrated at their inability to communicate with people in different areas. The Church Missionary Society explained:

> Since missionaries invested a year or more in language study, moving to a different language area was a waste of their resources. Aileen Armstrong learned six dialects, including Fuzhou, but this was a rare achievement. The language barrier also limited the mobility of Chinese church workers. The first generation of teachers and evangelists were nearly all from Fuzhou. This meant that they had to pick up another dialect if they were stationed some distance away; and they were not always capable of doing so.⁵

In addition to the myriad of Chinese vernaculars, several ethnic minority groups are found in Fujian, with 700,000 She people constituting the largest non-Han group, followed by more than 100,000 Hui Muslims and small numbers of Tujia and Miao. A

A Linguistic Babble

few thousand Gaoshan ("high mountain") people complete the ethnic composition of Fujian.[6]

As you will see in the chart below, the differences in vocabulary among the Chinese languages in Fujian are so great that they could be likened to the differences among European languages such as English, Spanish, German, and Italian.

Furthermore, within each of these broad groupings are found further dialect differences, while other Chinese languages that are predominantly spoken elsewhere in China are also spoken in Fujian, including Cantonese, Gan, Wu, Hakka, Putian, Hui'an, and Shaojiang.

Pronunciation of Common Words in some Fujian Chinese Languages

English	Mandarin	Min Bei	Min Nan	Min Zhong
we	wo-men	ngaui-koq-noung	gun	
you	nin	nu-koq-noung	lin	
they	ta-men	i-koq-noung	in	
one man	yige ren	so-a noung	tsit-e lang	
to fly	fei	hi	hui	shui
to speak	shuo-hua	koung-wa	kong-we	wo-shia
rice	fan	puong	peng	pum
five	wu	ngu	go	
sun	tai-yang	niq-t'ao	dit-t'ao	
blue	lan	lang	da	so

The National Language

After Mao founded the People's Republic of China in 1949, Communist officials assigned to Fujian soon encountered the same linguistic tangle that Christian preachers had struggled with for decades.

In 1974, while the Cultural Revolution was still sweeping China, a delegation of American linguists was invited to study the language of just one county, Datian, in central Fujian. The Chinese government hoped to show off the "great progress that had been achieved" by the Communists in their drive to make Mandarin the national language of all people in China.

However, the visiting linguists struggled to see the progress being spouted by their hosts, and noted that the small county "has three major and over ten minor dialects. People scattered by a blade of grass could not understand each other. A cadre from the north needed three to seven interpreters to make a speech."[7]

In recent decades, a much higher percentage of people in Fujian have learned to speak the national language, as Mandarin is used almost exclusively in education and in most media. The traditional languages remain strong, however. Most households have become bilingual, using their own variety among themselves and their neighbors, but speaking Mandarin with outsiders.

To conclude, here is a brief summary of several of the main Chinese languages spoken in Fujian, with insights into some of the historical and cultural differences that have helped shape them into the proudly distinctive people groups they are today.[8]

Min Bei (Northern Min)—8.2 million speakers in China

Min Bei is spoken in eight counties around Jian'ou in northwest Fujian, within an area encompassed by the Min River Valley and the river's tributaries. The rugged mountains that separate the area from the rest of China caused Min Bei territory to remain isolated from outside influences for centuries, although the people looked across the sea and had contact with the Japanese and Taiwanese for many generations.

The Min Bei language developed so differently from Min Nan that one scholar noted, "Although both exist in Fujian, Min Bei and Min Nan are too different to be treated as if they constituted a single sublanguage. They have only a few phonetic features in common.... Both also have many more tones than Mandarin."[9]

Other Chinese tend to view Min Bei people as somewhat mysterious and think their language is impossible to learn. Today, more than one million Min Bei people live in Malaysia, Brunei, Indonesia, and other nations of Southeast Asia, where they are often referred to as the "Hokchiu." The New Testament was translated into Min Bei in 1934 but has fallen into disuse.

Min Dong (Eastern Min)—10.6 million speakers in China

The main Fuzhou dialect is part of the Min Dong language. Visitors from other parts of the country are often so confused upon arrival in Fujian that it has been said, "Chinese from elsewhere, on first hearing the language spoken in the city of Fuzhou, often refuse to believe that it is a form of Chinese at all."[10]

Hundreds of thousands of Min Dong speakers are also found scattered throughout Southeast Asia, especially in Malaysia, Singapore, Indonesia, Thailand, and Brunei.

Min Dong speakers are often treated with suspicion by other Fujian language groups, and when the Guomindang (Nationalist) forces fled the mainland and took control of Taiwan in 1949, one of the main objections of the Taiwanese people was that the Nationalists tried to force them to speak Min Dong. Most of the Chinese population on the island at the time were Min Nan speakers. Missionaries began translating the Scriptures into Min Dong in 1852, and the full Bible was finally completed more than three decades later in 1884, though it enjoyed only limited use and has been out of print since 1905.

A Linguistic Babble

Min Nan (Southern Min)—22.6 million speakers in China

The most widely used of Fujian's languages, Min Nan is spoken by over 40 million people around the world, including all the countries of Southeast Asia, Taiwan, Hong Kong, and in diaspora communities throughout the Western world. They have played a significant role in the economies of all the places they settled and were key contributors to the establishment of the city of Bangkok, Thailand.

In Southeast Asia, the Min Nan are often called "Hokkien"—which is the pronunciation of the word "Fujian" in their language, while those living in Cantonese areas are referred to as "Hoklo." Wherever they have settled—including Singapore, Malaysia, and Taiwan—the Hokkien, Amoy, Teochew, Hui'an, and other communities are noted for maintaining their distinctive cuisine and customs.

Missionaries first began translating individual books of the Bible into the Amoy (Xiamen) dialect of Min Nan in 1852, but nearly a century elapsed before the full Bible was finally completed and printed in 1933. It is still used by Christians in Taiwan and other nations today.

Min Zhong (Central Min)—3.6 million speakers in China

The smallest of the four main Min languages, Min Zhong is spoken in the Sanming and Yong'an prefectures of central Fujian. Min Zhong people also possess their own customs, including a distinctive style of opera. When the Communists came to power, Fujian had 20 forms of local opera and 115 opera troupes operating throughout the province. Although Mao disbanded the troupes, they proved so important to the cultural expression of the people that the government soon relented, and they were revived.

Despite having a population that is approximately the same size as that of countries like New Zealand and Norway, no Scripture has ever been translated into Min Zhong.

Putian (Xinghua)—3.0 million speakers in China

The fascinating Putian language is spoken by over three million people in a relatively small area of eastern Fujian Province. The town of Putian (now Xinghua) was founded in AD 567, and today their language is only spoken in Fujian within an oval valley about 34 miles (55 km) wide and 62 miles (100 km) long. The Putian language is so distinctive that it is said, "Persons fluent in both Min Nan and Min Bei cannot understand them."[11]

Even the famous evangelist John Sung, whose ministry grew to such prominence in the 1930s that he was nicknamed "China's greatest evangelist," struggled to preach the gospel in his home province because of the linguistic diversity. It was said that Sung, who was a native of Putian,

> sometimes spoke in his Putian dialect in parts of Fujian, but in others he used an interpreter, as he did in Cantonese-speaking areas and throughout the rest of China, until he finally became proficient in Mandarin near the end of his preaching career. In some places he used English and was interpreted into a local language by missionaries.[12]

Today, thousands of Putian people are found in Singapore and Malaysia, where they are also known as the Hinghua. The full Bible was translated into Putian in 1912, using the Roman script, but few people still have access to it.

Hakka—44.2 million speakers in China

The Hakka people, whose name means "guests," inhabit a wide area of south China, with at least three million found in western Fujian Province.

A Linguistic Babble

The ancestors of the Hakka are believed to have originated in north China, before being forced to migrate southward where they encountered other groups that didn't want to share their land. As a result, rivalry between the Min Nan and these unwelcome "guests" frequently led to bloodshed.

Today, Hakka people possess a very strong sense of shared identity. When a non-Hakka woman marries into a Hakka family, she is required to learn the language, and the Hakka proudly boast that they would "rather surrender the ancestral land, but never the ancestral speech."[13]

Nestorians in Fujian

A Nestorian monument that was unearthed at Quanzhou in 1906.

In 635, Nestorian missionaries from Syria are recorded to have traveled down the Silk Road into Xinjiang and onward to Chang'an (now Xi'an), which was China's capital at the time. The Nestorian scribe Malech later reported,

Nestorians in Fujian

> For 150 years this mission was active.... One hundred nine Syrian missionaries have worked in China during 150 years of the Chinese mission.... The missionaries traveled on foot—they had sandals on their feet, a staff in their hands, and carried a basket on their backs. In the basket was the Holy Writ and the cross. They took the road around the Persian Gulf; went over deep rivers and high mountains, thousands of miles. On the way they met many heathen nations and preached to them the gospel of Christ.[1]

The Nestorian influence is known to have reached far more widely than just the areas around the nation's capital and even spread even to distant Fujian Province. The respected historian, Arthur Moule, wrote that when the authorities were building the walls of the city of Quanzhou in the eighth century, they dug up a large cross, which

> was placed respectfully on the side which faced toward the east, at the height of six feet. Such was the awe, and even the traditional faith, with which the inhabitants of the country regarded it that, according to some, the city would not be destroyed as long as that precious symbol of salvation and life remained in it.[2]

The Nestorians ministered in relative peace until 845, when the emperor issued an edict against religion. Although the edict was primarily aimed at reducing the influence of Buddhism, Christians were also caught up in the conflict. Approximately 2,000 Nestorian monks and nuns were forced to abandon their spiritual vocation, which dealt a heavy blow to the fledgling church in China at the time.

After the persecution of 845, the Nestorian enterprise in China faltered, and the faith appears to have been stopped in its tracks. By the end of the first millennium, few traces of their presence remained. Nearly three centuries later in 1292, however, the famous explorer Marco Polo and his uncle, Maffeo, shared a tantalizing account of a meeting they had in Fuzhou during their visit to Fujian. When an Arab merchant told them about a group of believers in the province with their own unique religion, the Polos were eager to visit them and investigate for themselves.

They soon found the community were not Muslims, nor were they "fire worshippers" (Zoroastrians). After an extensive investigation, they concluded the people were Christians, and must have been a remnant of the Nestorian movement, for the first Catholic missionaries did not arrive in Fujian for another quarter of a century. One account records:

> They had books, and Maffeo and Marco read them and began to interpret the writing and to translate from word to word and from tongue to tongue, so that they found it to be the words of the Psalter [a volume containing the Book of Psalms and other writings].
>
> They asked them whence they had that religion and order. And they answered and said, "From our ancestors." They had also in a certain temple of theirs three figures painted who were three apostles of the seventy who went preaching through the world. And they said [the three men] had taught their ancestors the religion long ago, and that the faith had already been preserved among them for 700 years, but for a long time they had been without teaching and so were ignorant of the chief things.[3]

The Polos thought about ways they could help those forgotten believers and advised them to contact the Nestorian metropolitan in Beijing: "Explain to him your state, that he may come to know you and you may be able freely to keep your religion and rule."[4]

Long before the final collapse in 1368 of the Yuan (Mongol) Dynasty that had shown favor to Nestorian Christianity, Nestorian influence in China had greatly waned. What had started as a movement of great spiritual vitality had become bogged down in compromise and political alliances. Although information from that era is hard to come by, anecdotal evidence suggests that many Nestorians had become a less than godly

A painting believed to depict a drunk Nestorian monk in China.

representation of Christ, with priests accused of drunkenness and immorality.

The end of 700 years of Nestorian influence in China coincided with the arrival of Catholic missionaries. In Fujian, all memory of the Nestorians appears to have completely vanished by the time the first Catholics arrived, with only occasional archaeological discoveries providing reminders of their long presence in the province. The most noteworthy discovery occurred in 1906, when four ancient Nestorian crosses and a monument were unearthed near the coastal city of Quanzhou.

Early Catholics in Fujian

A Catholic Gospel tract on the life of Christ, published in Fujian in 1635.

Early Catholics in Fujian

After the demise of Nestorianism, the next representatives of Christianity in Fujian Province were Catholics, who by the 1320s had established churches in various towns. When the Italian Franciscan friar, Odoric of Pordenone, visited Fujian between 1323 and 1327, he reported, "Passing through many cities and towns, I came to a certain noble city that is called Zayton [Quanzhou], where we friars have two houses."[1]

At the time of Odoric's visit, the Bishop of Quanzhou was another Franciscan, Andrew of Perugia, who had arrived in the city in 1318. Some years earlier, a wealthy Armenian woman was grieved that there was no place of Christian worship in Quanzhou. Subsequently,

> The Armenian lady . . . attending only to the promptings of her zeal and piety, and determining to devote her immense riches to the salvation of souls and the glory of God, built such a magnificent church there that the archbishop, Montecorvino, gave it the name of a cathedral and raised the province into a diocese.[2]

Encouraged by the early progress of his mission in Fujian, Andrew requested new recruits be dispatched from Europe to help strengthen the work and reap the harvest. Four men were chosen to join the work, but before they reached China their ship blew off course and they were cruelly put to death by a fanatical Muslim governor off the coast of India.[3]

Undeterred, Andrew soldiered on alone, and he noted in 1326, "We are able to preach freely and unmolested. . . . Of idolaters a very large number are baptized, but having been baptized they do not walk straight in the path of Christianity."[4]

Andrew of Perugia died in Quanzhou in 1332. Remarkably, his tombstone was discovered more than six centuries later in 1946.

The Catholic mission in Fujian Province continued for several more decades, but its success was relatively short-lived, and the work in Fujian came to an abrupt end in 1362 when the newly-appointed Bishop of Quanzhou, James of Florence, was murdered while traveling through Central Asia.

The Second Catholic Wave

More than two centuries passed with no known Christian presence in Fujian. While several famous Catholic missionaries, including Matteo Ricci, impacted the Chinese court in Beijing during this period, no records exist of activity in faraway Fujian Province.

François Pallu (1626–1684), who served as the vicar apostolic in Fujian Province in a time of great upheaval against Catholics.

A long time passed until a leading government official, Shen Que, composed a "thunderous manifesto" against secret societies, which was implemented throughout the whole Chinese empire in the seventeenth century.

As a result, throughout China churches were ransacked and "[a]ll the Christians who could be seized were loaded with chains and dragged to prison. The greatest severity was shown to the catechists.... They were insulted and treated in the most shameful manner to induce them to confess imaginary crimes."[5]

The Jesuit missionary Giulio Aleni entered Fujian in 1625 and spent the next 25 years winning many converts among the upper classes of society. It was said of Aleni, "For four months he personally visited all the scholar officials of the capital city, Fuzhou, and spent another eight months visiting all the other officials in the province. More than 50 scholars wrote testimonials praising Christianity."[6]

When persecution broke out in 1638, Aleni fled to Macao. The officials in Fujian assumed they had seen the last of him, but he secretly returned the following year and continued to serve Christ covertly in the province until he died at Nanping in 1647.

Around the same time that Aleni was carrying out his mission, the Franciscans and Dominicans also sent workers to Fujian, and a burgeoning Catholic community emerged, especially in and around Fu'an in the north of the province near the Zhejiang border. Fu'an has remained a Catholic stronghold to the present time, with an estimated 20,000 Catholics in Fu'an and nearly 100,000 in the entire Ningde Prefecture today.[7]

Because of the imperial edict suppressing religion, for many years Catholics in Fujian were hunted like animals. The first recorded martyr in the province was a Spanish Dominican named Francisco de Capillas, who was put to death at Fu'an in January 1648.

Early Catholics in Fujian

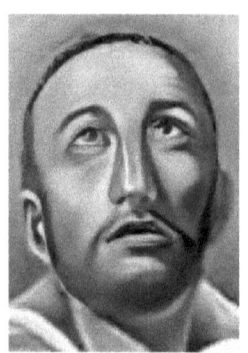

Francisco de Capillas
CRBC

Capillas was born in Spain in 1607, and as a young man he expressed a desire to see God's kingdom established in the far-flung corners of the world. As a result, in February 1632, aged just 24, he set sail for the Philippines, where he served in northern Luzon for nine years before transferring to Fujian Province in 1642.

His ministry was to preach and disciple Chinese believers, as well as to administer the affairs of the mission. One of his fellow priests said Capillas "would go to a hospital every day after prayers to serve the sick, with much love and care embrace them, console them, feed them, and even fix their beds."[8]

When an anti-Christian riot broke out at Fu'an on November 13, 1647, many Chinese believers were seriously injured. As soon as he heard this, Capillas set out to help them. As the Spaniard hurried along a path, he was captured by a group of soldiers and thrown into prison. Despite his dire surroundings, Capillas radiated great joy and he wrote,

> I am here with other prisoners and we have developed a fellowship. They ask me about the gospel of the Lord. I am not concerned about getting out of here because here I know I am doing the will of God. They do not let me stay up at night to pray, so I pray in bed before dawn. I live here in great joy without any worry, knowing that I am here because of Jesus Christ.[9]

On January 16, 1648, Francisco de Capillas was taken from of his prison cell and decapitated. Two months passed before local believers found his remains and buried them.

The Paris Missionary Society was the next Catholic group to establish a work in Fujian. Maigrot de Crissey, who was based in Fuzhou, baptized 80 converts in 1687 and a further 75 in 1688,[10] but the work was severely damaged by infighting among the Chinese converts, and it experienced only moderate growth into the eighteenth century.

A portrait showing de Capillas in prison just before his martyrdom.

The Dominican Martyrs of 1747–48

After the death of de Capillas in 1648, almost exactly 100 years elapsed before the next major persecution of Catholics in Fujian. During that time the Christian community was small and scattered throughout the province, with a total of just 3,700 believers reported in the whole of Fujian in 1663.[11]

By 1722, the Dominicans had established 37 churches in Fujian, overseen by nine missionaries.[12] However, two years later the new Yongzheng Emperor in Beijing issued an edict banning Christianity, and a fresh persecution of Christians was launched.[13]

The Governor of Fujian, Jueluo Manbao, sent this advice to the emperor, which foreshadowed the anti-Christian approach of the Communist Party more than two centuries later:

> The Europeans who are at the court are useful there for working on the calendar and other services, but those who are in the provinces have no use whatsoever. . . . The temples that have been built must all be transformed into buildings of public use. This religion must be rigorously forbidden. Those who have been blind enough to follow this religion must be obliged to correct themselves immediately. If they continue to assemble for praying, they must be punished according to the laws.[14]

In 1724, seven of the nine foreigners residing in Fujian decided to go into hiding and to secretly continue their ministries. Remarkably, some of the missionaries managed to evade capture for more than 20 years, as local converts helped them stay one step ahead of the authorities. Often, services were held in the dead of night to avoid detection, and the foreigners were disguised as Chinese peasants whenever it was deemed necessary to move them to a new location.

When a later Viceroy of Fujian learned that a group of Spanish missionaries had defied the imperial edict and were still carrying on their work in the 1740s, he was enraged and launched a fierce manhunt to capture and put them to death. Their heroic testimonies are summarized here:

Born in the town of Tarragona in 1680, Sanz was named Joseph at birth, but he decided to change his name to Pedro

Martyr when he joined the Dominican Order. Perhaps this humble Spaniard knew the kind of death by which he would later glorify God.

After serving in the Philippines, Sanz arrived in Fujian Province in 1715, where he found a flourishing Christian community that was attracting many new converts.

In 1730, while in hiding, Sanz was appointed Bishop of Fujian and he was smuggled to Fu'an County—the very place where Francisco de Capillas had been beheaded for his faith a century earlier.

Pedro Martyr Sanz
CRBC

For the next 17 years, Sanz hid in Christians' homes, secretly ministering to believers. The Chinese authorities presumed that he and the other missionaries had fled China, but when rumors began to circulate that the priests were in hiding, a large manhunt was launched to flush them out. Sanz and the other missionaries decided to surrender, believing it was not worth endangering the lives of their protectors.

The act of surrender did not lessen the punishment against Sanz, and he was brutally tortured. While in prison at Fuzhou, Sanz learned of his pending execution in a letter from a Chinese convert, who wrote, "Your Excellency will soon be crowned with the palm of martyrdom. We cannot hold back our tears. But now we ask your blessing and intercession before God."[15]

After reading the letter, Sanz prostrated himself on the floor of his cell and recommitted himself to Jesus Christ. For three days, Pedro Martyr Sanz prayerfully prepared his soul to meet the Lord, and on May 26, 1747, an executioner's sword separated his head from his body.

Early Catholics in Fujian

Joachim Royo Perez
CRBC

One source said that Sanz had converted many Chinese to Christianity, including prison guards and even the executioner who beheaded him. They were all convinced of the truth of the gospel by the joy and calmness he displayed in facing death.

Joachim Royo Perez sailed for Fujian in 1715, spending his first two years in the city of Quanzhou. When the edict against Christianity was issued, Royo adopted "a hidden life, serving his people by night and often spending much time hidden in secret rooms, tombs, and cemeteries."[16]

In July 1746, Royo was discovered by enraged officials and imprisoned at Fuzhou, where he remained behind bars for the next two years. Other inmates reported that he spent most of his time in prayer and preaching the gospel to the other prisoners and the guards.

Finally, on October 28, 1748, the 57-year-old missionary was put to death by suffocation. The men who were ordered to end Royo's life declared,

> He received us with joy. We felt a deep remorse about being forced to carry out the order for his execution, because we revered him as a very good and innocent man. He constantly preached to us about the Christian religion, and in prison we always saw him praying to God with a joyful countenance. Oh, he was indeed a holy man.[17]

Born in Granada, Spain, in 1694, Juan Alcober joined the Dominican Order when he was just 13. He was sent to the Philippines in 1725, where he worked among Chinese immigrants in the town of Binondo. This work allowed him to study the Min Chinese language and prepare for ministry in Fujian, which he commenced in 1728.

After the edict was issued against Christianity, Chinese believers courageously sheltered Alcober in their homes, and he constantly moved about to avoid detection. On one occasion, soldiers were closing in on a village where Alcober was hiding, so an ingenious plan was devised to place him inside a coffin and stage a mock funeral. The "mourners" carried the coffin straight past the unsuspecting soldiers.

Juan Alcober
CRBC

On another occasion Alcober was disguised as a peasant water seller, enabling him to visit believers in various villages. Troops came to the place where he was hiding, so he climbed into a tree. As the night wore on, the missionary quietly said his evening prayers, and was surprised to hear someone else praying. His colleague Francis Serrano was hiding on a different limb in the same tree!

Alcober was finally discovered and sent to prison in Fuzhou in June 1746. For two years he was tortured mercilessly, and he hoped death would come quickly. One of the last things he wrote was, "Awaiting the blessed hope and the coming glory of our Mighty God."

The sentence of death by strangulation was finally carried out on October 28, 1748, and he died alongside his colleague, Francis Diaz. Later, one of their executioners described the martyrdoms of Alcober and Diaz:

> When I received the order to kill the two Europeans, I called two guards and my brother to help me carry it out. As we approached them, we saw them praying. They urged us to follow the law of

God. We tied a rope around their necks and began to spin them around until they strangled to death. They died praying, welcoming death peacefully.[18]

Francisco Diaz del Rincón was the "baby" of the five Spanish martyrs killed in Fujian in 1747 and 1748. He was just 35 at the time of his death, yet he had already spent 12 years in Asia as a missionary.

Francis Diaz del Rincón
CRBC

As a child, Diaz told his father he wanted to go to China to preach the gospel. In 1736 he undertook the long and dangerous sea journey to Asia, arriving in the Philippines sick and frail. After recovering he traveled to Fujian Province, where he found the mission in turmoil because the government was searching for the other missionaries.

Not being fluent in the language, Diaz was forced to rely on the help of local believers to survive. He was granted permission to return to the Philippines if he wanted, but he chose to remain in Fujian regardless of the consequences.

In 1746, a group of soldiers searched for Diaz. Frustrated by their inability to locate his hiding place, they captured some Chinese women to find out where he was, but they refused to speak, preferring to suffer than to betray a servant of God. He was finally captured, taken just outside the Fuzhou prison gates, and suffocated to death on October 28, 1748. Some brave Christians risked arrest by retrieving his remains to give him a proper burial.

Born in 1691, Francis Serrano Frias was considered a holy and virtuous man. In 1725 he arrived in Fujian, where he gained the respect of all who knew him. It was said of Serrano, "He was gifted with endurance to the extreme—a tremendous personal vitality. In those difficult times, he often had to disguise himself as a peasant and cross forests and rivers at night in order to encourage the Christians."[19]

Serrano's success in concealing himself from the authorities for more than two decades finally ended in June 1746. He was imprisoned at Fuzhou and tortured for 28 months. The interrogators were desperate to obtain the names of the Chinese believers who had protected him, but despite suffering brutal beatings, Serrano refused to divulge any information.

Francis Serrano Frias
CRBC

In those days, when a criminal was sentenced to death, he was branded across his face. Serrano wrote, "Our hearts exulted. We were branded as slaves of Jesus Christ. Since our great Lord accepts us, these heads of ours are no longer ours any more, but the Lord's. He can take them whenever He wishes."[20]

On the night of October 28, 1748, Francis Serrano was put to death by suffocation. He had lived his 57 years to the full, spending 23 of them preaching the gospel among the people of Fujian.

After killing the five Spanish Dominican missionaries in 1747 and 1748, the Fujian authorities may have assumed the churches would fall apart, but the seed of the gospel had been deposited deep within many Chinese men and women, and they continued to trust Christ and encourage one another in the faith.

In 1663, the number of Catholics in Fujian had numbered just 3,700,[21] and despite waves of horrific persecution and martyrdom, when the next survey of the size of the Catholic churches took place in Fujian in 1866, it was found the number of believers had grown to 30,000.[22]

Early Catholics in Fujian

By that time the spiritual landscape had changed dramatically in Fujian, and the Catholics—who had labored alone for Christ for more than 500 years—were now joined in the province by the first Evangelical missionaries.

1830s and 1840s

In almost every account of Evangelical mission history, the accolade of being the first Protestant foreign missionary is given to William Carey, the "father of modern missions," who arrived in India in 1793. The first Evangelical missionary in China is invariably said to be Robert Morrison, who arrived in 1807.

It is peculiar that historians completely overlook the fact that the Dutch Reformed Church sent missionaries to Taiwan (then considered fully a part of China and under the control of Fujian Province) as early as the 1650s, with 5,000 tribesmen on the island soon becoming Christians. Those early believers met a grisly end when Dutch rule of Taiwan was deposed and all the Christians were massacred in 1661.[1]

Karl Gutzlaff — China's Most Hated Missionary

The first recorded Evangelical Christian to set foot in today's Fujian Province specifically may also be the most hated. The German pioneer Karl Gutzlaff visited coastal areas of the province between 1831 and 1835. Gutzlaff wore Chinese clothing and dispensed both medicine and Gospel literature wherever he went.

The reason that Gutzlaff was such a despised figure in Chinese history (and, indeed, among many of his fellow missionaries) is not solely because of his preaching of the gospel, but because of the unwise actions he took, which aligned Christianity with the opium trade that ruined millions of lives throughout China.[2]

1830s and 1840s

In the 1830s, the only way a foreigner could travel up and down the Chinese coast was on British vessels that also promoted the drug trade. One historian explained,

> Missionaries, like all Westerners in the Canton area before the Opium War, were dependent on the opium trade and could hardly avoid participating in it, at least passively. Opium clippers transported salaries, mail, and reports for missionaries, merchants, and foreign service personnel. Religious tracts awaiting distribution

Karl Gutzlaff dressed as a Chinese sailor.

were stored at the opium depot of Lintin. The dominant opium dealer, Jardine-Matheson, served as banker and money changer for missionary and trader alike.³

While many missionaries reluctantly took advantage of the service to get to their destinations, Gutzlaff unwisely took things several steps further and became a paid interpreter for the Jardine-Matheson Company. For a time, Gutzlaff tried to downplay the crucial role he played for the company, only telling supporters back home about his evangelistic endeavors.

It appears that Gutzlaff justified his position by claiming the gospel was finally going forth, and that the mode of transportation was therefore of minor importance. Options for traveling in China were extremely limited at the time, and the choice was either to take passage on board the opium ships or not go at all.

It was said that Gutzlaff accepted his role with Jardine-Matheson because he "found irresistible the chance to preach the gospel and distribute literature among villagers along China's coast, and furthermore, he would be provided with three times as many religious tracts. . . . Besides, he needed the income."⁴

With the benefit of hindsight, there is little doubt that the actions of Karl Gutzlaff and others like him seriously damaged the cause of Christ in China, where Chinese perceptions that Christianity is closely linked with Western imperialism still linger nearly two centuries later.

Later missionaries found their witness for Christ rejected because of the perceived connection between Christianity and the drug trade. Irishman John Wolfe lamented that locals often told him, "You destroy us with your opium, and now you insult us with your offer of peace and salvation."⁵

In October 1856, missionary Francis McCaw shared an incident that occurred when he was preaching on a street corner in Fuzhou and a man asked him if he had any opium:

"No," I said, "I don't use it, nor do the true worshippers of Jesus use it either."

"What countryman are you?" was his next question. "Englishman," I answered. "And you do not smoke opium? Do not your countrymen bring it here?"

He then turned to the crowd, with an air of triumph, raising his hand and shaking it aloft, soon enlisting all the audience on his side; and to make the scene more ludicrous—to say nothing worse of it—in the midst of all the confusion an old woman, apparently above 60, came forward, and clenching her hand, shook it up at my face in desperate rage.

I remained quiet for some time, until the noise abated. Then I addressed them on the subject and told them that I came here to teach them a religion which condemned all such evil drugs and practices.[6]

Despite his misguided zeal, Gutzlaff's accounts of his journeys up and down the Fujian coast in the 1830s make both fascinating and disturbing reading. After arriving at Xiamen, he observed,

It is a general custom among the people to drown a large proportion of the newborn female children. This unnatural crime is so common among them that it is perpetrated without any feeling, and even in a laughing mood; and to ask a man of any distinction whether he has daughters, is a mark of great rudeness. Neither the government nor the moral sayings of their sages have put a stop to this nefarious custom. The father has authority over the lives of his children and disposes of them according to his pleasure. The boys enjoy the greater share of parental affection. . . . There is also carried on a regular traffic in females. These facts are as revolting to humanity as disgusting to detail. They may serve, however, to stimulate the zeal of Christian females to promote the welfare of one of the largest portions of their sex, by giving them the glorious gospel of our Savior—which alone restores females to their proper rank in society.[7]

Gutzlaff and his crew soon ran into trouble, as customs officials boarded their ship and demanded they depart and stop spreading their religion among the people. Undeterred by the threats, Gutzlaff went ashore after receiving an invitation to visit a temple. This incensed the officials even more, and as a result,

> Those poor people who happened to come into the neighborhood of the ship were treated most barbarously. After being severely beaten on board the war-junks, so that we might hear the lamentations of the sufferers, they were then exposed in the pillory with a *cangue* about the neck, and a label inscribed with their crime; not of [interacting] with barbarians, or going aboard, but of *looking* at the barbarian ship. Thus, the mere sight of us was contaminating![8]

Although most people would be discouraged by this initial foray into Fujian Province, the ever-optimistic Karl Gutzlaff was far from deterred, and he boldly distributed even more Gospel literature in Xiamen before finally pulling anchor and heading up the coast. He wrote,

> We often conversed with the common people about the things which concerned their eternal happiness; we gave them books, exhorted them to read them with diligence, and we left this kindhearted people with a deep impression.
>
> Today we distributed more books than usual. They were at first cautious in taking them; but seeing that we asked nothing in return, they made no scruple to accept them, and with gratitude.... It is highly desirable that a Christian mission should be established here.... The facilities for disseminating the divine Word are greater in this place than in any other part of China.... Though I have [spoken] with thousands of Amoy [Xiamen] men, I have never met with one Christian among them.[9]

The final journey Gutzlaff made in Fujian appears to have been in 1835, when he and American Congregationalist missionary

Edwin Stevens were able to travel 38 miles (61 km) up the Min River from Fuzhou to the city of Minqing, where soldiers opened fire on their vessel and caused them to retreat toward the coast.

Gutzlaff was not the only Evangelical missionary to share the gospel along the Fujian coast at the time. In August 1835, Edwin Stevens and Walter Medhurst—a famous linguist who helped translate the first Bible into Chinese—commenced a two-month tour along the coast of China, "taking a cargo of 20,000 volumes of Scripture and tracts for distribution."[10]

After visiting Shandong Province in the north, the duo turned south and made their way past Shanghai and Zhejiang to Fujian, where the winds turned unfavorable and they were forced to shelter on an unknown island. Stevens wrote,

> Strong winds bound us here four days, unable to move or reach the shore until the last day.... Swarms of the people met us at landing, and everyone welcomed us, too eager to receive our books. We walked over much of the island during the day and left in all its villages some portions of the Scriptures or other books, with none to hinder or forbid us.
>
> We anchored in the fine harbor of Dongshan.... Five minutes sufficed to bring together many hundreds of smiling people, another minute taught them our object of coming, and half an hour sufficed to distribute 100 volumes.... They could scarcely have scrambled for them more eagerly and violently.[11]

The First Resident Missionaries

The honor of being the first Evangelical missionary permitted to reside in Fujian belongs to the 38-year-old American David Abeel, who served with the Dutch Reformed Mission. Abeel, a native of New Jersey, and fellow American William Boone, traveled to the coastal city of Xiamen on February 23, 1842.[12]

David Abeel (left), who in 1842 was the first Evangelical missionary to live in Fujian; and Elihu and Eleanor Doty, who arrived a few years later.

Abeel discovered his mother had died just after he arrived in Fujian, but he remained in Xiamen for the next several years, based just off the coast on the island of Gulangyu. He befriended a leading official named Xu Jiyu, who was later appointed governor of Fujian. Abeel was later joined in the work by William Pohlman and Elihu Doty, who had been serving in Borneo (a large island now shared by the nations of Malaysia, Indonesia, and Brunei).

Sadly, David Abeel's missionary career was cut short due to tropical diseases taking a toll on his health. Before sailing for New York, where he hoped to recover, he admitted, "I am doubtful which home I shall reach first." He died of pulmonary tuberculosis in September 1846, aged only 42 and having never married.[13]

John Stronach and his wife, Margaret, were sent by the Church Missionary Society from their home in Edinburgh, Scotland, to Singapore in 1837. They relocated to Xiamen in 1844, and two years later John was joined in the mission by his older brother Alexander and his sister Catherine, creating a unique situation of three siblings serving as missionaries in China at the same base.

John was one of the missionaries who worked on the first ever translation of the Bible into Chinese. The role required him to relocate to Shanghai, so he handed the Xiamen work over to Alexander. Decades later, John Stronach recalled the beginning of his work in Fujian: "In 1844 I was sent up to China and began a missionary work in Amoy [Xiamen], having acquired the language to such an extent that I could at once begin to preach to the inhabitants. . . . In 1844, when I went there, there was not a single convert in all the large province of Fujian."[14]

In 1848, a gardener named Wu Tu and his son were baptized, becoming the first Chinese Evangelical Christians in Fujian. Soon, several others were baptized and a small fellowship was formed.

1850s

Carl Fast and Anders Elquist

A sketch of Carl Fast.

The second Evangelical martyr in China and the first to die in Fujian Province was Carl Josef Fast, whose career had barely commenced when pirates killed him on the Min River in October 1850.[1]

Earlier that year, Fast and Anders Elquist had arrived in Fuzhou. They were the first two Swedish missionaries sent to a foreign land, but the lives of these promising young Christian men were brief and tragic.

After spending much time trying to secure a permanent residence in Fuzhou from which to launch their mission work, Fast and Elquist were finally granted permission to rent a house near the city wall. One day, after visiting a British ship docked at the mouth of the river to exchange money for their work,

> [t]hey were suddenly attacked by a Chinese piratical craft, filled with armed men, who had put off from one of the villages along the shore. During the encounter, Fast was mortally wounded and fell from the boat into the river, which was at once his deathbed and his grave. His remains were never recovered. Elquist, when his friend had fallen, threw himself into the river, and by diving under the water succeeded in reaching the shore, having received several wounds.[2]

After swimming to shore, Elquist wandered in the hills above the river for two days before he was rescued by a passing ship and taken back to Fuzhou. His physical wounds, coupled with the mental and emotional trauma of the incident, were too great to overcome. He tried to continue his missionary work, but his health deteriorated and he was forced to return to Sweden in 1852.

Under God's blessing, a significant breakthrough occurred in 1855, seven years after the first Chinese Evangelicals in Fujian had believed the gospel. That year, 77 new converts were baptized in Xiamen. Although the number of Christians was still miniscule, the seed of the gospel had been planted, and a massive harvest was later produced for the kingdom of God.

Today, the whole of Xiamen Prefecture contains 4.8 million people, of whom nearly 600,000 (12.3 percent of the population) are professing Christians (418,000 Evangelicals and 174,000 Catholics).[3]

The Church Missionary Society — A Decade of Funerals

The London-based Church Missionary Society (CMS) consisted of believers from Presbyterian, Anglican, and Congregational backgrounds. They sent their first two workers—William Welton and David Jackson—to Fuzhou in 1850. Almost immediately the fledgling mission suffered a series of blows, as a combination of severe spiritual attacks and tropical diseases combined to wreak havoc upon the workers.

Jackson soon transferred to Shanghai, but Welton labored on alone, operating a medical dispensary from a rented room in a Buddhist temple. In November 1851, a crowd of Chinese attending a kite-flying festival attacked Welton's dispensary, destroying the furniture and carrying off everything they could lay hold of. The missionary barricaded himself inside the temple, and thankfully, his life was spared.

Welton labored alone until 1855, when he was joined by Francis McCaw and his wife and by Matthew Fearnley, but just a few months later the work suffered a further setback when Mrs. McCaw fell ill and died. The remaining trio struggled on, and it was said of their medical work:

> [t]he dispensary, besides exerting a powerful influence in giving them favor in the sight of the people, was made a means of disseminating gospel truth. A Chinese tract, directing the reader to the 'True Physician,' was given to every patient; and for three or four years from 2,000 to 3,000 cases were treated annually. The way of life must have been made known very widely by this instrumentality.[4]

The CMS workers in Fuzhou were greatly encouraged when the first two Chinese converts, Huang Qiude (Fuzhou dialect: Wong Kiu-Taik) and Deng Danbin (Tang Tang-Pieng), were baptized. The first Evangelical church in Fuzhou was established near the south wall in 1856.

Just as it appeared the CMS work was making progress, William Welton's health broke down. He returned to England and died in March 1857, just prior to his fiftieth birthday. Further heartbreak occurred a few months later when Francis McCaw contracted a fever and perished, only 26 months after he arrived in Fujian. The surviving missionaries soldiered on in great difficulty, shocked by the frequent deaths of their colleagues.

Meanwhile, 160 miles (257 km) further south in Xiamen, a woman named Wang Yixi (Hokkien: Un Hese), became the first known female convert in Fujian in March 1855. When news spread that Wang had been baptized and had joined the ranks of the despised "foreign devils," a huge backlash occurred in the community. It was bad enough that a small number of men had embraced Christianity, but now that the first woman had succumbed too, it was feared that soon the "Jesus doctrine" would spread like a virus and affect everyone.[5]

Huang Qiude

A crucial early church leader in the capital city was Huang Qiude (Fuzhou dialect: Wong Kiu-Taik), who was employed as a landscape painter when a close friend, Hu Nanmi, converted to Christ and joined the Methodist church in the city. Huang's testimony is worth retelling here:

> After much prayer and frequent earnest entreaties, Hu persuaded Huang to read the Scriptures and attend the public services; and very soon the result was manifest. Huang's mother, who was tenderly attached to her son, was warned that he was in danger and ought to be looked after. "What is wrong?" she exclaimed. "My son has always been industrious and dutiful. What has happened?"
>
> "He attends the foreign church." "Impossible," cried the old lady. "It cannot be that my son would do such a thing." On questioning him, however, she found, to her horror, that it was only too true.
>
> She kept him closely confined to the house and tried in every way to shake his determination by weeping, scolding, and

1850s

Huang Qiude, a key early church leader in Fujian.

threatening by turns. It was all to no purpose and her wrath was intensified by continually hearing him praying, "Lord, bless my mother!" and invoking the hated Name of Jesus.

"Mother," said Huang, "I cannot stop praying." "Leave the house, then," she exclaimed. "I disown you forever as my child,

> and when I die, do not dare to join with the family in celebrating my funeral." ...
>
> Huang went and lived with his friend Hu and rapidly grew in knowledge and grace. One day his mother sent to bid him come to her. He could only think it was a plot to seize and kill him, but after a painful mental struggle, he went, and his mother asked if he was still determined to be a Christian. "Mother," he said, fully expecting some sudden assault, "I am." "Then," said she, "if you will not change your mind, I shall change mine. You may be a Christian, and you may live at home."[6]

Overwhelmed with joy, the 23-year-old Huang fell to his knees and thanked God. He was baptized a few weeks later. At his baptism he took the name Qiude, meaning "Seeker of Virtue."

For some time, Huang Qiude continued to work as a painter, but eventually he served as an effective evangelist with the American Mission. In 1870 he became the first ordained Chinese Anglican minister in Fujian and proved brilliant at debating the scholars and presenting a clear message of the merits of Jesus Christ. Tragically, he died in 1895 after falling off a ladder and fracturing his skull. It was said of Huang,

> Hundreds came regularly to hear him. . . . He was deeply acquainted with the Confucian learning and was able to meet and expose the arguments of both Daoists and Buddhists with telling power, combined with Christian meekness and tact. He was a perfect gentleman in his bearing and a true Christian in his character.[7]

Xi Da, the Pirate Fighter

Another jewel in God's crown during the early decades of the Evangelical enterprise in Fujian was a much loved former soldier named Xi Da (Hokkien: Sok Tai).

1850s

A sketch of Xi Da.

In his vocation, Xi was charged with stopping the many pirate ships that wreaked destruction along the Fujian coast and across the Taiwan Strait. During one battle he was shot in the eye, which led him to seek treatment at the mission hospital in Xiamen.

Although the operation was successful, he permanently lost his sight in that eye and was plunged into despair to the point of wanting to commit suicide. While convalescing in the hospital, Xi attended the daily chapel meetings where he heard the gospel for the first time. Until that point, he had considered Christianity a cursed tool of imperialism and had wanted nothing to do with it.

When Xi bowed his knee to Jesus and committed his life to follow the Lamb of God, others advised him to keep his faith secret so he could retain his job as a soldier. Xi Da, though, "had found a great faith that had uplifted his whole life, and it was not a thing to be hidden away or to be ashamed of."[8]

1850s

Sometime later, several soldiers from Xi's regiment decided to enter a chapel to mock the Christians during a Sunday service. They were shocked when their own leader stood up and shared his testimony, and they hurried back to the camp to report the incident to the colonel.

From that time on, Xi Da's position became untenable. The military commanders could find nothing in his character to justify dismissing him, so they sought to hasten his death by sending him on a dangerous mission with no backup against the most murderous pirate fleet. As his ship drew alongside the main pirate ship, Xi saw that

> [h]er decks were crowded with half-naked men, bloodthirsty and savage-looking, and on whose faces murder was written large and plain.... To his horror, he found the support ships were being kept back purposely, so that he would have to bear the brunt of the coming fight all by himself.

Descending quickly into his cabin, he knelt down, and lifting up his eyes to heaven, he said, "Oh God, the enemy is behind

A sketch of the missionary graveyard in Fuzhou, 1858.

me, and the enemy is in front of me. Deliver me this day, for Christ's sake."[9]

God answered His servant's prayer, and a great deliverance occurred when many of the pirates panicked and jumped into the sea, where they drowned. Despite this victory, Xi knew he must leave the military. He exchanged pirate-hunting for soul-winning, and for years the powerfully built war hero preached the gospel to thousands of people in the busiest part of Xiamen.

The attrition rate in the early years of Evangelical work in Fuzhou was extraordinarily high. One account from 1858 summarized the difficulties missionaries had experienced since the first missionary had arrived just 12 years earlier, as they struggled to establish a beachhead for the gospel in the city:

> Their lives were short, yet long enough to exhibit bright examples of the power of Divine grace, and to prove the depth, strength, and maturity of their Christian character and experience. They finished their course with joy, none regretting their consecration to the work of missions, and each leaving some inspiring sentiment to encourage the church, and to urge others to enter their labors.
>
> Such has been the force that has been sent into this great heathen city since its first occupancy in 1846. In all, 36 male and female missionaries have come, of whom 10 have died, 13 have been compelled to retire by failing health and other causes, and 13 still remain connected with the various missions.[10]

1860s

At the dawn of the new decade, the Evangelical missionaries in Fujian were feeling more encouraged as they saw an increase in the number of conversions. Gifted Chinese Christian leaders began to lead the church and carry the gospel among their communities.

The work of the Dutch Reformed Mission proved effective in Xiamen and surrounding districts, with 292 church members counted in 1861.[1] The following year, the Reformed Mission and the English Presbyterians published a combined report from Xiamen that listed 407 believers in five churches under their care.[2]

Having had a 500 year head start before the first Evangelical arrived in the province, the Catholics continued to dominate the Christian landscape in Fujian, with one study estimating there were 30,000 Catholic believers throughout Fujian in 1866,[3] compared to just a few thousand Evangelicals.

George Smith

Although an indigenous Chinese church had emerged in Fujian by the late 1850s, the Church Missionary Society's work in Fuzhou City was in tatters. George Smith, who arrived in 1858, was the only CMS worker remaining in the province at the start of the 1860s. Unable to speak the local dialect, Smith was alone for his first year among the

George Smith

hundreds of thousands of lost people in the city. The CMS had been working in Fujian for more than a decade but had no fruit to show, lamenting that all their efforts had left them "without one single conversion or prospect of such a thing."[4]

A motion was put forward to close the CMS mission and send new recruits to other parts of China. It was obvious, the leaders of the home board argued, that God was not with them and the work in Fuzhou would be better left to others to carry on. Decades later, John Wolfe summarized the desperation felt at the time:

> The missionaries had labored there without a single convert being brought to Christ. They went there, they labored, they prayed, and they shed bitter tears. Some of them during that time died and were buried there, without a single shadow of a sign that any influence whatever had been brought to bear upon the people of that great city.
>
> The friends at home got discouraged and wished to give up the Fujian mission, but one solitary missionary [George Smith] said, "You may give up the mission, and you may sell off the premises, but I am determined to stay here as long as I live."[5]

Smith's heroic stand of faith was accepted by the CMS board, and they agreed to keep the mission open for an undetermined period.

Remarkably, the Church Missionary Society rose from the brink of defeat to become the most successful mission in Fujian, with thousands of Chinese Christians in dozens of churches. None of it would have occurred without the defiant stand taken by George Smith, who refused to give up in the face of overwhelming odds.

By 1863, the prospects of the CMS had markedly brightened. A small group of believers had been formed, and that year saw 13 baptisms and another five converts waiting their turn. The missionaries exulted, "Crowds of attentive listeners attended the services. Books and tracts in large numbers were eagerly purchased, so much so that free distribution was suspended. The colporteurs sent to the surrounding villages met with a most encouraging reception."[6]

The breakthrough the CMS had prayed and labored for so long was finally taking place, and the missionaries were deeply encouraged, thinking the worst was behind them. Then, in October 1863, disaster struck when George Smith suddenly died. Even though his length of service was brief, Smith's faith and determination proved to be a watershed in the history of Christianity, not only in Fuzhou but throughout the whole province.

Ye Hanzhang

Ye Hanzhang

The southern city of Xiamen quickly emerged as the engine room for Evangelical Christianity in Fujian, with a succession of dedicated church leaders coming from the city and its environs.

Ye Hanzhang (Hokkien: Iap Han-Cheong) was ordained to the ministry in March 1864, at the age of 32, and he went on to give more than 40 years of sterling service and wise leadership to the body of Christ in the Xiamen region.

As a young boy, Ye had worked at a shop next to the home of Dutch-American missionary John Van Nest Talmage, who was one of the most effective nineteenth century missionaries in Fujian. Ye often slipped away to hear Talmage preach, and the seed that was planted in his heart later helped him repent of his sins and take a firm stand for Christ.

When news emerged that Ye had become a Christian, his family strongly opposed him and did all they could to win him back to the beliefs of his ancestors.

He refused to give in, however. When a riot erupted in 1850, the Ye family's property was destroyed, and they were left homeless and destitute. Talmage took them into his home, providing food and daily necessities free of charge. This act of kindness broke all resistance to the gospel, and Ye's parents also repented and placed their trust in Jesus Christ.

For 18 years, Ye Hanzhang pastored the Zhushu Church in Xiamen, wholly supported by the local believers and not by any mission funds.

In 1883, the second phase of Ye's ministry commenced when he accepted a call to take the gospel to the town of Xiaoxi, 70 miles (113 km) southwest of Xiamen. Ye oversaw a rapid expansion of the work there, with one source saying, "He proved even more successful in this parish than in his former one. From one organization it grew to four; from four church buildings to 12; and a membership of 121 to 332, not considering the hundreds of inquirers and adherents."[7]

Once, while he was teaching on the Beatitudes, a man suddenly rushed forward and slapped Ye hard on the cheek, challenging him to turn the other cheek also. Without hesitation, the man of God turned his face and allowed the assailant to slap him again. The congregation was in an uproar and tried to seize the man, but Ye remained completely calm and told them to let him go, satisfied that the believers had received a sermon illustration they would never forget.

Ye's decades of faithful service were not without severe testing and bitter experiences. Three of his sons and two daughters died before reaching adulthood, and he struggled with loneliness after his beloved wife passed away in 1899.

Ye Hanzhang died in 1912 at the age of 80, but his legacy endures. Today, this humble man of God has descendants from the third to the seventh generation living around the world in the United States, Canada, the Philippines, Australia, and Sweden.

Xie Xi'en

One of the key early Evangelical church leaders in Fujian was Xie Xi'en (Fuzhou dialect: Sia Sek Ong).

Born in 1839, Xie was teaching in his village school when he first encountered Christianity. Gradually convinced of the truth, he renounced the idolatry and ancestor worship of his community. His stance was sorely tested when his little son fell sick, and all his relatives came to plead with Xie to abandon his faith. He refused and later reflected on that time:

> In this affliction I discovered that I had the root of the Truth in my heart. . . . The more they tried to persuade me, the more my heart was fixed. When the child finally died, they heaped reproach upon me for doubting the power and efficacy of the idols. I heard all their severe words patiently and gained the victory.

1860s

Xie Xi'en

> I decided to forsake all the cherished joys of this world. . . . I knelt, confessed my sins, and prayed. . . . Some hours later, I was walking to and fro when a voice seemed to say to me, "The Lord has heard your prayers and forgiven your sins." It seemed to be above me, at my side, and within me. My sorrow disappeared and peace and joy unspeakable filled my soul.[8]

Xie went on to become a pillar in the house of God. For many years he provided clear and godly leadership, and the family of believers continued to grow in grace and in number.

Nathan and Sarah Sites

Nathan and Sarah Sites

A native of the US state of Ohio, Nathan Sites (whose Chinese name was Xue Cheng'en, meaning "inheritor of grace") and his wife, Sarah, served as Methodist Episcopal missionaries in Fujian for 34 years, from their arrival in 1861 to the time of Nathan's death in 1895.

In the 1860s, much missionary activity was learned by trial and error. This led to some comical situations, including an incident in 1866 when Sites went to preach the gospel in Lujiao village, dressed all in white and with a white pith helmet on his head.

In Chinese culture, white is associated with death and mourning and is the predominant color worn at funerals. The people of Lujiao ran from Sites, thinking he was a ghost. One source noted, "To the villagers the missionary in his pith helmet may have resembled a demon spirit, who was always pictured dressed in white and wearing a conical white hat."[9]

After terrifying the people of Lujiao, Sites and a colleague traveled to the nearby village of Banzhong, where they preached on a street corner. A local scholar took offence at the foreigner's message, rapping Sites on the head with his wooden pipe and asking, "Who are you that you dare to make yourself equal to Confucius?"

The crowd stood back to witness the confrontation and were amazed when Sites apologized in a gentle voice saying, "'Please forgive me if I have spoken wrongly.' His humble attitude astonished the onlookers, and word about the visitors spread."[10]

Left for Dead

The Sites' time in Fujian was divided between the capital city, Fuzhou, and the interior city of Nanping, 113 miles (184 km) up the Min River. Periodically, Nathan faced severe trials, the worst when he was brutally beaten by a mob while constructing a church building in Nanping. In a book written by Sarah 17 years after her husband's death, she recalled the incident:

> The literary guild of the city, with the approval and sympathy of the prefect and other officials, had sworn to abuse and put out of the city any foreign missionary who came preaching the "Jesus doctrine." A pre-concerted and carefully organized plan was now afoot to bring a band of notorious assassins from an adjoining town to carry out their purpose.
>
> Nathan was struck over the head, in the face, and about the body. One fiend with a sharp, two-pronged, hardwood fork, thrust him in the face, aiming to put out his eyes. He cut a cruel gash under each eye, and at this time Mr. Sites thought his eyes were indeed out. Though blinded by the stunning blows and the blood, he broke out of the house and through the crowd for some distance, when he was surrounded and lifted off his feet and thrown upon his face to the pavement. His boots were pulled off and his feet tied with a rope.
>
> Now he was powerless, lying with his face towards the stone pavement. Moving his face a mere few inches out of the pool of blood which had flowed from the wounds below his eyes, he felt

an assurance that God had not forsaken him, while every breath was a silent prayer that deliverance might come.[11]

God spared the life of Nathan Sites that day, but the assault left him with deep scars on his face for the rest of his life. He and Sarah were also called to bear other scars. In those days, missionaries customarily sent their children back to their home country when it was time for them to gain an education. However, the Sites couldn't bear the thought of being separated from their daughter, Belle, so they had delayed for years their return to America for a furlough.

Finally, Belle moved to the United States when she was 18, but a short time later, a heartbreaking telegram reached Nathan and Sarah in Fujian, informing them that their beloved daughter had suddenly died. Feeling isolated on the other side of the world, Nathan and Sarah grieved deeply and prayed for the comfort of the Holy Spirit. Before long they resumed their work, albeit with heavy hearts.

Pretty Near Heaven

By 1895, Nathan and Sarah Sites were again living in Fuzhou, where they faithfully shared Jesus Christ with everyone they met. As the work grew, many of society's most desperate people encountered the gospel. One day a notorious opium dealer, Lau, came storming up to the gate of the mission compound clutching a container of poison, intending to pour it into the Christians' newly dug well.

Lau loudly demanded to be let in, but the Chinese believers barricaded the gate. Nathan saw an opportunity to display the love of God to a sinner, and he opened the gate, put his arm around the angry man, and invited him inside for tea and cake. Several visits later, Lau surrendered his life to Jesus Christ and was completely set free from his drug addiction. From that time on,

> [t]here arose a saying among the natives that all Dr. Sites had to do was to put his arm over a man's shoulder and that man would become a Christian.... After years of faithful discipleship, Lau was asked to explain his salvation. "Man cannot save man," he answered, "but that man walked daily with God and through him came the power of God to me."[12]

The mission's emphasis on reaching the lowest rung of society caused explosive growth, and church membership increased seven-fold in two years. One Sunday, after listening to hours of testimony from former drug dealers, prostitutes, and gamblers, Sites remarked, "Pretty near heaven this, isn't it?"

That evening, after returning home, Nathan developed a fever. When no improvement had occurred for two days, the local Christians lovingly carried him down to the river and placed him on a boat to take him to the city hospital. As the believers prayed for him, Sites raised his hand and blessed them. It was his final act of ministry in Fujian. The next morning the 64-year-old pioneer was taken to his heavenly home after 34 years of faithful service in the province.

More than 500 Christians, all dressed in white, attended the funeral service at the Fuzhou cemetery, where Sites was laid to rest alongside many other missionaries who had invested their lives sharing the good news of Jesus with the people of Fujian.

An intriguing story later emerged of a Chinese preacher in another district, who died two days after Sites. News of the missionary's passing had not yet reached the district, but as the preacher lay in a semiconscious state he suddenly sat upright,

> clapped his hands, and looking radiantly happy, he said to the sorrowing friends who stood about him, "Do not mourn for me. I have seen into heaven. I came near the gate and saw within it a

vast company, all clothed in white. The first one I recognized was Teacher Sites. He stepped from among the crowd and grasped both my hands, exclaiming, 'Oh, my brother, I am glad you have come.' Then he led me just inside the gates of that beautiful city; but I came back only to tell you what I have seen and to say goodbye."[13]

After passing through a period of grief for her departed soulmate, Sarah Sites continued to serve God through her gifted writing. She died in 1912 after completing a book about her husband's life and ministry.

John Wolfe — "The Fujian Moses"

John Wolfe

After a succession of missionaries in Fujian's capital city died or were forced to leave the field throughout the 1850s, the progress of the gospel stalled. Few residents of the city had received a clear presentation of the claims of Christ.

Right at the point when the Church Missionary Society was considering throwing in the towel in Fujian and focusing their attention on other parts of China, God sent an Irishman who would become His instrument to propel the gospel forward not only in Fuzhou but throughout the entire province.

Born in County Cork, the 30-year-old John Wolfe arrived in Fuzhou in May 1862 to commence a career of sterling service for Christ. Almost as if to make up for all the short-lived workers whose bodies lay in the city graveyard, the Holy Spirit equipped and protected Wolfe for a great length of time. When he was

John Wolfe — "The Fujian Moses"

finally laid to rest in Fuzhou at the age of 83, he had spent a remarkable 53 years of his life serving God in Fujian.

Wolfe came to be so highly regarded by Chinese believers that they nicknamed him "The Fujian Moses" as a mark of deep respect and because of his long beard, which they supposed made him similar to Moses in appearance. By the end of his long career, Wolfe had been appointed archdeacon of Fuzhou and vice president of the CMS. Decades later, one source described Wolfe as "the chief instrument in the remarkable ingathering in Fujian Province."[1]

After commencing work under the leadership of George Smith, Wolfe's plans took a sudden detour when Smith died the following year. Wolfe was suddenly thrust into leading the mission.

Wolfe fell gravely ill after a riot in 1864 left several Chinese believers severely injured and the CMA chapel, mission school, and dwellings were destroyed. He was sent to Hong Kong for treatment, and gradually recovered. Far from destroying the work of the gospel, Wolfe found that the anti-Christian riots had performed

> a real service to the work by bringing Christianity prominently before people of all classes. Men who had hitherto not known—or not noticed—what was going on, began to inquire what this new doctrine really was. Crowds flocked to the rebuilt chapels; false and gross reports which had been circulated were discredited; the notion that Christians could only be abhorred by all right-thinking folk for their vile and wicked lives was corrected . . . and one of the converts said, "It is much easier to be a Christian now than it was 12 months ago before the riots."[2]

Two additional key events took place in Wolfe's life in 1864. While in Hong Kong he married Mary Ann Maclehose, and in their first ten years together they had six children (three boys and three girls). All three girls later served Christ as missionaries in Fujian.

In November 1864, the work in Fuzhou was further strengthened by the arrival of missionary Arthur Cribb. He and Wolfe became close co-workers, forging a fruitful and long-lasting partnership for the gospel.

By 1867 the number of Chinese converts in the city had grown to 50, and for the first time the good news was being spread in the villages surrounding Fuzhou. Wolfe was a hard worker who found it difficult to slow down, but in 1869 his health broke down, compelling him to return to Ireland for two and a half years.

The Wolfe family returned to Fujian in December 1872, finding the sea journey to China was weeks shorter than before due to the opening of the Suez Canal. With John's health greatly improved, he immediately set out on an extensive journey throughout the province to check on the work that had taken place during his absence.

At almost every location he visited on his 338 mile (548 km) trip, Wolfe was greatly encouraged and reported, "More than 150 baptisms were registered in the interval; the total number of adherents of the church, including candidates for baptism, rose from 360 to 800 and that of the communicants—the best index of spiritual life—from 150 to 280."[3]

Revival in Luoyuan

One of the engine rooms of Evangelical progress in Fujian was the sleepy town of Luoyuan, located 43 miles (70 km) north of Fuzhou City. Nestled in a deep valley surrounded by high mountains and hemmed in by the sea, the people of Luoyuan first heard the gospel when Wolfe and a Chinese evangelist visited in November 1865. The first baptism took place the following year, and soon a trickle of men and women were pressing into the kingdom of God.

One of the wealthiest merchants in the town was a man named Xie. His only son, Song, was a notorious evildoer who was despised by the townspeople. He had brought such disgrace to the family name that Xie was at the point of disinheriting his son. One day, "by chance," Song walked by the chapel as a local evangelist was preaching. He had never heard the gospel before, but

> [t]hen and there the truth laid hold of his heart, and he gave up his sins forthwith and yielded himself to the Redeemer, of whose love and power he had heard. His neighbors would not appreciate the inward spiritual change, but they did see at once the difference in his outward life. It became a common subject of speculation among them, and it brought great numbers to inquire and to buy tracts and books. The old father could not at first believe in the reality of the reformation, and . . . although himself a zealous idol-worshipper, he could not oppose his son adopting a religion which had worked in him such a change. The son, however, became intensely anxious for the salvation of his father.[4]

On one of John Wolfe's visits to Luoyuan, Song came to his room in deep distress. Falling on his knees next to the missionary's bed, he cried out in prayer for his elderly father's conversion. Song refused to be baptized until his father became a believer, saying they must enter God's kingdom together.

With some difficulty he convinced his father to come and meet Wolfe, who wrote,

> I found him very dark and ignorant, but not at all disposed to prevent his son becoming a Christian, and at the end of a long conversation I could only elicit from him the old story, "The doctrine is very good, but it will not do for me; I will do what my fathers did before me."
>
> They both returned home, however, and about two hours later the son returned almost breathless with joy and informed us

that his father had decided to be a Christian. The incense vendor had been round to the shop as usual with his wares to sell for the approaching festival, but his father refused to buy any and sent him away, saying, "I have decided to worship no more idols; I want no more of such vain and foolish things. I have determined to become a Christian and worship the true God."

Of course, we were all delighted and returned hearty thanks to God on his behalf. The old man was present at evening prayers, and at the baptism, and he then remained the entire evening talking about religion.... The report that this old man believed spread like wildfire, and scores came to the chapel inquiring for books.[5]

The Holy Spirit transformed both father and son so powerfully that they became men of strong faith and prayer. Xie displayed such spiritual growth that within six months he was exhorting others to follow Christ wholeheartedly as he taught the Scriptures to them.

Through instruments like Xie, Song, and others, the fire of the Holy Spirit spread from Luoyuan and touched many villages throughout the region. This letter from Wolfe introduced Christians around the world to the movement:

The work has grown to an extent which has exceeded my most sanguine expectations. The Lord has done great things for us, whereof we are glad. There appears to be quite a movement towards Christianity in this district. I was almost overpowered on Sunday to witness the large number who came asking for admission into the church of God.

This movement extends over a wide extent of country and, without any apparent immediate cause, was simultaneous in places and villages over 10 miles (16 km) apart. The evangelist at the station has not been able to leave the chapel for months because of the flow of inquirers constantly pouring in to learn about the salvation of their souls.

John Wolfe — "The Fujian Moses"

There were about 90 candidates on the books, besides a large number who were earnestly seeking and receiving instruction. I at once decided to visit all the candidates at their own houses, and thus be better able to judge their state and fitness to be received into the church. . . . I was much interested and greatly encouraged by these few days' visiting. I found a deep spirit of earnestness pervading the minds of these people. I found no traces of idolatry in their houses. I found the prayer book and hymn book well read and their little children able to repeat many of the hymns and prayers.

The Bible was in every house, and though most of them could not read it, all endeavored to make as much use of it as they could. Their little ones of about four years old were taught to pray, and I have heard the children of this age and over talk of Jesus, and of God, and of prayer, as subjects with which they seemed familiar. They could tell you that Jesus was the Savior of the world, that He loved them, and that God was the Great Being who made the world and everything, and that it was wrong to worship idols.[6]

With hundreds of people converting to Christ and abandoning their old way of life, it was not long before trouble arose in the Luoyuan area. In 1874, all fury broke loose when scholars and soldiers mobilized to try to put a stop to the spread of the "foreign religion." Chapels and Christian homes were ransacked, and believers suffered severe beatings. In a summary of the persecution it was noted,

Some were beaten, some robbed, and some dragged before the magistrates upon false charges and compelled to purchase their liberty by heavy payments. One man had a dying thief laid at his door by the district policeman, who then accused him of murder. Another was kept in prison for many months and died there.

It seemed like a return of apostolic days to meet these fine sturdy old Christians, who have suffered the loss of all and endured stripes and imprisonment for the Savior's sake in the course of the last six or seven years—manly men, too, with glistening eyes as they told of a Savior ever present in their hours of distress.[7]

God's people in Luoyuan survived the onslaught, and gradually the church regained lost ground. By 1880 there were 280 believers in the city, 223 of whom had been baptized.[8]

From the beginning, the seed of the gospel found fertile soil in Luoyuan, and the fame of Jesus Christ has continued to expand until the present time, with an estimated 35,000 Christians in Luoyuan County today out of a population of 200,000 people.[9]

As revival fires continued to blaze across northern and central Fujian, John Wolfe was amazed, as the results were far greater than he had ever imagined. This 1880 summary included figures just from the work of the Church Missionary Society:

> Year by year the work of the Lord has prospered in the hands of our missionary brethren. . . . The number of Christian adherents has steadily risen from 1,648 in 1876, to 2,323 in 1877, to about 3,000 in 1878 and 1879, and to 3,556 at the close of 1880, the total having more than doubled in four years, notwithstanding many falling away and a good many deaths.[10]

The She People

Although approximately 700,000 She (pronounced "Sher") people are the largest ethnic minority group in Fujian, they rarely feature in Christian accounts of work in the province, and they remain a largely unreached people group today. For centuries the She have chiefly dwelt in the mountains, with a language and set of customs unique to themselves.

The She worship a host of deities and spirits, including Pan Hu, the dog-king they believe was the forefather of their race. Until recently, the She people reportedly "worshipped the totem of this legendary animal and held a large festival in its honor every three years."[11]

John Wolfe — "The Fujian Moses"

As with many firsts in Christian work in Fujian, the first Evangelical to share the gospel with the She people was John Wolfe in 1866, when he visited the town of Fuding in northeast Fujian, which serves as a gateway to the She community.

Wolfe expressed optimism that a good work would unfold among the She people, but a decade passed until the first two She men were baptized. One of the men died soon after, and many She people attributed his sudden demise to the fact he had embraced the foreign religion. Medical mission work was undertaken in the area, and the dam finally burst in the early twentieth century, "with 30 of 33 families living in Buangsang village resolving to give up their idols and worship the one true God. By the end of 1903, Fuding boasted a church membership of 456 believers."[12]

The breakthrough among the She, both then and now, occurred as part of the general growth of the Chinese churches in the districts they inhabit, rather than as a result of targeted outreach to the She people. For generations the She have been in a process of assimilation into Han Chinese culture and language.

John Wolfe (back, center) and a group of Chinese pastors in 1894.

John Wolfe — "The Fujian Moses"

John and Mary Ann Wolfe remained in Fuzhou for the rest of their lives. When Mary Ann went to her eternal reward in December 1913, she had been married to John for 49 years, all of which had been spent serving God together in Fujian.

Almost exactly two years later, "The Fujian Moses" also fell asleep in the Lord, aged 83. His body was laid to rest next to his beloved wife in the Fuzhou cemetery.

After John Wolfe's death, Chinese and European church leaders decided to commemorate his life by building a cathedral in his memory, and in 1927 the Christ Church Cathedral (Cangxia Church) was opened in Fuzhou. He is still fondly remembered by many Christians throughout the province today.

1870s

The 1870s arrived with the Catholic Church still dominating the Christian landscape in Fujian, especially in the north of the province. One source estimated there were 30,000 Catholics in Fujian in 1873.[1]

By comparison, only two Evangelical mission agencies were laboring in Fujian at the start of the decade, with the following statistics:

Evangelical Mission Statistics For Fujian, 1870[2]

Mission	Baptized	Adherents	Schools	Students
Church Missionary Society	271	633	2	65
Methodist Episcopal Church	931	2,139	6	129
Totals	**1,202**	**2,772**	**8**	**194**

A time of intense persecution for Christians in Fujian suddenly erupted in 1871, as a plot designed to destroy all missionary work in South China was launched. Known as the Shan Xinfan plot, riots broke out in July 1871 after

> [t]housands of inflammatory [anti-Christian] placards appeared, scattered in every direction.... Under this persecution, the converts gave unmistakable evidence of the grace of God that was in them. The Christians were driven from their homes and robbed of clothes, money, and property, yet not one denied the faith.[3]

One widow, who had only placed her trust in Jesus two years earlier, was targeted by the rioters, but she refused to be

Catholic believers kneeling in prayer in the church courtyard.

intimidated. When they threatened to destroy her house if she didn't renounce Christianity, the elderly woman held her Bible aloft and boldly declared, "This Book teaches us the religion which foreigners believe; that same religion I believe. . . . Sooner than give up the religion of Christ, I would cheerfully permit the officers to behead me."[4]

Trouble at Zhedu

The Church Missionary Society first opened a station in the town of Zhedu in 1875. From the start, the Chinese believers there suffered a great deal of opposition from the locals, who believed that Christianity upset the spirits they and their ancestors had served for centuries.

In January 1876, a leading woman in the community died, and the town leaders blamed the Christians for upsetting the spiritual harmony. They seized the mission chapel and turned it into an idol hall, hoping that the angry spirits would be placated by being worshipped inside the church building. When the Christians resisted, they were badly beaten and their Bibles and other books were burned. A short time later, when another person died of fever, the community leaders

> raised the cry that the Christians were the cause of the fever and that the idols were angry. One Sunday morning, as the Christians were quietly engaged in worship, the leading gentry, with the constable beating a gong and followed by a mob, proceeded to the chapel, dragged the Christians away, and beat them most violently. They threatened to kill them unless they renounced their faith and returned to the worship of idols.[5]

Not only did the believers give no thought to the demands that they recant, they showed faith and courage by returning to the chapel the very same afternoon, where they continued to worship God. This act was perceived as a direct provocation by the authorities, who raced to the chapel and dragged each believer from the building, beating them brutally. During the attack one man, Ling Zhe'ang, was beaten to death.

Ling's relatives demanded the magistrate come to the village to examine the body and open a murder investigation. The law required him to come immediately, but he purposely delayed his visit, so that by the time he arrived five days later, Ling's body had decomposed. The magistrate took one look at the corpse and announced it was clear that Ling had committed suicide by drinking poison.

Lin Jiniang — A Hand-Picked Servant of the Lord

One of the earliest and most loved Chinese Christian women in Fuzhou was Lin Jiniang (Fuzhou dialect: Chitnio Ling), whose unique testimony was a blessing to countless women in the province.

1870s

Lin Jiniang (Chitnio Ling), who was raised in Singapore and sent to Fujian in God's service.

Born in Singapore to a family that had never heard the gospel, Lin heard about the Chinese Girls' School (now St. Margaret's School), but when she asked her father if she could attend he flew into a rage, claiming that Christians were evil-doers and the only way she would ever attend the school was if he died and could not stop her. Shockingly, within two months both of Lin's parents had perished, and the orphaned girl was accepted by the matron of the school.

1870s

The Chinese Girls' School had been founded decades earlier, when Maria Dyer[6] visited Singapore on her way to China in the early 1840s. Walking along the streets, she was horrified to see a pitiful group of young girls auctioned as slaves for the wealthy people of the city. Dyer was determined to help, and in 1842 she started a facility to care for homeless girls, which became the first and only girls' school in Singapore for decades.

The school accepted the most destitute girls in Singapore. Many were orphans who had been abused, while others had been abandoned or sold into slavery. When Lin arrived at the school, Sophia Cooke was in charge. Hailing from the English town of Norfolk, Cooke served 42 years at the school, and such was her influence that it came to be popularly known as "Miss Cooke's School."

In 1877, after some months at school, the truth of the gospel touched 12-year-old Lin Jiniang's heart, and she believed in Jesus Christ and asked to be baptized. When her extended family heard of her conversion, her aunt threw herself to the ground in a fit of rage and told Lin that her brother would kill her if she went ahead with the baptism. When her family realized she could not be persuaded to change her mind, they cursed and denounced her. The young girl recalled,

> Some of them begged me with their eyes full of tears. . . . They came again and again to the school, day by day, so many times, till they got so tired of me and quite vexed, and never would come to see me again. My aunt was so sad that she cried until one of her eyes became quite blind. . . . My brother, friends, and relations said they would have nothing to do with me anymore.[7]

Several years later, three Western missionaries from Fujian visited Singapore and spoke to the girls, pleading with them to consider becoming missionaries to the province, where few people had ever heard the name of Jesus Christ. Lin's heart was touched, and she told God she was willing to surrender and go to China if that was His will.

Over time, the number of students at the school greatly increased and its good reputation spread. Girls were well-educated, taught to read Chinese and speak English, and were trained in household chores such as how to sew and cook. At the same time, young men in faraway Fujian Province were turning to Christ, but no suitable wives could be found for them. The missionaries asked the school if they would consider sending some of their best young women from Singapore to Fujian to marry some of the young Christian men.

Lin was one of the first four women sent to Fujian in 1888, in a journey that took five weeks by ship. She first met her husband at the wedding ceremony. Her husband, Ling, was considered one of the finest young Christian men in the province. He took his bride to Jian'ou in remote north-central Fujian, but their marriage was short-lived.

Although it produced a little son, the union had lasted just two years when Ling and two other evangelists were captured and barbarically tortured by an infuriated mob. Ling never recovered from his injuries, and soon afterward, as his grieving wife put it, "He went to glory in heaven and won the Crown of Life."[8]

Few of the Christians in Jian'ou today know about the sacrifice that Ling made so long ago, but his death was not in vain. Today, approximately 60,000 of the 450,000 residents of Jian'ou profess Jesus Christ as Lord and Savior.[9]

Now a widowed single mother in nineteenth century China, Lin Jiniang did not succumb to anxiety, but rededicated her life to the Lord and continued to serve Him. She was appointed to lead the Church Missionary Society's school for women at Fuzhou, where the Chinese girls deeply respected her. New missionary recruits also found her advice and help invaluable when they arrived in China, for Lin was uniquely able to straddle both the

Chinese and Western cultures, and she spoke both Chinese and English fluently.

In 1895, Lin wrote a letter to friends in England, saying, "I know you are all praying for China, but please pray specifically for Fuzhou City. Though the walls are great, and the people are strong, we have a King who is stronger than they. He can break down these walls. We must have great faith, for there is nothing too hard for Him."[10]

Lin added to her family by adopting a little girl, and she often took her son and daughter with her to preach the gospel in the suburbs and villages surrounding Fuzhou. Lin would play an accordion, which attracted a crowd of amazed onlookers, and then the children would sing.

Lin Jiniang, the orphan who was rejected by her family, went on to become a key figure in the Fuzhou Christian community. By trusting in God alone, she overcame countless persecutions and trials and strengthened the faith of countless women over a 30 year period.

The three other girls who had traveled from Singapore with Lin had differing experiences. Two were heavily persecuted and died due to the stress of their lives in Fujian, while the third

The students and staff of the women's Bible school at Fuzhou. Lin is in the middle.

Singapore girl, Lie En (Grace Lie), went with her husband to Korea, where she is believed to be the first foreign missionary to take the gospel to the women of that country.

The Fire Spreads

In 1864 the good news of Jesus Christ was first proclaimed in the town of Lianjiang, 30 miles (49 km) northeast of Fuzhou, and by 1871 a total of 34 adults and 18 children were listed as baptized church members. When John Wolfe visited in the mid-1870s, the work had regressed: "He found the church entirely scattered—some dead, others expelled, others again standing aloof. . . . It was a heavy trial of faith to have to begin the work again almost anew."[11]

Undeterred, the great Irish missionary refocused his efforts and things quickly turned around in Lianjiang. In 1876 he wrote, "The work has taken a fresh start. Several of the old converts have returned and three new ones have been baptized."[12]

The leadership of the Lianjiang church was handed to a Bible teacher named Hu Waiying and his wife Artu, who had received a Christian education in Singapore. They did such a good job that by 1881 it was reported, "There have been 20 baptisms in the city in the last two years. Seven towns and villages in the district have been occupied, and the number of Christian adherents has risen to 141."[13]

The early believers at Lianjiang did well not to give up after the prospects looked grim for the gospel there, and today the county boasts more than 150,000 Christians,[14] with the Three-Self Church reporting in 2009 "[a]t least 50,000 adults, or 10 percent of the total population are registered Christians."[15]

Just 15 miles (24 km) north of Lianjiang, separated by a range of hills, sits the town of Danyang. John Wolfe first established a base there in 1867, and a few months later he joyfully reported,

> The interest of the people in the Word of God is remarkable. Our evangelist complains that he has no time to himself for private reading or improvement from the continual flow of inquirers and learners. Several placed themselves under regular instruction, gave up idolatry, and observed the Lord's Day. In October the first baptism took place.[16]

The first convert at Danyang was a prominent man of the town, who believed the gospel as soon as he heard it. He soon attracted others to the faith, starting with his own family members. In March 1868, "[t]wo of his sons and four of his grandchildren were baptized, and in September ten other persons, all through his instrumentality, notwithstanding that he was in a very feeble state of health. He might be seen staff in hand, tottering from house to house, persuading people to come to Christ."[17]

The testimony of a farmer and his wife in Danyang is noteworthy:

> The husband received the truth several months ago and told his wife of his determination to become a Christian, and at once he destroyed all his household images. The wife, seeing this, became frantic with rage and grasped a large sword-knife and attempted to stab her husband.
>
> This act of his wife enraged the husband, and he attempted to beat and injure her. For months peace had utterly departed from this dwelling. . . . The husband began to learn more of Christ and exercised more patience; and this . . . resulted in her conversion and brought a deep and a blessed peace to this once miserable dwelling.[18]

After seven years, the number of believers in Danyang stood at only 26 baptized members and 11 enquirers, but a solid foundation had been laid, and God's grace gradually spread to many of the town's inhabitants. Today, Lianjiang County (which includes Danyang) boasts one of the highest Christian populations in

1870s

Fujian, with 30 percent of residents confessing Jesus Christ as Lord and Savior.

In the small town of Qibu, located south of Ningde City, John Wolfe reported the outbreak of a revival in 1875, coupled with strong persecution:

> On the occasion of my visit to this place in November last I baptized seven deeply interesting men, who made an open confession of their faith in Christ surrounded by a mob, which literally howled for their death.
>
> This mob threatened to pull down the chapel, and one of them struck a severe blow on me. A friendly heathen warned our evangelist of a design on the part of the gentry to come and pull me out of the chapel at night and set fire to the house. This caused us some little anxiety, but we knelt down and committed ourselves to the care of our Heavenly Father and then lay down calmly and enjoyed a peaceful sleep.
>
> One of those whom I baptized that evening made a very deep impression on my mind. He was 80 years old and perfectly blind. He showed a marvelously clear perception of the atonement by Jesus. He stood up in the congregation and leaning upon his staff, related the history of his conversion to Christ. It was deeply affecting. At the age of 30 he was a devout worshipper of idols, but he soon found out their worthlessness and abandoned them forever.
>
> For many years he worshipped nothing and was in agony to know what to do. He then worshipped the rising sun, but this brought no peace to his heart. He then worshipped the moon and stars, but peace did not come. At length, in the deepest distress, he gave up the worship of the sun and moon and cried out to the true God.
>
> The old man heard about Jesus and believed at once with his whole heart. "Now," he said to me on the occasion of his baptism, "I can die in peace; I have found a Savior." I am expecting great things in this village.[19]

1870s

Breakthrough in Putian

Putian has long been a key location in Fujian and the home of a unique language that differs from other Chinese varieties in the province.

Evangelical work in Putian commenced in 1862, but the people were slower to embrace the gospel than in many other parts of Fujian, with their distinctive language proving a difficult barrier for both the missionaries and their Chinese converts to overcome.

Gradually, Putian became a center of light to many surrounding villages and districts. A great number of Putian people migrated to Southeast Asia in the late nineteenth century. Today they form sizeable communities in Malaysia and Singapore, where they are also known as the Hinghua.

The first conference of Chinese Christian women at Putian.

1870s

The first known believer in Putian was a man named Lin Zhenzhen, an opium addict who stopped to rest outside a chapel in Fuzhou in 1862. After hearing the gospel proclaimed, he surrendered his life to Christ and was baptized, and the power of the Holy Spirit completely delivered him from the scourge of the drug.

Within five years, Lin had established the first Evangelical church in Putian. As he shared the gospel he was often beaten by people, but he continued to proclaim the truth of God's Word, leading many to the faith until he went to be with the Lord in 1877.

In 1873, eleven years after the gospel was introduced, a significant breakthrough occurred in Putian, with missionary John Mahood reporting, "Some of the people who were once the chief opponents of Christianity in this great heathen city are now publishing abroad the tidings of salvation."[20] Later that same year he wrote,

> It has been a year of remarkable progress. Upwards of 100 persons, mostly Buddhists, have joined the city congregation. . . . We have had to enlarge the church to accommodate the numbers that come. It seats now over 300, and every seat is occupied, and many have to stand about the doors.[21]

The Church Missionary Society had gotten off to a shaky start in Fujian, but through great faith and dogged perseverance, they had weathered the storm. In 1865, fifteen years after the first CMS missionaries had arrived in the province, the mission counted just 35 believers in their fellowships, but the gospel soon flourished in a remarkable way, as the table on the following page demonstrates:

The Church Missionary Society — Church Members in Fujian, 1865–1889[22]

Year	Believers	Communicants[23]
1865	35	19
1868	227	167
1871	450	230
1873	1,075	270
1874	1,360	443
1876	1,648	700
1877	2,323	850
1889	7,562	2,142

1880s

A sketch of three pastors from Gutian in 1880.

The three main mission agencies working in Fujian at the start of the 1880s were the awkwardly-named American Board of Commissioners for Foreign Missions (ABCFM), which was a mission established by the Congregationalist denomination; the Church Missionary Society (CMS); and the Methodist Episcopal Church.

The three groups signed "comity" agreements with each other, agreeing not to overlap into areas where another mission was operating. Their combined statistical reports for 1880 showed 2,934 baptized Christians in all of Fujian from a total of more than 6,600 "adherents" (which included non-baptized believers and inquirers).

Thirty-one schools had also been established by missionaries to provide a Christian education to the youth of Fujian. These proved highly popular, and the number of schools exploded in the following years, laying a powerful foundation that future generations of Christians in the province have benefited from.

In 1880 there were 31 Christian schools with 430 students enrolled throughout Fujian, but by 1900 the numbers had mushroomed to 579 schools with 11,708 students.[1] Incredibly, this means that over the 20 year period a new Christian school opened in Fujian on average every two weeks.

One mission agency that was conspicuous by its absence in Fujian was the China Inland Mission, founded by the great Hudson Taylor. Impressed by the inroads being made by the existing mission groups in Fujian, they chose to focus on other more needy provinces of China. Consequently, the CIM never had any significant presence in Fujian, with their one small station in the far north of the province administered from a base across the border in Zhejiang Province.

Evangelical Mission Statistics for Fujian, 1880[2]

Mission	Baptized	Adherents	Schools	Students
American Board (ABCFM)	215	215	10	172
Church Missionary Society	1,251	3,556	2	65
Methodist Episcopal Church	1,468	2,841	19	193
Totals	**2,934**	**6,612**	**31**	**430**

The Catholics, meanwhile, divided Fujian into two administrative regions in the 1880s—one for speakers of the Xiamen

(Amoy) dialect and another for all other people in the province. Both regions were administered from Fuzhou City.

Statistics for Catholics in Fujian in the late nineteenth century are scarce, but in 1890 one source listed a figure of 36,090 believers in 51 churches.[3] That number included Taiwan, which at the time was administered by the authorities in Fujian Province.

Suffering Saints

The 1880s continued to see strong growth for Evangelical churches throughout Fujian, with many remote areas of the province hearing the gospel for the first time as it gradually spread from town to town and village to village.

Along with encouraging stories of salvations and healings, violent persecution was experienced in many places, as local authorities worked to dampen the embers of revival, which threatened to burst into flame.

Many stories emerged of how the Chinese Christians stood firm in the faith despite massive pressure to recant. From the town of Jinjiang, near Quanzhou, came a stirring testimony of the sufferings endured by a local evangelist named Chen Renshui (Hokkien: Ting Ing-Soi).

The trouble in Jinjiang started in 1879, when local community leaders grew jealous of the growing influence of Christianity and began to discriminate against believers. Their land and food was seized, and residents were forbidden from having anything to do with the Christians. Then, one day,

> Chen, passing through a village, was set upon by an immense crowd, instigated by these chief men. He was terribly beaten and then dragged off, no one knew where, and shut up in some place. . . . His bravery all through was something remarkable. . . . Even when he saw a knife in their hands and believed they were going to carry out their threats to kill him, he boldly told them

they could not kill his soul, and that if it were God's will that he should die, he was only too ready and rejoiced to go.

Chen Renshui never recovered from the effects of his ill-treatment. He grew weaker and weaker and died just as the year 1880 was closing. . . . His one sorrow was that he had done so little for the One who had suffered so much for him. He often used to talk of the joy of going to heaven, and one day when the end was fast approaching, he said, "It is not death. Living is death; dying is life."[4]

Persecution from family members was also common throughout Fujian. In the city of Ningde a Christian woman, who was aptly named Naixin ("Patience"), suffered terribly at the hands of her unsaved husband. The missionaries wrote of her trials in 1886:

> Her husband will not let her go to the chapel and will not permit her to read any of our books. He has taken some from her and destroyed them before her eyes. When I was there some of the Christians told me that this woman wanted me to call on her husband, but as an older Christian said it might bring more blows to the woman, I decided not to go. So, I wrote on a slip of paper, "Come unto me (Matt. 11:28) and be not afraid, for God loves you." . . . A few days after my visit, she and her two daughters-in-law joined in the service.
>
> On her return home, Naixin's husband asked why she had disobeyed him by going to worship God. He then struck her and knocked her down. She said, "If you beat me till I am dead I shall not fear, for I shall then go home to God." This aggravated her husband still more, and he took up a chopper and, holding the iron, struck her with the handle on the shoulder. He might have gone further but was hindered by some who were present.
>
> Two days after this, she said, "Although my husband struck me with the chopper the other day, you see I am all right now. Praise the Savior! . . . Please ask all the missionary ladies and our

native sisters to pray for me and my house and to ask God to turn the heart of my husband."[5]

Instead of quick relief, however, Naixin had to endure many more beatings at the hands of her brutal husband for years. Somehow, she endured by clinging to God, and an 1888 mission report said of this dear sister,

> Last September, the husband of this woman beat her so severely as to confine her to bed for 17 or 18 days. For the greater part of that time, she ate very little and cried bitterly. Amid her sufferings she thought of the words, "A man's foes shall be those of his own household." She thereupon prayed that the Savior would strengthen her and make her willing, if necessary, to be beaten to death by her husband rather than deny Christ.
>
> When she recovered, she went to the chapel. At this, her husband was greatly exasperated, seized a shoe and threw it at her, saying, "If you will go to worship God, I shall beat you till you die." Naixin replied, "If you kill me, I shall be saved, but I will not give up going to the chapel." Her husband, seeing that she was determined, desisted from beating her. . . . She is now 65 years old and was baptized. Her two daughters-in-law also were subsequently baptized.[6]

The pain and misery that many of the Christians at Ningde endured was a shining example of true faith amid overwhelming difficulty. The church in the city grew, until a new building was erected that could seat 200 worshippers. Today, the large Ningde Prefecture contains more than 2.6 million people. Of those, approximately 400,000, or about 15 percent of the population, confess Jesus as Lord and Savior.[7] They owe much to the stubborn faith and perseverance of early Christians like Naixin, who patiently refused to give up her faith in the face of overwhelming suffering.

Principalities and Powers

In the 1880s, many Western missionaries were forced to examine their faith as they grappled with the reality of the spiritual realm in Fujian. Less than 20 years had elapsed since Charles Darwin's theory of evolution swept the Western world, and many missionaries had been trained to rationalize and trivialize the supernatural. On the field, however, God's servants often encountered situations that were not easily explained by human reason.

In 1880, one of the CMS workers in Fuzhou wrote of a rural woman who was demon-possessed. In a dream she was told that if she wanted to be set free, she should go to Fuzhou and learn the doctrine of Jesus. She turned up at a missionary's home with her husband and four children, begging to learn about Jesus.

The powers that had long dominated her life refused to let her go easily, and an intense spiritual battle ensued for her soul, during which she was physically seized and afflicted. She moved into the mission school where she studied the Bible for a year. After her conversion and baptism, she learned to read and became a "Biblewoman," traveling around the area sharing the gospel and testifying that Jesus Christ has the power to deliver even the most sin-bound person.

James Collins, an Irish Anglican and the first missionary of the Dublin University Fujian Mission, arrived in the mountains of northwest Fujian in 1888. After settling into his new job, he soon found that the demonic realm was very real, and to be successful he would need to learn to battle it. Collins wrote,

> You can't walk a few yards among the heathen with your eyes open without feeling how greatly they are in bondage to Satan. If you laugh at a Chinaman for worshipping wood or stone, he says, "I do not worship the idol but the devil it represents." Here, you do not feel that you are working so much for any special society,

but for God against His enemies and against the devil, who has enslaved people whom Christ died to free.[8]

A Decade of Bloodshed and Growth

By the end of the 1880s, the body of Christ in Fujian was able to reflect on a decade of bloodshed and hardship but also of unprecedented growth. The Church Missionary Society had consolidated its position as the largest and most fruitful mission group in the province, with more than 7,500 adherents, including 4,007 baptized church members.[9]

Considering that a proposal had been put forward to close the CMS mission in 1860 due to its complete lack of fruit and that they only had 35 believers by 1865, the growth of the CMS was staggering, as the Spirit of God set the scene for an even greater harvest to follow.

1890s

Zhong Fu and the Fateful Journey

In the nineteenth century, it was extremely rare for a Chinese person to travel to Europe. Oriental culture was still a thing of great mystery and fascination to people in the West. Zhong Fu (Fuzhou dialect: Tiong Ahok) was the wife of a wealthy Fuzhou merchant named Zhong Heling, who owned stores all over the city. Introduced everywhere as "Mrs. Tiong Ahok," she was the first Chinese Christian woman to travel to the United Kingdom, where she spoke to amazed audiences.

Although it seemed that the crowds often came to gaze at her tiny, bound feet, Zhong pleaded with the British churches to send more workers and to spare no effort to bring the gospel to all people in China.

Born in 1850, Zhong and her husband had little interest in the gospel until she shared her misery at being childless with a visiting missionary, Miss Foster. Although the couple had an adopted son, it was considered a disgrace at the time not to have given birth to a biological son of her own. She asked if God had ever answered anyone's prayers for a son. After Foster read the biblical story of Hannah to her, Zhong cried out in deep anguish of soul to the living God.

The Lord graciously answered her prayer, and a year later Zhong gave birth to a little boy. Her shocked neighbors nicknamed the child "The Christian-Doctrine Little Boy," but he grew up using the English name Jimmy.

1890s

After the birth of her son, Zhong Fu became a wholehearted follower of Jesus Christ. She was baptized in 1884 and never wasted an opportunity to share the gospel and her testimony with women in Fuzhou and the surrounding countryside.

In the late 1880s, missionaries Robert and Louisa Stewart had scheduled a visit to their homeland in England, and they asked Zhong if she would consider accompanying them. She consented and in 1890 she became the first Chinese Christian woman to visit England after enduring a months-long terrifying journey marred by constant sea sickness.

Zhong Fu with her son Jimmy and adopted son.

1890s

They traveled around the United Kingdom and Ireland for four months. Zhong shared in nearly 100 meetings with Louisa Stewart interpreting for her. Zhong often stretched out her pleading hands on the platform and said, "It is entirely for the sake of Christ's gospel I have come. To have an opportunity to speak to people about the needs of the Chinese women is all my heart's desire. Come over and help. Kindle hot hearts! It is very important."[1]

Zhong Fu with Robert and Louisa Stewart in England in 1890.

1890s

A Sad Conclusion

Zhong intended to stay much longer in the United Kingdom, but news reached her that her husband had fallen ill, and she made the difficult journey home, expecting to find him fully recovered. She disembarked in Fuzhou full of joy, only to be given the news that her husband had passed away a few days earlier.

To make matters worse, due to the months of delay as she traveled home, her adopted son had managed to seize much of the estate for himself, and she suddenly found herself reduced to poverty. Zhong's neighbors compounded her misery by mocking her incessantly, saying her husband's unexpected death was punishment for offending their ancestral gods by becoming Christian.

Zhong Fu now had two sons to raise: her beloved son Jimmy, who was a constant blessing, and her adopted son, who brought her much grief and pain. Later, Jimmy contracted pneumonia and died when he was just 23. He was a dedicated follower of Jesus Christ, and as he lay on his deathbed, Jimmy "suddenly pointed to a corner of the room and said, 'Look! There are God's angels. I see them. They have come to fetch me!'"[2]

His mother thought that Jimmy was delirious, but after he calmly described the other people in the room, she realized he was in his right mind and asked him to pray that he might live. "No, no," Jimmy answered, "I am going home!" and he closed his eyes and died.

Later, Zhong Fu joined with the missionaries to open a school for girls, many of whose parents were leading officials in Fuzhou. Later, she moved to Beijing to live with her adopted son and his wife, but they abandoned her in her old age. She was seized as payment for the evil son's debts, and the shock broke her health. Zhong soon died and her body was sent back to Fuzhou for burial—a grim ending to a life lived passionately for God.

A Fruitful Trip Down Under

Robert Stewart.

In 1892, Robert Stewart received an invitation to speak at mission meetings in several Australian states and New Zealand. Louisa was due to give birth to their seventh child, but Robert saw it as a priceless opportunity to mobilize workers from the bottom of the world, so he went alone. Three weeks into the sea voyage he received word that Louisa had given birth to a son, Evan, and everything was going well back in Fujian. In one of the typical addresses on his tour, Stewart told the audience,

> "There are now nearly 100,000 believers in a land of 400 million, and there is still only one missionary for every 250,000 people." He held a graven figure up in his hand and described how families in every house prayed to idols like this for protection. He also showed them a very small shoe and explained how infant girls

were cruelly hurt and deformed by foot-binding. He told of the towers outside cities containing a small hole and pit into which newborn girls were frequently cast.³

On April 24, 1892, Robert spoke at an Anglican church in Melbourne, where sisters Eleanor and Harriet Saunders were deeply touched by the message and offered their lives to advance the cause of Christ in China. So effective was Stewart's tour that many women in Australia and New Zealand indicated their interest in going to the mission field.

Louisa had been instrumental in women's work in Fujian, establishing a Christian hospital and a boarding school for girls in Fuzhou that resulted in numerous conversions to Christ. By 1893, the Stewarts felt the work in Fuzhou had matured to a point that they could hand it over to local leaders, and they were appointed to develop the work in the inland town of Kucheng (now Gutian).

By 1895, statistics for the three main mission organizations in Fujian revealed how Christian education had emerged as a major part of their strategy to win people to Jesus Christ, with more than 300 schools already functioning throughout the province.

Christian medical graduates in Fuzhou, 1895.

In the 15 year period since 1880, the number of baptized Christians in Fujian had tripled, while the number of Christian schools and students had increased tenfold.

Evangelical Mission Statistics For Fujian, 1895[4]

Mission	Baptized	Adherents	Schools	Students
American Board (ABCFM)	1,102	3,748	55	1,477
Church Missionary Society	3,062	13,111	169	2,399
Methodist Episcopal Church	4,898	11,411	81	1,271
Totals	**9,062**	**28,270**	**305**	**5,147**

The Gutian Massacre

Accounts of God's work in Fujian in the final decade of the nineteenth century tend to be dominated by one event, which occurred in the summer of 1895 near the mountainous town of Gutian, about 80 miles (130 km) northwest of Fuzhou City. The massacre of 11 defenseless missionaries—including six single ladies, two children, and a baby—sent shockwaves throughout the world and helped shape the Christian landscape in Fujian Province for years to come.

The Evangelical church in Fujian had grown by leaps and bounds since its inception in the 1840s, and by the mid-1890s knowledge of the gospel had spread throughout the province. It seems that to curb the growth of the church, Satan launched a

The site of the Gutian Massacre. The single women were staying in the house on the left, with the Stewart family and Nellie Saunders in the house on the right.

series of attacks on God's children, culminating in the barbaric massacre in 1895.

One of the more unique—in both name and vision—of the dozens of Evangelical mission agencies working in China at the time was the Church of England Zenana Missionary Society (CEZMS). This was a mission exclusively for females, with the stated goal of reaching women and children in the heathen nations of the world. The CEZMS appointed their first missionary to China in 1883, and many new recruits arrived in the following years.

Irish missionaries Robert and Louisa Stewart led the work in Gutian and were responsible for watching over the dozen single ladies who served in the mission.

To counteract the searing heat of the summer months, the missionaries at Gutian were in the habit of retreating to the nearby hill village of Huashan ("flower mountain"), which enjoyed a more pleasant climate due to its 2,000-foot (610-meter) elevation. At the time of the massacre, the missionaries were enjoying a much-needed spiritual and physical break from their labors. Four of the Stewart children were with them at the retreat: their two daughters, Kathleen and Mildred, and two little sons, Herbert and Evan.

As the Stewart family and seven single female missionaries enjoyed their conference in the last week of July 1895, it was reported, "Day after day they gathered in close communion, refreshing one another's souls in the study of God's Word. Utterly wearied in body, they had been so uplifted in spirit that those who were present say that they were like 'days of heaven on earth.'"[1]

At the final service on July 31, the missionaries rededicated themselves to the Lord's service with these words: "Here we offer and present unto Thee, O Lord, ourselves, our souls and bodies, to be a reasonable, holy, and lively sacrifice."[2]

Herbert and Evan Stewart.

A secret Chinese society known as the Vegetarians had been stirring up trouble throughout the countryside. Little was known about this sect, apart from the obvious fact that they abstained from eating meat. They were not a religious group as much as a motley collection of anti-government rebels.

None of the Vegetarian sect's prior behavior suggested they were interested in attacking Christians, so nobody predicted what unfolded on the morning of August 1, 1895, when, without warning, more than 100 men descended on Huasang, "and in a few minutes nine missionaries were dead, two small children fatally wounded, a fifth lady left for dead, and both houses in flames."[3]

At quarter to seven in the morning, Kathleen Stewart and the other children were excitedly picking flowers for little Herbert's birthday picnic later that day when a mob suddenly descended from the woods. The children rushed towards the trail to see what they thought was a procession, but Annie Gordon, who was reading the Bible under a tree, saw the men's spears and shouted for the children to run away. Kathleen managed to escape the murderers' grasp and rushed into the bungalow to her parents. When her assailants chased after her,

> [s]ome entered the bedroom occupied by Mr. and Mrs. Stewart, and striking down Mrs. Stewart, who was at the door, next killed her husband, telling him that their object was not to obtain money but to take his life. Poor little Herbert they wounded terribly, and they attacked and killed the nurse, Helen Yallop, who was bravely trying to hide the baby under her clothes.[4]

Several days later, Kathleen, who was just 11 years old at the time, detailed the tragic events that had unfolded:

> The men broke open our door and entered our bedroom. First, they pulled off all the bed clothes, opened the drawers and took what they wanted to, smashed windows and things, then began beating Mildred and cut her with their swords. Afterwards they left the room. One man saw me under the bed as they were going out and gave me a knock on the head with a stick.
>
> We next saw Topsy Saunders with her cheek very much cut, being walked backwards and forwards by the men who were asking her questions, and if not answered quickly they dug a spear into her. One thing we heard them ask was about her money, and she told them they had taken all she had.
>
> Next, we saw Nellie Saunders lying by the bedroom door moaning (and writhing from a fatal spear wound). From the window we saw men outside the back door beating and killing the other missionary ladies. Four were outside; one woman's head I saw quite smashed up in a corner. It was an awful sight.
>
> Very soon I heard a rushing noise like water. I went out to see what it was and found our house on fire. I went back to Mildred and told her, and she got up and went through the servants' rooms to the nursery where we found Herbert covered with blood, Lena lying on the ground with the baby beside her, and Evan sitting in his cot crying. I screamed at Lena. She did not answer. I tried to lift her up but could not. I took the baby first and laid her down outside, then went back for Evan. We then all (including Mildred

and Herbert) went down past the ladies' house, which was also in a blaze, into the little wood.⁵

Robert and Louisa Stewart were dead, and three of their children were severely injured. Herbert and the baby later died, while Mildred survived after spending a long time in a critical condition, her knee having been sliced open by a sword.

The Vegetarians set the buildings alight with kerosene, believing they had killed all the foreigners, but a few had fled into the woods, where they waited until the murderers left. The shocked survivors didn't know what to do. The next day it was decided they should leave immediately for the safety of Fuzhou on the coast.

Leaving at three o'clock in the afternoon, the group undertook a "terrible and difficult march all through the night, during which the little birthday boy, Herbert, so terribly wounded, "fell asleep" and joined his parents. "How glad Father and Mother will be to see him!" said brave, suffering Millie, when told of his death.⁶

The traumatized survivors finally arrived at the hospital in Fuzhou that Louisa Stewart had helped to build, and doctors treated their wounds.

Looking back, Mildred Stewart said she was aware of the miraculous presence of God during the long journey to Fuzhou. She remembered how none of the survivors, despite carrying life-threatening wounds, felt any great pain until they reached the hospital. Without the divine intervention of the Holy Spirit, nobody involved with the Gutian Massacre would have survived the ordeal. One writer remarked,

> The heroism of these children at such an awful moment was undoubtedly inspired. Consecrated to God for China from their birth and trained in the atmosphere of self-sacrifice and holy courage, they followed in their now sainted parents' footsteps. . . . Not one word of reproach or resentment did they utter. Little

Mildred, sorely wounded and her parents and friends cruelly murdered, could not settle to rest, for she wanted to pray and to plan that those gaps in the ranks might be filled up.... So earnestly did she long that the people who had dealt so cruelly with her family would be led to the Savior![7]

On August 6, the entire foreign community in Fuzhou turned out for the funeral service of the victims. The Christian world was shocked to the core by news of the Gutian Massacre. It was as unexpected as it was brutal, causing another mission group to lament more than a decade later,

> The doing to death of that band of devoted missionaries at their summer retreat in the hills was such a ruthless and dastardly act that it aroused the indignation of the whole civilized world. No fewer than nine faithful servants of Christ passed through fire and sword into His presence that bright summer morning in 1895, slain by the people whom they had come to help and save.[8]

The Single Ladies

Most of the martyred missionaries were single women, whose consecrated lives are worth exploring in greater detail.

Annie Gordon

Annie Gordon was instantly hacked to pieces by the Vegetarians' swords. She had struggled with loneliness since arriving in China, yet she felt happy and fulfilled to be obeying the Master's call.

The band of wicked men also butchered Eleanor (Nellie) Saunders and her sister Elizabeth (Topsy), who came from a strong Christian family in Melbourne, Australia.[9] When their widowed mother was informed of her daughters' deaths, she took it as an honor from God and even greeted two friends who called to comfort her by asking, "You've come to congratulate me, haven't you?"[10]

Remarkably, despite her advanced age, Nellie and Topsy's mother moved from Australia to Gutian, where she served in place of her two slain daughters. Historian A. J. Broomhall remarked, "No clearer demonstration of forgiveness, love, and heroism could have been given. Within a few months of the massacre there were more Chinese inquiring about Christ in the province of Fujian—including the Gutian district itself—than ever before."[11]

Hessie Newcombe

Hessie Newcombe was still in bed when the Vegetarians staged their early morning attack. As the bloodthirsty mob surrounded the house, the terrified missionaries "all gathered in Flora Stewart's bedroom and finding escape through the windows impossible, as the spear-men were guarding them, they quietly knelt in prayer with Hessie Newcombe leading."[12]

Of the 11 missionaries and children who were killed at Gutian in 1895, perhaps none was so fondly remembered as the young English rose Elsie Marshall. Her life of just 24 years had touched so many people that a biography titled *For His Sake* was written soon after her martyrdom.[13]

From an early age, Elsie had taught the children's Sunday school class at her church. She read every missionary book she could lay hold of, and it was through their influence that she longed to serve God in some faraway unreached corner of the world. In November 1891, Robert

Elsie Marshall

and Louisa Stewart visited Elsie's hometown and shared about the need for female missionaries to come and help reach the desolate women of China. Her heart stirred within her, and she offered her life to serve in China with the CEZMS. Little did she know that less than four years later she would be slaughtered for Christ alongside the Stewarts.

As the summer of 1895 commenced, Elsie was so involved in the work that she asked her leader, Robert Stewart, if she could delay coming to the retreat until August. Stewart, with her well-being in mind, declined her request and told her to come with the other missionaries in July. The massacre took place on August 1. The last letter Elsie Marshall wrote home before she was martyred spoke of the upcoming spiritual retreat:

> I know He has some very precious lessons to teach us. One thing, I think, is to look on and see how God works. Another thing is not to be too much engrossed in the work itself to forget the Master, but to remember that if He likes to call us away to other work, He is at liberty to do so. We are His bondslaves, just to go here and there as He pleases. He has made me so glad to leave it all with Him now, and there's not a shade of worry.[14]

Flora Stewart

Elsie was barely awake when screams rang out that fateful morning. She was one of the four women hacked to death after being dragged from the house. Elsie was seen "clinging to her Bible to the very end, though the hand with which she grasped it was nearly severed."[15] She finally fell as savage blows rained down on her, and she went to be with Jesus.

Flora Stewart, who was also known as Lucy, does not appear to be related to the Stewarts who led the Gutian mission. At the time of the attack, Lucy was still in bed and had yet to dress for the day. The mob entered her room, and after stealing everything of value, they dragged her outside and slashed her to death.

Although there had been numerous slaughters of Catholics in China over the centuries, the killing of 11 missionaries (including children) at Gutian was the first massacre of multiple Evangelical missionaries in the 88 years since Robert Morrison had arrived in China.

It was later revealed that the Vegetarians had carried out the attack to annoy and provoke the government in Beijing. Their leader had devised three potential plans, one of which was to attack the missionaries at the Huashan retreat center. The men decided to cast lots, asking the spirits to show them which of the three plans they should launch. They were persuaded by a fortune teller, a man nicknamed "Long Finger Nails," to attack the missionaries. Then,

> [f]or three successive nights the lot fell on Huashan, and a band of 120 men were told to carry out the evil plan. After it was over, the murderers threw off all disguise and their pretended Vegetarian vows, had a feast of pork and chicken, and took a new name for their society.[16]

A Wave of Blessing

Both the Christian and secular worlds were outraged at the Gutian Massacre, and cries for vengeance were made. However, the missionaries would not entertain such thoughts, and they refused to accept any government compensation for the loss of lives. At a special memorial service held in London on August 13, "not one bitter word was uttered; nothing but sympathy with the bereaved, pity for the misguided murderers, thanksgiving for the holy lives of the martyrs, and fervent desires for the evangelization of China."[17]

The Gutian Massacre

If the massacre was a demonic plot hatched by Satan to destroy the church in Fujian, it backfired spectacularly. When news of the slayings spread throughout the province, thousands who had previously been indifferent or opposed to the gospel now became sincere inquirers as they sought to understand why so many foreigners had left the comforts of their home countries to invest their lives in this remote corner of the world.

Within a year or two the work in Gutian, where the martyrdoms had taken place, was said to be "spoiling for want of reaping,"[18] while in Fuzhou, John Wolfe reported the churches in the city were overflowing with people, noting, "I have never seen anything like this in all my years here."[19]

Mildred Stewart before returning to China in 1910.

Amazingly, four of the Stewart children ultimately returned to serve God in China, despite their parents and siblings having spilled their blood and having their lives snuffed out there.

In a remarkable demonstration of forgiveness and the grace of God, Mildred Stewart continued to love the Chinese people, and despite having a permanent limp from the sword cut to her leg, she joined her brother James in missionary work in Sichuan Province.

When she left for China in 1910, a family member remarked, "It was even more wonderful that she bravely went out to the wildest part of China when she . . . could remember clearly all the terrors of her childhood. Wonderful isn't it, the power and courage God gave. I never knew her to show any sign of fear."[20]

Decades later, Mildred and her husband Reg moved back to England, where she was diagnosed with phlebitis—a condition better known as deep vein thrombosis today—that caused searing pain in the veins of her damaged leg. At the time, blood-thinning medicine was not used, and the only method to treat her pain was for Mildred to rest in bed with her leg elevated.

Having been slashed with a sword and left for dead in Fujian when she was just 11, Mildred continued to be salt and light to her generation. She lived an abundant life as a disciple of Jesus Christ until she was suddenly called home after suffering a stroke in 1956, at the age of 75.

Flora Codrington

By God's mercy, the only missionary who survived the Gutian Massacre of 1895 was Florence (better known as Flora) Codrington. She was terribly disfigured and mutilated in the attack, but heroically refused to surrender her call, and after a time recovering in England, she returned to Gutian. She spent many more years serving Christ in China, becoming a senior member of the mission.

When the bloodthirsty murderers approached the mission house, four women ran out the back door only to find themselves surrounded by dozens of armed men. As the terrified women huddled closely together, one source recalled, "Miss Codrington called out to the others not to be afraid: 'Sisters, never mind, we are all going Home together!' Acting on the advice she gave the others to fall at the first blow and to lie still, in hope of being left for dead, she fell, terribly wounded in the face and neck, arm, and thigh."[21]

After a time recovering from the terrible physical and mental scars inflicted on her by the murderers, most people assumed Flora would remain in England, but she knew that God had called her to China, and even the slayings of her co-workers could not prevent her from returning to Fujian at the start of

1897. When she reached her mission base, the local Christians came out to welcome her with great emotion. Flora recalled the special moment:

> As we neared Shaxian, the stir of excitement increased. Christians from all the different villages in the district met us and surrounded or followed our chairs, and as we passed along the streets, greetings resounded on all sides. Our chairs were put down in the marketplace, and there the little children clung round us, and with their dear dirty little arms in ours, we entered the familiar old house. There, such a sight met us. . . . To see the women's faces and to feel the clasp of their hands was more than sufficient reward for coming back to them.[22]

Flora Codrington served in Fujian until the 1930s. She wrote several children's books, culminating with a 1934 book titled *Hot-Hearted*,[23] which was a collection of inspirational testimonies about Chinese Christian women she had been honored to know and serve alongside.

Flora Codrington (second row, third from left) and her women's Bible class at Shaxian.

1900s — The Putian Revival

A women's Bible class at Dongdai, led by missionary Amy Oxley.

Five years had passed since the Gutian Massacre, and as a new century dawned over Fujian, thriving, evangelistic churches were operating in nearly every part of the province.

In the summer of 1900, the Boxer Rebellion erupted across northern China, with thousands of missionaries and their Chinese converts massacred in the demonic onslaught. In Fujian, believers continued their work with little disruption, even after two provincial officials, Xu Cheng and Yuan Zhang, received a telegram from the wicked Empress Dowager Cixi in Beijing ordering, "All foreigners are to be decapitated."

Risking their lives, the two officials changed one character of the edict so that it read, "All foreigners are to be protected," and Fujian was consequently spared the death and destruction that wreaked havoc in other parts of China. For their act of rebellion, Xu and Yuan were executed.

In 1904, the China Inland Mission stated that there were considerably more than 40,000 Evangelical believers in Fujian.[1] This number—which represented a huge increase over previous estimates of 6,600 adherents in 1880 and 28,200 in 1895—was confirmed by statistics supplied by the three main mission agencies in Fujian at the turn of the century:

Evangelical Mission Statistics For Fujian, 1900[2]

Mission	Baptized	Adherents	Schools	Students
American Board (ABCFM)	1,959	4,349	92	2,058
Church Missionary Society	4,327	21,478	212	3,354
Methodist Episcopal Church	6,995	16,541	275	6,296
Totals	**13,281**	**42,368**	**579**	**11,708**

These figures meant that for the first time in Christian history, the place of the Catholic Church as the dominant Christian force in Fujian was under threat. A 1907 survey found there were 51,299 Catholics throughout the province meeting in 173 churches.[3]

The Evangelical enterprise, which had almost drawn alongside the Catholics numerically, would soon shoot far ahead of them as a growing number of gifted Chinese pastors and evangelists emerged to take the leadership reins of churches across Fujian.

The first years of the new century also witnessed a surprising event, when the first known Chinese missionaries were sent overseas from Fujian to spread the gospel. At the time, China was considered one of the neediest and most challenging mission fields in the world, so when reports emerged of Chinese believers heading overseas, not everyone was impressed.

One of the pioneer missionaries was Wang Naixiong (Fuzhou dialect: Uong Nai Siong), a Methodist pastor from Fuzhou. He promoted a radical plan not only to send a few individuals to proclaim Christ, but to transplant entire Christian communities to a new country to be the salt and light of the gospel. Wang left Fujian in 1901, taking about 1,000 believers with him to Sarawak (now in East Malaysia), where they established a Christian community that reached out to both Chinese people and tribal groups in the area.

The Putian Revival

Although encouraging growth had occurred in various parts of Fujian, the church needed a breakthrough in order to reach the teeming millions who were still enslaved by vice and idolatry.

After some small breakthroughs for the gospel were experienced there in the 1870s, the Putian district, known in the local dialect as Hinghua, was the scene for a powerful outbreak of

A group of Putian pastors whose churches experienced powerful revival.

heaven-sent revival, which commenced in the summer of 1907 and continued to 1909, sweeping thousands of people into the kingdom of God and forever changing the spiritual direction of that part of Fujian.

The little-known Putian revival is rarely mentioned in the annals of great Christian movements of the twentieth century, so most Christians around the world are unaware of it. If not for the efforts of American Methodist missionary William Brewster (who also translated the Bible into the Putian language), few details of this great move of the Holy Spirit in Putian would survive. Brewster wrote a 56-page account of the revival, but because it was published in China, few Western Christians were aware of its existence.

Although Putian was the epicenter of the revival, its influence spread far and wide, impacting remote parts of the province. Because of the rapid development of transportation in the years preceding the revival, the gospel was able to spread much more quickly. It now took just a few hours to travel from Putian to Fuzhou, whereas previously it had taken three or four days.

Although God had brought a steady trickle of people into the Putian churches since the 1860s, the trigger-point for the movement came when news of the mighty revival that swept the Korean Peninsula a few years earlier reached the missionaries and Chinese church leaders in Putian. In July 1907, a group of 100 Chinese preachers met in the city for their annual mid-year retreat and conference. One of the delegates recalled,

> There was unusual heart-searching and persistent prayer, especially at the meetings before breakfast. One young man particularly made a most humble confession of having cheated in one of his examinations and of unchristian feelings toward his brethren. The meeting was prolonged for a day or two more than had been originally planned, with much profit to many.[4]

God's Chosen Vessels

As the Spirit of God began to stir the hearts of Christians in Fujian, He also laid a burden on the heart of an elderly, blind Christian woman 8,000 miles (13,000 km) away in Houston, Texas.

Sarah Wilson, whose daughter Minnie was a missionary in Putian, had been shut off from society for several years due to her infirmities. Sarah, who never set foot in China, helped pray in the Putian revival at the same time God began to deal with the sins and compromises of believers in the district. One letter from Sarah to her daughter told of her certainty that a victory had been won in the heavenly realms, and the results would soon follow on the ground in Putian. She wrote,

> I have been praying much, especially for over a year, that the Spirit might be poured out in awakening, convicting, converting, and sanctifying power. I feel like it must come for His sake. It may come to you before my letter gets there. My soul has got so full I had to quit writing and praise the Lord our God, and then pray a while, before I could write more.[5]

In the early days of the revival, the heartrending confession of sin by a man named Na, who worked as a missionary's assistant, deeply shocked other believers and caused them to examine their own lives. Many people confessed their sins and got right with God.

Although he had never led a church, the Holy Spirit set Na apart for the ministry, and despite protesting his inability to perform such a role, he was appointed to pastor a church with 1,500 members, so sure were the other leaders that God's hand was involved in the appointment.

Na proved a good fit for the position, and every day he cried out in prayerful dependence on the Lord. Whereas many missionaries and Chinese church leaders had fallen into a spiritual slump and were satisfied with the status quo, Na hungered for

1900s — The Putian Revival

God's presence. He spent days in prayer and fasting, asking the Lord to send revival to Putian, and his prayers were answered.

Startled by a Roar

When the revival broke out in Putian, the impact was dramatic and far-reaching. The leaders of the boys' school had grown concerned at the flippant attitude of most of the students, but one afternoon a missionary was startled by a roar emanating from the church. Not recognizing the sound, he rushed over to see what was happening, and found

> [t]he boys of the school were there with their head teacher and the pastor. The students were all sobbing and praying together, but there was no confusion or hysteria. They were convicted of sin and were praying for pardon. Each was pleading audibly for himself. After a while, the pastor urged them to be quiet while he pointed to the cross for relief. One after another told in simple language the story of his sins, and each had his own individual account to give.
>
> About a year earlier, two improper anonymous letters had been written and sent to a student in the girls' boarding school. An investigation pointed to two of the students in the boys' school as the guilty parties. While they denied it, the evidence seemed conclusive, and they were punished.
>
> At this meeting the guilty boy—who was not one of the two who had been punished—confessed, and in heartbroken contrition, he begged forgiveness of his innocent companions, whom he had grievously wronged by keeping silent while they were punished for his sin.[6]

The convicting power of the Holy Spirit spread, and a female teacher at the girls' school publicly confessed that she had stolen four dollars that rightfully belonged to the school. After writing a letter confessing her sin and repaying the money, that very night

1900s — The Putian Revival

Items handed in by penitent people during the Putian revival, including drug paraphernalia and a chain used to bind slaves.

she fell ill and passed into eternity a few days later. When news of her death circulated, the fear of God fell upon the churches as people realized they could not risk facing the Judge of all the Earth with unconfessed sin in their lives.

As the impact of the revival spread to every church in Putian, one pastor wrote,

> The revival in this place is truly increasing more than I can tell you. Early every morning more than 200 are in the meeting, and at every service there are people confessing their sins with weeping. Some confess to having stolen, others to a lack of respect and poor treatment of parents. Many confess to smoking tobacco and drinking wine, and others to using opium, gambling, and all the vices. Both men and women have confessed to adultery with loud weeping, smiting their breasts in grief.[7]

One of those present at a prayer meeting was the treasurer of the mission. He rose to his feet, and with tears in his eyes confessed that he had kept 20 cents that was left over after bills were paid and that he had pocketed the money even though he knew it was wrong.

Although the monetary value was small, his confession had a huge impact. People were gripped with the fear of God and began to cry out, confessing their sins. Restitution was made, stolen money and goods returned, and items used for sinful purposes were brought to the church to be destroyed.

Before long, a room in the church was filled with opium pipes, cartons of cigarettes, bottles of liquor, pencils and books stolen by students, and countless other items that the Lord put His finger on and demanded be put right. A bottle of poison was discarded by a church member, who admitted he was waiting for an opportunity to kill an enemy.

Among the more unusual items handed over was a long chain belonging to the leader of a secret gang called the Gun and Knife Society. He explained that he had used the chain to bind many people they had kidnapped for ransom and revenge, and he no longer wanted any connection to the accursed thing.

The crowd at an early morning prayer meeting outside a Putian church in 1909.

He surrendered his life completely to God and later joined evangelistic teams that preached the gospel throughout the district.

A Spirit of Prayer

Like all genuine heaven-sent awakenings, a spirit of fervent prayer and intercession characterized the Putian revival. When Pastor Na announced a morning prayer meeting commencing at six o'clock, 30 to 40 members came. By seven o'clock, 200 people had crammed into the church. As the meeting continued, the crowd doubled again, until 400 believers were pleading with the Lord Jesus to bring revival to their city.

The intensity of the revival increased as more of God's people prayed and received a burden to rescue the lost for Jesus. In one church, more than 100 prayer meetings were held in a 50-day period, as people sought relief for their anguished souls by making peace with the Creator.

Every church in Putian was overflowing with joyful believers and earnest seekers. An eyewitness reported,

> The people came by the thousands, where we had at first expected hundreds.... The seats were so close together that it was necessary to stand in prayer. The congregation on Saturday night numbered 4,800. Sunday night there were four simultaneous meetings aggregating between 6,000 and 7,000.
>
> For five successive mornings, at half past five o'clock, between 2,000 and 3,000 Chinese Christian men and women gathered for prayer.... And such praying! Three thousand voices blended into one. At a little distance it sounded like the roar of a storm—yet there was no confusion. It was orderly, harmonious noise.... As the voices died down, usually one specially led of the Spirit would continue the petition.... The very atmosphere seemed charged with divine power.[8]

1900s — The Putian Revival

The Blessing Spreads

After several months of God cleansing His people, a shift in focus took place as renewed believers gained a fresh burden for the salvation of the two million people in the densely populated areas in and around Putian. The city was home to countless opium addicts, some of whom were former church members. The power of God was present to deliver men and women, and hundreds were set free from the vice. The Methodist hospital in Putian filed this report:

> Most of them realized that repentance must include all their sins, not merely this one that had enslaved them. They had prayer meetings together night and morning, and as the pains of the cracking chains would come upon one and another, he would call upon his companions to help him with prayer. . . . Hundreds of these men were saved from the living death of this fearful bondage.[9]

A group of drug addicts seeking deliverance during the Putian revival.

The revival spread southwest of Putian into the Xianyou District, where there were just two fellowships at the time. A meeting in May 1909 prompted this report:

> The revival has very greatly increased. Yesterday the church was crowded, as the voice of praise and the cry of penitent confession mingled together. There were many who came forward to praise God for salvation, and more than 100 men and women confessed their sins with weeping. To our surprise, the church was again full in the afternoon. . . . We have great hope that both churches in Xianyou will receive together the baptism of the Holy Spirit.[10]

William Brewster noted two main characteristics of the Putian revival. First, it was almost totally led by the Chinese. The foreign missionaries participated and gave counsel when asked, but almost all preaching and decision-making was done by local church leaders. Second, the revival was a spontaneous movement. Brewster observed,

> There was no prearranged plan or program to be carried out. No evangelist had been sent for. It was the work of the Holy Ghost sent down from heaven. Even after the meetings were in full swing, they were planned for only from day to day. Seldom were leaders appointed more than two days in advance, and they were not publicly announced even from one meeting to another. The people did not come to hear some favorite preacher, but to be taught of God by whomsoever He chose to use as a messenger.[11]

It's difficult to say if the Putian revival ended at a specific time. By 1910 the remarkable events that had characterized the early stages of the movement had become less frequent, but thousands of people were still being saved each year, and hundreds of strong, evangelistic churches had been established throughout the region.

Today, the entire Putian Prefecture—which contains 2.7 million people—is home to approximately 420,000 professing Christians, three-quarters of whom are Evangelical believers.[12]

The fruit of the life-changing Putian revival was seen in Fujian for generations. In one of the churches a small boy, just eight years old, had his first experience of Jesus Christ, and a seed of faith and revival was inserted deep within his heart. That little boy was John Sung (Mandarin name: Song Shangjie). He grew up to become China's greatest evangelist of his generation.

Amy Oxley-Wilkinson

Amy Oxley, aged 25.

One of the most effective missionaries in Fujian during the first half of the twentieth century was Amy Oxley, who came from a wealthy Australian family. After surrendering to Christ, she exchanged her privileged upbringing for a life serving sick and blind people in Fujian, making an impact that has endured to the present day.

Born in 1868 at Camden in New South Wales in a home described as "the most valuable estate in the county,"[1] Amy was the daughter of John Oxley, an influential magistrate and a representative in the first state parliament.

Her great grandfather, Samuel Marsden, is famous for his early pioneer gospel work in Australia, and he came to be known as "the apostle of New Zealand" and is reputed to be the first person to preach the gospel there, serving as the first missionary to the Maori people in 1813. Marsden is also thought to have introduced the first sheep into New Zealand.

Amy's life was forever changed when she was 24, after Irish missionary Robert Stewart preached during his 1892 trip to Australia. Realizing a life of true faith in Jesus Christ meant denouncing her own plans and submitting to God's will, Amy applied to join the Stewarts in their work in Fujian but was shocked when she heard that the entire Stewart family and seven other missionaries had been brutally slain in the Gutian Massacre.

The incident became the talk of Western society, with many lamenting the young women who had "wasted their lives" in faraway China, when they could have made a name for themselves at home. This sentiment made Amy more determined than ever to serve in China, and she arrived in Fujian in January 1896 to begin her service as a medical missionary. By the end of the year, she was already seeing dozens of patients each day at a clinic in the coastal town of Dongdai, approximately 43 miles (70 km) from the provincial capital, Fuzhou. In one letter home, Amy described a Christian leper she treated:

> At the Fuzhou Leper Asylum, I saw a man with a glory and a brightness in his face that could not possibly have been there unless God had been shining upon him. There are two tiny places where his eyes had been, for now he is blind. There is a small round hole where once there was a nose, his lips are drawn far apart, and both top and bottom rows of teeth were showing. And yet I have never seen such a wonderful face, for truly love, joy, and perfect peace are written there. . . . I have never realized in quite the same way how God's indwelling presence can so wonderfully transform a human being.[2]

Although she went to China to meet people's medical needs and to share the gospel, by the end of her first year, God deeply touched Amy and directed her attention to the plight of blind children. She recalled,

> In my homeland, I had passed the blind on the other side of the street, for I had no special interest in them. Now my heart was stirred to its depths on many occasions when blind children were brought to me in our dispensary. What could I do? . . . Going to a village one day, I stumbled across a helpless blind boy cowering in a ditch. He told me his father wanted to kill him but seeing I was coming, had left him for me.[3]

For the next few years, Amy continued her medical work as she pondered how to specifically minister to blind children. The answer came in September 1898, when a powerful typhoon badly damaged the mission buildings at Dongdai. While rebuilding work was underway, she visited a blind school run by the Presbyterians at Xiamen, 185 miles (300 km) to the south.

The visit had a profound impact on Amy. She learned to read Braille so she could teach the blind how to read, and after returning to Dongdai she gained her first student, a young boy named Xiao Lingkai, whose mother had come to Amy months earlier with this desperate plea: "He is my only son. I am a widow, and he is blind. Do good deeds, open his eyes, and help him to see."[4]

Struggles at Home and a Surprise

In June 1899, Amy read that an English doctor, George Wilkinson, was coming to open a new medical mission in Fuzhou. She was glad to know another pair of skilled hands would soon be joining the work.

In the summer of 1900, Amy took her first furlough home to Australia after six years in China. Her trip brought many

Amy and her school for the blind at Fuzhou. The banner says, "They shall see His face."

surprises, and she experienced what missionaries today often call "reverse culture shock." She no longer fit into Australian culture, and she found many Christians to be superficial.

On New Year's Day, 1901, Amy was expected to celebrate the founding of the Australian Federation, when six states were combined into a commonwealth for the first time. Her heart was grieved when she learned of the simultaneous introduction of the White Australia Policy, which discriminated against non-whites who wished to migrate to Australia, with a special emphasis against her beloved Chinese people, who were loathed and feared by a large part of the population.

One of the more positive things to come from Amy's visit home was a long poem, "The Blind Chinese Boy," composed by a preacher named William Yarrington, who was inspired after hearing Amy speak about the work in Fujian. For years, parts of the poem were used to bring awareness to the needs of the blind in China. The first and last stanzas of Yarrington's poem said,

> I am a lonely Chinese boy;
> I have no happiness or joy,
> But full of misery and pain
> I often cry and weep in vain,
> For I have none to love or care
> For all my sorrow, or to share
> My burden, and to give relief,
> And comfort in my childhood grief.
>
> They tell me that though I cannot see
> There yet is joy awaiting me.
> That one day, through God's loving grace
> I shall have sight and see the face
> Of Jesus Christ, the Savior dear
> Who suffered so much sorrow here. . . .
> And then my pains will all be past
> And I shall dwell with Him at last!"

Amy was excited to return to Fujian, where George Wilkinson had arrived during her absence. Like most single lady missionaries at the time, Amy did not expect to marry, as she was fully dedicated to serving the Lord and His people. From the moment she met Wilkinson, they were attracted to each other. As Amy never shared any hint of a romantic connection in her letters, her friends and family back home were shocked when she casually announced,

> I am engaged to be married to Dr. George Wilkinson, a man whom I have met at all times of the day and night in connection with the medical work for six months. As the days have gone by, I have found out what a true and good man he is. A most considerate Christian, a thorough missionary, and a clever doctor, I can see how wonderfully God has been working out His plan and purpose. . . . He has shaved off his beard, and he looks very much younger. He is 36 years old and I am 35, so that is just right.[5]

Amy Oxley-Wilkinson

The marriage between Amy Oxley and George Wilkinson was presided over by the veteran Fujian missionary, John Wolfe. Amy soon became pregnant and gave birth to a girl on April 7, 1905. Little Isabel was the joy of their lives. The ministry continued to flourish, with Amy and George finding their service was more fruitful because of the complementary nature of their God-given gifts. A baby son, Marsden, was added to their growing family.

The years rolled on, and the First World War disrupted missionary work for several years. However, when Amy returned to Fuzhou in 1918, she was thrilled to learn that the number of blind boys in the school exceeded one hundred.

Amy and George's selfless work among society's most vulnerable members did not go unnoticed, and the president of the Republic of China conferred on Amy the highest honor available to a foreigner in China at the time—the Order of the Golden Grain. This honor had previously been given to only one Westerner. The *Church Missionary Gleaner* understood the rarity of Amy's award, and covered the ceremony on their front page:

> The streets were decorated, and the governor's band marched for miles displaying the official board which was to be presented. Altogether it was a gala day, as more than 1,000 guests flocked to witness the formal presentation of the gold medal and the honorary board, and to offer their own congratulations.[6]

A Change of Direction

In keeping with mission policy of the era, Amy and George's children were sent to England for their education. It was a heavy blow to Amy, who missed them terribly. When news arrived that the relatives who had taken responsibility for Isabel and Marsden no longer had the resources to finish their schooling, Amy and George were faced with a difficult decision.

George, Amy, and the children reunited in London.

In 1921, after more than two decades of sterling service for Christ in Fujian, George resigned from the mission. When his resignation letter arrived at the Church Missionary Society headquarters in London, they did all they could to change his mind, but George and Amy were determined to take care of their children, and they caught a boat to England where they were joyfully reunited as a family.

Soon after arriving, a plan was put in place for eight blind boys from the school in Fuzhou to travel to England to be part of an exhibition in London. The *Straits Times* in Singapore covered the boys' curious journey from Fujian:

> Eight boys from the school arrived in England, having traveled by Japanese steamer via the Suez Canal. . . . Each boy is a trained musician and can play and sing English and Chinese music. All can speak English to some level quite fluently. They were

accompanied by their Chinese teacher . . . and by a coolie who cooks all their food in native fashion.[7]

The exhibition was a tremendous success, with more than 250,000 people flocking to it. Many wanted to see and hear the blind Chinese boys, who played melodious songs while seated in a replica Chinese street. The bishop of London attended and was moved to remark,

> These lads are a little bit of the real China. . . . As you look at them, you have to realize that they are representative and symbolic of many thousands of the blind in China for whom in the past practically no provision has been made. They are living testimonies of what the coming of the Lord Jesus Christ means to the vast populations of the East. Once unwanted and neglected, they have been cared for, educated, and saved in the wide and true sense of the word.
>
> The performance, consisting of vocal and instrumental music in English and Chinese, was received with the utmost appreciation by a large audience. . . . Mrs. Wilkinson is anxious that English audiences should understand and feel the force of the gospel message which these young men are singing, and certainly their songs do linger in the mind.[8]

At the conclusion of the exhibition the boys, with Amy acting as their translator, commenced an extensive five-month tour that visited 130 cities and towns of the United Kingdom. The impact of those meetings meant that donations for the blind school secured its future for years to come.

Although Amy's desire was always to reflect attention on the Lord Jesus Christ and His transformative work in the lives of the boys, many people wanted to honor Amy for her work. Among her admirers was Queen Mary, to whom Amy and the boys were presented during the exhibition in London.

Amy Oxley-Wilkinson

The Blind Band that toured England in 1922.

When Amy waved goodbye to the young men at the dock in February 1923 as they started the long voyage back to Fujian, her heart was burdened. Most of them she had known from their infancy. She had acted as their mother and had taught them to read, write, play music, and to become disciples of Jesus. Now that her family was settled in England, Amy didn't know if she would have the opportunity to visit her beloved Fujian again.

The years continued to advance, and although Amy and her family were physically safer than during their decades in China, they were nevertheless subjected to continual spiritual testings as they sought to be a light for God in the midst of a dark world. When the Second World War broke out, Amy and George were in their 70s, and the stress of those years weighed heavily on them. By the end of the war, many of their friends and siblings had died, and George's health had deteriorated, with Alzheimer's disease slowly consuming his mind.

By the late 1940s their son Marsden had migrated to Australia, and daughter Isabel was married and living in Hong Kong. Amy felt lonely, and when she was diagnosed with advanced liver cancer at the age of 81, she knew her time was short. During her final few weeks in palliative care,

> [o]ne of the things that occupied her mind and prayers was the fate of her school in China. If victorious, the Communists had threatened to eradicate Christianity and expel missionaries from the country. This could lead to persecution of the boys, especially those who had spent time in the West, and ultimately to the closure of the school.[9]

Amy Oxley-Wilkinson fell asleep in the arms of the Lord on June 6, 1949, less than four months before Mao Zedong proclaimed the advent of the People's Republic of China. She was 81 years old. Tributes for her life and service to the people of China flooded in from around the world.

George Wilkinson went to his eternal reward two years later and was buried next to his beloved wife of 47 years in the Tunbridge Wells Cemetery.

Epilogue

Authors Robert and Linda Banks, who wrote a gripping biography of Amy Oxley-Wilkinson, shared a touching story that occurred on Christmas Eve 1980. It took place soon after China had opened its iron gates just slightly to the outside world after three decades of oppressive rule, during which many Christians in Fujian had been killed or imprisoned for their faith. They wrote,

> A man, whose family had emigrated from southeast China shortly before the Communist revolution, had just returned to Fuzhou, the capital of Fujian Province. After dining in a downtown restaurant, he started to walk home. It was cold and wet that night, with a wind blowing down from the surrounding mountains. As he wandered through the historic area, the man looked for any reminders of his childhood. Glancing at buildings he used to

pass, including where a large church once stood, little remained of an earlier time.

As he walked on, he heard an unusual sound carried by the winter wind. Someone further down the street was playing the flute to a tune he knew well: "Joy to the world! The Lord is come. Let earth receive her King!"

As he approached, in the half-light he could just make out an aged, blind beggar dressed in rags. He recognized the man's face immediately.

"Excuse me," he said in the local dialect. "I am the son of Pastor Ding, who used to be well known in this area. You might not know me, but surely you remember my late father?"

The old man lowered his flute, looked bewildered for a moment, then shook his head decisively. "No, sir. I am a humble beggar, blind and useless throughout my life. I am the refuse of this socialist state and a burden to the people. I swear I don't know of any pastor or foreigner. I am sorry."

"But how can this be?" the other man said. "I remember you. I heard you playing and singing in the Blind Boys' Band when I was a child. Weren't you one of Mrs. Amy Wilkinson's students? In fact, one of the nine who traveled with her to England?"

Starting to utter something, the blind man suddenly fell silent. The deep furrows on his face and bent frame told of the hardships he had endured over the years.

Overcome by a flash of inspiration, the pastor's son started to sing tentatively in English, "Amazing grace, how sweet the sound, That saved a wretch like me. I once was lost, but now am found. . . ."

The old man unexpectedly began to cry and through his tears joined in the song—open faced, sounding like a young man, and with the voice of an angel.

". . . Was blind, but now I see!"

The two embraced and held each other for a long time into the night.[10]

Today, the Communist authorities of Fujian have taken over the school for blind boys that Amy Oxley started after stumbling across a blind boy in a ditch more than a century ago. Remarkably, the current president of China, Xi Jinping, personally supported the building of a new campus for the blind school when he was the secretary of Fuzhou's Municipal Party Committee in the 1990s. Although the atheistic system has driven Christian content at the school into the private realm, music remains a key emphasis of the school.

A century after Amy Oxley-Wilkinson left China, her godly and loving influence can still be seen today through the lives of the thousands of blind children who have been cared for in Fuzhou.[11]

1910s and 1920s

American missionary Elizabeth Perkins and a common mode of travel in Fujian in the 1910s.

Revolution

The 1911 Revolution—which brought an end to more than 4,000 years of dynastical rule and ushered in the Republic of China—resulted in great upheaval throughout the country, but in Fujian many Christians were excited, thinking the change would help spread the gospel more quickly and usher in the kingdom of God. Their optimism proved misplaced, however. Instead of China becoming a Christian country, in the 1920s a new force, Communism, appeared on the scene and began to fill the political and social void.

Even before the rise of Communism, the change of government structure had created unforeseen challenges for the body of Christ in Fujian, with one historian noting, "The province declared its independence from the Manchu dynasty in November 1911, and from that time on, missionary work was never as easy as it had been in the first decade of the century. From about 1918 there was increased unrest in country districts."[1]

At the dawn of the new decade, the statistics for the Evangelical church in Fujian were revealing. By 1910, the three main mission organizations in the province reported only minimal gains over the decade since 1900, with the Church Missionary Society reporting an actual decrease in the number of adherents connected to their churches. The Methodist Episcopal Church took over as the dominant Evangelical mission in Fujian, almost doubling their number of baptized believers during the first decade of the twentieth century.

Evangelical Mission Statistics For Fujian, 1910[2]

Mission	Baptized	Adherents	Schools	Students
American Board (ABCFM)	1,994	2,896	75	2,611
Church Missionary Society	4,841	11,379	175	4,038
Methodist Episcopal Church	12,470	32,756	210	4,834
Totals	**19,305**	**47,031**	**460**	**11,483**

Testing the Spirits

In the 1920s it was not popular for Christians to openly talk about demonic possession or activity. Supernatural incidents were often downplayed, and strange occurrences were explained away by rational reasoning.

As God's children sought to extend Christ's kingdom to all parts of Fujian, they often found themselves unable to progress until concerted prayer and spiritual warfare was waged against the demonic strongholds that had been entrenched over Fujian society for centuries.

In 1925, missionary Margaret Barber shared a remarkable testimony from Xiamen, in an article titled, "Testing the Supernatural." It serves as an example of the complex layers of demonic activity that Christians often encountered when they shared the gospel in Fujian's idolatrous strongholds:

> Last autumn, near Xiamen, in a preacher's house one night, a voice was heard in the ceiling and a light appeared. The voice professed to be that of the former preacher who had lived in that house and had died there 20 years ago. It soon became known all over the countryside that the old pastor was speaking from the roof of his former dwelling, and crowds flocked day by day.
>
> The utterances were extraordinary and full of Scripture. Exhortations to live a holy life were frequent, and people of evil character dared not go, because no sooner were they seated, than the voice would address them by name and ask them to repent of their sins. In most cases, sins known only to the person and the spirit addressing them were revealed.
>
> The spirit never becomes visible, but often a brilliant light is seen hovering over the house. . . . Many Chinese Christians have been utterly deceived. They well know the supernaturalism of heathenism, but it has never entered their heads that a demon could manifest himself in a Christian church, use Scriptural terms, exhort to goodness instead of evil, and press the reading of the Bible.[3]

An Extensive Survey

In 1922, after years of gathering data from every part of China, the monumental book *The Christian Occupation of China* was published. It found that for the first time, Evangelical church members in Fujian had surpassed Catholics.

The Catholics, who first worked in the province in the thirteenth century before recommencing their efforts in 1696, now numbered 61,712 believers in 348 churches,[4] while Evangelicals totaled 86,094 church members.[5]

Fujian, therefore had the highest number of Evangelical Christians of any Chinese province at that time, surpassing Guangdong (78,519) and Jiangsu (70,084).[6]

Two years earlier, in 1920, the individual mission returns from Fujian for the three main mission agencies revealed substantial increases over the previous decade, with the number of Christian adherents growing from 47,000 to 72,600. More than 18,000 students attended over 600 Christian schools throughout the province, helping establish the next generation of disciples of Jesus Christ.

Statistics for the Three Main Evangelical Missions in Fujian, 1920[7]

Mission	Baptized	Adherents	Schools	Students
American Board (ABCFM)	3,145	8,974	143	4,909
Church Missionary Society	7,054	20,153	207	5,799
Methodist Episcopal Church	21,259	43,523	252	7,349
Totals	**31,458**	**72,650**	**602**	**18,057**

New Leaders Emerge

The 1920s concluded with the church in Fujian going through a consolidation period as it tried to hold on to the gains of the previous decades that had propelled Fujian to become the province with the highest number of Evangelical Christians in China.

1910s and 1920s

Andrew Gih

God, in His foreknowledge, knew that His people in Fujian would come up against a powerful adversary in the following decades, and He desired to fortify His church so that it would be able to withstand the approaching onslaught.

To help strengthen the body of Christ, the Holy Spirit raised up several highly influential believers, whose ministries not only impacted Fujian Province, but ultimately millions of believers around the world.

One of the key leaders to emerge in Fujian was Andrew Gih (Mandarin name: Ji Zhiwen), a prominent Chinese evangelist who made a great impact for God. Formerly employed as a post office official in Shanghai, Gih changed his vocation and established the largest and most effective team of evangelists in China, called the Bethel Worldwide Evangelistic Band. This led to Bethel bands leading hundreds of thousands of Chinese to Christ in China and among the Chinese diaspora in Southeast Asia.

When Gih visited Xianyou in 1928, missionary W. B. Cole attended the meetings and reported,

> In a meeting for women, with between 200 and 300 present, the Spirit was manifest with power. Many were in tears and sobbing out confessions of sin. The meeting lasted from two o'clock until after five. Many came into the joyful experience of salvation. . . . Now I am asking the Lord that the revival may go on until it reaches every nook and corner of the work.
>
> We now have many young men and some older ones too who have had a deep experience. They are on fire for Christ. They are sanctified, and they believe in the Book. How the good Lord has answered our prayers.[8]

Margaret Barber

A young Margaret Barber.

A Hidden Giant of the Faith

On the surface, few people would consider Margaret E. Barber to be a key figure in the history of Christianity in Fujian Province. She was not well known outside her circle of friends, she rarely traveled or spoke in her home country, and she never wrote a book, although she did compose many poems and hymns. During her time in China, Barber lived a simple life of faith, with little financial support.

While Barber (whose Chinese name, He Shou'en, means "recipient of peace and grace") hosted a Bible study at her modest home near Fuzhou, most of her ministry was hidden from public

Margaret Barber

view as she engaged in intercessory prayer. Despite her relative obscurity, Barber was considered a giant of the faith by some of China's most prominent Christian leaders of the era, and consequently, her life is worth examining.

Born in the English town of Suffolk in 1866, Barber traveled to Fuzhou in 1899 as an Anglican missionary affiliated with the Church Missionary Society, where she was part of the burgeoning mission community under the leadership of John Wolfe. For the first seven years she taught at the Tau Su Girls' High School in the city, and she joined evangelistic teams that traveled around the countryside sharing their faith. In those early days it was said of Margaret Barber

> [a]t first, she felt awkward in preaching the gospel, because she could not speak much Chinese. Therefore, she hired Pastor Lee from the Anglican denomination to teach her the Fuzhou dialect, and before long she could speak. Because she wanted to save souls, she went with Pastor Lee to preach the gospel in Lianjiang County. The Spirit of the Lord was with them and a young man believed in the Lord. Then a group of older women received the Lord Jesus' salvation, left their idols, and turned to God. Some even gave their lives to the Lord and became Barber's co-workers.[1]

In November 1899, Barber wrote home about a disabled Chinese woman who had found Jesus Christ in Ningde:

> Yesterday a chair stopped before our door, and when I went to see who had arrived, I saw a poor deformed woman, a cripple of about 30. . . . In answer to my greeting she said, "I have come to learn about Jesus." . . . I told her about the importance of speaking to Jesus often, when she interrupted with, "But I am told that when Christians pray they must kneel. And I cannot kneel. If I put my head down and close my eyes, will that do?" Soon afterwards we all met together and prayed for her, and as we prayed, she cried quietly to herself.[2]

After this initial contact, the disabled woman tried to attend all the meetings she could, desperate to know the true and living God. The light of the gospel gradually illuminated her heart and she submitted her life to Christ. Two years after first meeting Barber, the woman was a baptized, whole-hearted believer, causing another missionary to say,

> She came in for just one week's special preparation. It was such a pleasure to teach her, she was so anxious to learn. It was, too, very sad to see her sit from early morning till night on her tiny stool, utterly unable to help herself or move unless someone lifted her bodily. She is very patient. Her knowledge of Chinese characters astonished me. As I referred her to different passages in her Bible, she could read them very well indeed. . . .
>
> I know that for some time her New Testament, prayer book, and hymn book have been her only companions, and she spends much time reading them. I asked, "How is it that you know characters as well as you do? If you come across characters you do not know, who teaches you?"
>
> "The Holy Spirit does," was her reply, "I have no one else."[3]

Margaret Barber enjoyed sharing God's Word with Chinese women, and in one letter home she provided an insight into the women in her class:

> There were 20 women in my station class who were nearly all converted. Not long ago, 13 of these dear women were baptized after several months of probation, and in every case the testimony was that they were changed women.
>
> One elderly woman, not the least bit handsome, all her front teeth having gone, was found on the hillside, looking for poisonous weed to end her existence. Her husband and son were dead, and she felt she had nothing to live for and had twice been rescued from the river. The women in the class helped her, and begged her to come and learn about Jesus, so she came, stayed, and is now very happy.[4]

Ten Accusations

Although on the surface everything seemed well, behind the scenes Margaret Barber had been at loggerheads with a few fellow missionaries. Her main protagonist was the principal of the girls' school, who accused her of ten different faults. Although details of the charges were never made public, one source said,

> Because she had the rich life of Christ overflowing in her excellent living, many students were attracted and desired her instruction. This made the principal jealous, and he accused her of ten "illegal" matters.
>
> Barber quietly left the Tau Su Girls' High School. Even so, a list of her "crimes" was sent to the headquarters of the British mission. At that time, she learned to remain silent under the shadow of the cross. She would rather suffer misunderstanding than defend herself. She returned to England and continued to avoid vindicating herself until the brother responsible for the mission told her, "As your authority, I charge you to tell me the facts of what happened in China. Don't hide anything." Then she told him what had happened.[5]

Finding herself unable to remain under the auspices of the Church Missionary Society, Barber was unsure of God's plans, or if she would ever set foot in China again. While attending the Surrey Chapel in Norwich, she gained a new lease of life and was able to lay the burden of the conflict at the foot of the cross. Realizing her Heavenly Father had more for her to do in Fujian, she returned to China as an independent missionary without the support of a mission organization, but with the promise that God would supply all her needs.

Pagoda Anchorage

When Margaret Barber returned to China for her second term of service in 1909, aged 45, she was accompanied by her niece, Margaret Ballord, who was 20 years her junior. The two remained together until Barber was called to heaven 21 years later.

Barber had lived in Fuzhou during her first term of service, and it was assumed she would return to the city, but when their boat crossed the Min River, she looked out at a beautiful village called Pagoda Anchorage, and immediately felt that was the place the Lord had set aside for them, even though it took visitors over three hours to travel there from Fuzhou. The property was described as follows:

> Pagoda Anchorage was an obscure place near the sea, and there Miss Barber lived in a simple house. This was in sharp contrast to the fine house where she had lived the first time she was in China. To reach her house from Fuzhou, one had to take a steamship to Mawei, then a little boat to a nearby village, then walk along the path on the hillside to some old wooden houses. In one of the houses was her bedroom, where she would fellowship with the Lord. Other houses were for hospitality. Pagoda Anchorage to Miss Barber was like Canaan to Abraham. It was her "promised land."[6]

During her second stint in China, Barber rarely traveled, but invested her time in intercessory prayer and personal meetings with believers, whom she always exhorted to surrender their entire lives to God and to avoid any hint of compromise. Her stance was not understood by many believers, with one critic saying,

> Some of the Chinese young people who received help from her were worried about her. They wondered, "Why doesn't she go out and establish meetings and work in a bigger city?" Instead, she

lived in a small village where nothing was happening. It seemed that it was a waste for her to be there.

One brother almost shouted at her, "No one knows the Lord as you do. You know the Bible in a most living way. Don't you see the need around? Why don't you go out and accomplish something? You just sit here seemingly doing nothing. You are wasting your time, energy, and money. You are wasting everything!"

Was there waste? After all these years, it is clear. She was a seed of life sown by God in China. This seed surely went through loneliness, humiliation, and seclusion. But thank God, He made her blossom and bear fruit. Only God knows how many people received spiritual help from her directly and indirectly.[7]

A Holy and Generous Woman

Due to the hidden nature of her ministry, it was difficult for many to know what Margaret Barber was really like to be around. Some gleanings from friends provide insights into her personality and approach to sharing the Word of God. One woman, who was a teenager when she first spent time with Barber, recalled,

> She was neither tall nor short. She had a round face that gave the impression of being kind, weighty, godly, and sober. She was filled with the light of the Lord so that when people sat beside her, they always felt comfortable. While she was speaking, her tone was soft and full of joy. She always had a smiling face that caused people to forget the suffering of human life. She could speak the Fuzhou dialect fluently.[8]

A Chinese student, who later became a spiritual son and co-worker of Barber, recalled the first time he met Barber:

> The first time I met her, her eyes were like lightning, her hair was like silver, and her face was shining like an angel. Her countenance was lovely, just like a mother's. Her behavior was holy, her

dress was simple, and she was always smiling and kind. She was different from other foreigners in China. Her walk was sober. She not only had a good reputation, but also was a good pattern. Everything she did was for the Lord, for the glory of God.[9]

Although many Christians found Margaret Barber somewhat mysterious, those who knew her best told of her love and deep generosity. She wanted nothing more than to please her Lord and Master, and if that meant rebuking sin and wrongdoing, she would rather obey God than take the easy option and ignore her duty. The level of her generosity is reflected in this testimony from one who knew her:

> There was a sister who had three daughters and one son. They were very poor and could not support themselves any longer, so they sent a daughter, Liu, to the Lai family as a maid. Liu was very beautiful, and one member of the Lai family wanted to take her as a concubine. When the mother and daughter heard this, they wept together, because the Lai family would not release her unless a payment of $240 was made.
>
> Sister Barber heard about this matter. Her heart of love could not bear to allow Liu to become a concubine. She encouraged both mother and daughter to pray to God. Barber did not have much money at the time, so she prayed that God would provide the ransom for them. God indeed heard their prayer and sent $240 from abroad to ransom Sister Liu, who later married Brother Chu.[10]

No summary of Barber's life would be complete without mentioning her overwhelming passion for the return of the Lord Jesus Christ. She constantly spoke about it with others, pleading with them to be ready for that glorious moment. Her eager expectation is evident in the many hymns she wrote concerning waiting for the Lord's return.

A Famous Trio

Margaret Barber is best remembered for the impact her life had on the prominent Chinese church leader and author Watchman Nee. The two met in 1922, when Barber was 56 and Nee was a 19-year-old young Christian with a call to preach the gospel.

The duo developed a close friendship, and on many Saturdays Nee would travel out to the isolated village at Pagoda Anchorage to receive instruction and to pray with Barber. During those times, she introduced Nee to books by a host of Western Bible teachers, including T. Austin Sparks, Madame Guyon, J. N. Darby, and Jessie Penn-Lewis—all of whom would strongly shape his views and future ministry. Nee once shared about the deep influence Barber had on his life:

> I heard many brothers and sisters talk about being sanctified, so I began to study the doctrine of sanctification. I found approximately 200 verses concerning sanctification. I memorized them and put them in sequence. But what sanctification was, I still was not clear. I felt empty inside, until one day I met this elderly sister. She *was* holy.... That light caused me to push forward. I could not escape, and this caused me to see sanctification.[11]

Other Chinese believers to come under Margaret Barber's influence in those days included Lu Zhongxin (known as "Faithful Luke") and Leland Wang, who was a close friend of Watchman Nee. Wang went on to establish the Chinese Foreign Missionary Union and was used by God for decades both inside China and around the world.

In the 1970s, J. Edwin Orr, a well-known American-British revivalist, looked back on those pivotal times in Fujian and noted Barber's influence on the new generation of Chinese church leaders:

> Leland Wang, Watchman Nee, and Miao Shaoxun, known as Simon Meek, a famous trio, were among a team of young men

Margaret Barber (standing) with her niece Margaret Ballord in 1928.

in Fuzhou revived or converted through Margaret Barber's influence. . . . There, in the style of the Christian Brethren, they met for the breaking of bread. Leland Wang became a China-wide, then a worldwide evangelist. Watchman Nee became the organizer of the Little Flock, an indigenous fellowship of churches.[12]

Barber held little regard for human reputations, caring only about the measure of Christ in a man or woman. This lack of favoritism allowed her to speak truth in love to people regardless of their social standing or supposed office.

Called Home

For most of Barber's life she had been fit and healthy, but in February 1930 she contracted enteritis (inflammation of the intestine), and she was confined to bed with a high fever.

Despite being in severe pain, Margaret continued to pray for all her Christian colleagues by name. Once, a Chinese sister asked, "When you should be praying for yourself, why do you only pray for us?" She replied, "All of you co-workers are always on my mind. I am burdened, so I pray for you." After several days of sickness, she left this world. It is said that before she departed, she shouted, "Life, life!"[13]

Margaret Barber was buried in a cemetery at the top of the mountain at Pagoda Anchorage. Many believers grieved deeply when they heard news of her passing, with Watchman Nee writing,

> I feel most sorrowful concerning the news of the passing away of Miss Barber. She was one who was very deep in the Lord, and in my opinion, the kind of fellowship she had with the Lord and the kind of faithfulness she expressed to the Lord are rarely found on this earth.[14]

Margaret Ballord was shocked by her aunt's sudden death, but she continued to work in Pagoda Anchorage until 1950, when she finally returned to England after 41 years of service in Fujian.

Leland Wang

Leland Wang

One of the key church leaders to emerge from Fujian during the 1920s and 1930s was Wang Zai, who also went by the English name Leland. Of all the Chinese Christians God has used throughout history, Wang probably holds the distinction of being the only one called to be a preacher from the deck of a gunboat while he was serving as a Chinese naval officer.

Born in Fuzhou in 1898, Wang was given a Bible as a child, but he couldn't understand it so he used it as a stamp album instead. It was one of the few brushes with Christianity he had during his formative years, when he and his family lived in a compound with no Christians at all among the 200 people who lived there.

As a teenager, Wang possessed a fierce temper. On one occasion his uncle beat him for insolence, and the young man decided to get revenge by murdering him. He secretly put kerosene in his uncle's rice bowl, but he smelled the fumes before eating his meal and was spared. Leland received another brutal beating for his trouble.

The Wang family owned a small shop in Fuzhou, and often when the cash was counted, some of the coins would fall to the floor. Leland wanted those coins to buy candy, but he knew his father would severely punish him if he was caught stealing, so he came up with an ingenious plan to minimize the risk of being caught. He applied glue to the soles of his shoes and then walked around the shop, coming away with many coins stuck to the bottom of his shoes.

At the age of 14, Wang suffered a terrible broken ankle when he fell off a fence. He spent two months recovering in hospital and fell into deep depression as he contemplated the possibility of never being able to walk again. In a bid to obtain inner peace, he studied Buddhism, Daoism, and Confucianism, but none satisfied the inner longings of his restless heart.

After being released from hospital, Wang enrolled in the naval academy, and in 1920 he married Ada, who had given her heart to Christ while attending a Christian school. Their wedding ceremony created a furor in the community when Ada spurned Chinese custom by refusing to bow to her ancestors. Her relatives were enraged, but most later came to faith in Christ, saying that her courageous stance helped them realize the gospel was true.

Ada led Leland to the Lord, but after returning to the navy, he soon fell away from the faith and became heavily involved with gambling, drinking, and smoking. It was only after Wang started to read the Bible every morning that the truth of God's Word began to illuminate his heart. He later testified, "I came to see that Jesus was nailed to the cross for me. . . . From this time on I was full of peace and I preached the truth."[1]

Leland and Ada Wang

Leland Wang had finally experienced the inner peace he had long searched for, and he was bursting with joy. He recalled,

> Thank God for the happy day that fixed my choice on Christ! Confucianism teaches us the duty of life; Buddhism, the vanity of life; Daoism, the simplicity of life; but Christ gives us the eternity and glory of life. . . . My mother, who was a Buddhist, soon came to the Lord. One by one, others in my family came to accept Jesus as "the way, the truth, and the life."[2]

Later, Leland also had the privilege of leading his uncle (the one he had tried to poison with kerosene) to faith in Jesus, just before he passed away.

"No Bible, No Breakfast"

After realizing that by becoming a Christian he was now enlisted in the Lord's army, Wang knew he needed to display at least the same level of self-discipline as he did in the navy. He established a habit of rising at six o'clock each morning to read God's Word, but after faltering in his commitment, he came up with a novel plan to help him stay awake:

> I prayed for dedication and disciplined myself by hitting my hand with a stick once for each minute I was late in rising. I think the longest I overslept was 30 minutes—which was a painful experience! My wife and others thought this punishment a little crazy, but it got results. I only overslept a few times.
>
> Later I found an even more effective means of ensuring my early reading. If I did not read at least one chapter to start the day, I did not eat my breakfast. "No Bible, no breakfast" became my motto.[3]

The Scriptures became the heartbeat of Leland Wang's life, and the Spirit of God breathed on him and equipped him for fruitful service. After seeking God's will on the matter, in 1921 Wang resigned from the navy after serving for nine years.

Wang was asked to lead a church in Fuzhou, but he refused. Instead he became a street evangelist, going out to preach with a basket, a bell, and a selection of Gospel literature. He immediately began leading people to Jesus, and he discipled the new converts by studying God's Word with them every day.

In 1928 Leland Wang founded the Chinese Foreign Missionary Union, with a goal of preaching to the Chinese diaspora scattered throughout Asia. After initially sending out 12 missionaries, the ministry quickly grew from its humble beginnings.

For almost half a century, Wang preached throughout the world, establishing churches in the United States, Canada, Europe, and the Middle East. He was given the nickname "The Moody of China" and received an honorary doctorate from Wheaton College in Illinois in recognition of his long and fruitful service to God.

Leland Wang in 1954.

Leland Wang died in 1975, having studied God's Word every day since his conversion. The former naval officer is fondly remembered by Chinese Christians around the world as a humble vessel whom the Lord used to make a lasting impact for the kingdom of God.

1930s

Harry Caldwell, a Methodist missionary from Tennessee, after a successful hunt in Fujian in the 1930s.

The Handover of Power

In the late 1920s, the Nationalist government introduced new laws relating to foreign control. All school principals in Fujian were required to be Chinese, as were the majority of directors on school boards. Foreign missionaries now had no option but to hand over control, but many Chinese believers found it difficult to adjust to the new paradigm. A pastor reflected,

> I can say in all honesty that until the law made the change obligatory, it had never occurred to me that our Chinese could head our schools, nor do I recall any missionary ever suggesting such

a thing. As I look back, I am amazed at my own stupidity! . . . The idea had simply never previously entered my head.[1]

In what would prove to be the final detailed returns filed by the three major mission organizations in Fujian, statistics for 1930 revealed that while the number of baptized believers saw modest gains throughout the 1920s, the new education laws resulted in the closure of 125 Christian schools in the province and 3,000 fewer students enrolled compared to a decade earlier.

Evangelical Mission Statistics for Fujian, 1930[2]

Mission	Baptized	Adherents	Schools	Students
American Board (ABCFM)	3,348	8,358	88	3,680
Church Missionary Society	7,192	15,292	137	4,048
Methodist Episcopal Church	35,915	48,572	252	7,349
Totals	**46,455**	**72,222**	**477**	**15,077**

Despite the decline in Christian schools between 1920 and 1930, a comparison of the figures between 1880 and 1930, fifty years earlier, shows the tremendous impact the gospel had made on the people of Fujian.

The number of baptized Christians exploded from just 2,900 to over 46,000 in that period, with adherents rising from 6,600 to more than 72,000. Whereas there had been only 31 Christian schools in Fujian in 1880 attended by 430 students, by 1930 over 15,000 students were receiving a Christian education in nearly 500 schools scattered the length and breadth of the province.

The 1930s also saw the leadership of the church in Fujian being gradually transferred from foreign to Chinese control. The transition was very uneven, however, with some mission groups sensing the urgent need for change and implementing it as quickly as possible, while other groups encountered strong resistance from their workers.

Reflecting the stance of many foreigners at the time, one missionary said, "If Westerners are to withdraw from northeast Fujian, the church would in a generation or two simply flicker out."[3] Echoing that sentiment, in 1932 the Anglican bishop of Fujian, John Hind, did not hold back his grim view of the state of the churches under his control when he lamented, "The church is extraordinarily weak and . . . is in no condition to face up to the future if support and guidance are withdrawn."[4]

Although the transfer of power was painful for some, at a certain point the Chinese Christians realized that *they* could evangelize their own people and lead their own churches. Although the crucial pioneering efforts and sacrifices of the foreign missionaries were deeply appreciated during the early decades, a new era had dawned when foreigners and their funds were no longer needed to prop up the church in Fujian.

An Inferno Erupts

The gradual removal of foreign control of the Chinese church was part of broader anti-foreign sentiment that was sweeping China at the time. Banditry and lawlessness plagued Fujian, and society became so unstable that many cried out for a strong authority to restore law and order. As a result, millions of people became open to the claims of Communism.

In July 1930, Church Missionary Society workers Eleanor Harrison and Edith Nettleton were abducted by bandits at Zhong'an. The duo's ransom was originally set at $500,000, but when the payment was not forthcoming, the bandits cut off one of Nettleton's fingers and sent it with a new ransom demand to the provincial authorities.⁵ The CMS then authorized a representative to pay $10,000 in gold for the women's release.⁶

The bandits received the payment, but when government troops mobilized to secure the missionaries' release the bandits thought they had been betrayed and beheaded the two elderly women, both in their 60s, on October 4, 1930.⁷

As the decade progressed, China was locked in a fierce civil war, and chaos reigned in many places. The Communists, meanwhile, were winning millions of people to their side and were increasingly disrupting Christian work throughout the province. In Putian, where powerful revival had swept thousands into God's kingdom starting in 1907, the Communists had infiltrated the churches, and many Christians had scattered. Despite great challenges and danger, the gospel continued to advance in Putian. When the Bethel evangelists held an evangelistic campaign in the city in May 1932,

> [t]hey found a church, with 3,000 seats, covered with posters denouncing Christianity. The meetings began without interference on weekdays, but by the time a revival had moved 2,000 people, the Communists came to break up the meeting. There was such power in the service that they hesitated, interested despite themselves, and one of their number went forward, with others seeking peace with God.⁸

With society disintegrating, a swarm of Chinese voices blamed foreign influence for the nation's ills. Fujian became a tinderbox, with the slightest flicker of a flame likely to ignite a raging inferno.

The spark that set the province ablaze occurred in January 1927, when a group of students protested outside the gates of an orphanage run by Spanish Dominican nuns. The nuns had sacrificially taken care of dozens of abandoned girls who had been left to die by their impoverished parents. The problem was so widespread that a chiselled stone was erected on the waterfront at Nantai that said, "Little girls are not to be drowned here."

1930s

Orphans cared for by a Catholic mission in Fujian.

The Spanish nuns could not bear to let any babies perish, and news quickly spread around Fuzhou that they were willing to pay for the girls rather than see them killed—20 cents per baby. As a result, hundreds of girls were brought to the orphanage, many of whom arrived in such poor condition that they soon perished. The number of corpses mounted up as the nuns were overwhelmed and unable to find enough burial sites.

One morning, a Chinese worker carrying two covered baskets from the back door of the orphanage was accosted by the students and asked what his cargo was. The nervous man replied, "Fish," but when the students took the lid off a basket and discovered dead babies, they stormed the orphanage, where they discovered more bodies awaiting burial.

News quickly spread throughout the city that the long-held rumors that foreigners killed Chinese babies and used their eyes for medicine was true. Riots broke out, and many churches and other buildings were looted and burned to the ground.

Mobs marched on mission schools across Fujian shouting, "Down with Western imperialism!" Students and teachers were attacked, with some suffering stab wounds, while two female

British teachers at the Methodist School in Fuzhou had their dresses cut off by the attackers, causing them to roam the streets clothed only in their underwear.

Lin Puqi, the brother-in-law of Watchman Nee, was accosted by a mob as he walked home. They cursed him, accused him of being a "running dog of the imperialists," and bound him with cords as they dragged him onto a platform. When the mob demanded he renounce his faith in Christ, Lin replied, "Never! You can kill me if you want."

As a result of these and other incidents, the US embassy in Fuzhou ordered the evacuation of its citizens. On January 19, 1927, a total of 125 Americans made their way to the port and boarded the USS *Pillsbury* for the Philippines, while 149 more Americans remained in remote parts of the province, unable to evacuate.

When the curtain was drawn on the 1930s, Chinese believers were in charge of most churches, mission schools, and Christian hospitals and orphanages in the province. Although on the surface the transition of power had appeared calamitous, God had been working behind the scenes, strengthening His people for their new responsibilities. The handover of control from foreign to Chinese hands proved crucial for Christianity in the province. Within a relatively short space of time, a new government came to power that expelled all foreign missionaries from the country, but God had graciously orchestrated events so that His children in Fujian would survive the coming storms.

John Sung — "China's John the Baptist"

John Sung

The Little Preacher

Of all the figures to emerge over the course of Chinese church history, probably none has been as enigmatic as the Fujian native John Sung, who appeared for a short time like a blazing comet before passing into the presence of the Lord at the age of just 43. Decades later, mission leader Paul Kauffman wrote of him,

> God was to grant John Sung just 15 years of public ministry. Perhaps no evangelist in history accomplished so much for God in so short a time. He was a powerful, fearless preacher, a tireless zealot who never spared his own strength for his audience. His

John Sung — "China's John the Baptist"

exploits are still talked about today. He often ministered three times a day—not just talks, but powerful, anointed sermons.[1]

John Sung's impact on Christianity in China was so extensive that he features in many provinces in *The China Chronicles* series. Because Fujian was his home province, this chapter and the one following focus on the impact he made in Fujian and offers a detailed analysis of his life.

Born in Hong Chek village near Putian in 1901, John Sung (Mandarin name: Song Shangjie or Putian dialect: Song Siong Chat) was the sixth child and fourth son of a "warm-hearted Methodist preacher" named Song Xuelian, who loved to share the gospel with simple rural people. Song Xuelian was the youngest of four brothers who started a church in their village in 1886, just after they had embraced Christ.

On many occasions young John accompanied his father when he visited church members, and when his father was sick or out of town, the boy sometimes preached to the believers, repeating from his sharp memory messages he had heard at church.

Local people loved the small boy and gave him the nickname "little preacher." He also helped edit his father's *Revival* magazine, which was distributed throughout Fujian as a testimony to all the great things God was doing in the province.

In 1909, the Putian revival impacted the Sung family's village, and eight-year-old John was deeply touched by the Spirit of God. As he heard the story of the life of Jesus,

> [h]e broke down and began to weep, realizing as never before his own sinfulness. Conviction spread to the whole congregation and soon all were on their faces before God confessing their sins. Reconciliation and restitution followed. People who had been enemies for years became friends. A purified church became a witnessing church, and within a month or two there were 3,000 conversions. . . . This was the first time that revival had ever come to this church. . . . Among the mourners was Pastor Sung's little

son. His bitter tears, he later said, soaked through the lapel of his coat.[2]

A short time later, John's father suffered a severe asthma attack while traveling home. As he stumbled into the house, it was clear that he was close to death, struggling to get oxygen into his lungs. Mrs. Sung froze in shock, not knowing what to do, but John

> [p]oured out his heart for his father. Prayer was immediately answered, and the father made a speedy recovery and had no further recurrence of this complaint. How the family rejoiced at this answer to prayer! John could never doubt that God was both willing and able to hear the prayer of faith and to heal the sick.[3]

John also emulated his father's habit of keeping a daily diary, making extensive notes of his ministry experiences and what God had taught him and of the insights he gleaned from reading eleven chapters of the Bible each day. Later generations of Christians have greatly benefited from John Sung's diligent note-taking.

John Sung's father, Sung Xuelian, playing an accordion and preaching on the street.

Years later, Sung was traveling in north China when the only place he and his colleagues could find to ride on a train was on the roof. He climbed up the ladder, and a coolie threw his bags up to him one by one. But when there was just a briefcase left, the man suddenly grabbed it and sprinted out of the train station into the crowded streets. The briefcase contained one of several thick diaries Sung had meticulously compiled. He was devastated, and until his dying day expressed his disappointment at losing the precious book.

A Fiery Enigma

In addition to the good traits he inherited from his father, John also inherited his fierce temper, which was a source of consternation and confusion to Christians. Sometimes when he preached, Sung would suddenly have a burst of anger from the pulpit or verbally eviscerate an interpreter for making a mistake during a sermon. In his own words, John described his battle with anger during his childhood years:

> From external appearances I seemed to be a success, but I was a fake. Take my temper. I must have inherited from father an explosive temper. Whenever he got angry, he would roar thunderously and contort his face into a livid green, causing those present to flee. Once in anger I splashed hot soup on my brother's face. Naturally, father spanked me, but I retorted, "If you ever spank me again, I'll kill myself by jumping down the well!" Father put a lid over the well.
>
> Another time I had a disagreement with my father, and to show my gumption, I rammed my head into a porcelain water jug. Amazingly, the water jug cracked, but my head didn't.[4]

Parts of John Sung's story are so extraordinary and complex that some Christian historians to the present day have struggled to know how to view him. While God clearly used him to bring tens of thousands of sinners to the foot of the cross, his forceful personality and dramatic methods caused many to take offense. Some who met him considered him extremely rude, for he did not tolerate fools, and he had such a singular focus that anything that got in the way of fulfilling Christ's call was considered an unnecessary distraction. One commentator has said,

> Sung could be very stern and brusque. He was not a people-pleaser, though he did seek to please God. He had little time for small talk or polite pleasantries. More than one church leader took offense when he declined invitations to tea or lunch during his preaching campaigns. They did not know that he was spending hours on his knees in prayer and Bible study or in follow-up conversations with those who had repented or wanted prayer.[5]

Seven Years in Babylon

At the age of 18, John Sung begged his father to send him to study in the United States. His father hesitated, but when a letter arrived with an invitation for John to study in America, his father took it as a sign from God and sent his son on the long ocean voyage with just $6 spending money in his pocket.

After arriving, John found work scrubbing the floor and cleaning the windows of a fabric store for 25 cents per hour, and during the school holidays he took a second job at a factory, working the night shift from 6 p.m. to 5 a.m. He wrote to his parents, "You might think me overworked, but my body feels surprisingly robust and strong."

Sung was an extremely bright young man, and coupled with his relentless work ethic, he completed his college degree in three years, finishing among the top students in his class even though he had started the course with a limited grasp of English.

He then received a scholarship to attend Ohio Wesleyan University, where he enthusiastically participated in Christian activities, being appointed president of the campus YMCA. By the fourth year in America, a friend lamented, "John seldom went to the meetings and never attended church on Sundays. After he had studied three more years under 'American heathens' he did not believe anything that his parents had taught him."[6]

After losing his faith in Christ, Sung was a lost soul without a moral compass. Pride welled up in his heart after the local newspaper lauded him as "Ohio's most famous student," but the praise of men could not assuage his unhappiness. In desperation, John turned to the religion of his forefathers and began to chant Buddhist scriptures. Instead of finding peace, he said, "My soul wandered in a wilderness. I could neither sleep nor eat. My faith was like a leaking, storm-driven ship without captain or compass. My heart was filled with the deepest unhappiness."[7]

The Breaking Point

To make ends meet, Sung undertook all his studies while working several manual jobs, including heavy work at a steel factory. This demanding job precipitated his first health crisis, which he detailed:

> I hadn't worked there a full day before I got dizziness, heart palpitations, splitting headaches, and a high fever. Still, I persevered until I developed a huge hemorrhoid. The doctor said I must have surgery. Knowing I didn't have any money, friends had to vigorously persuade me to go to the hospital for surgery. Before surgery, I wrote a farewell letter to my loved ones.[8]

Sung was also diagnosed with tuberculosis, before modern treatments for the dreaded disease had been introduced. He had an operation for the hemorrhoid, but being a young man who lived life at maximum speed, he ignored the doctor's orders to recuperate slowly. He discharged himself from the hospital early, throwing himself back into his studies and work before he had completely healed.

This was the start of major health struggles that he experienced for the rest of his life. As a result, his condition worsened and became a chronic affliction known as anal fistula, which plagued him until it ultimately led to his death at an early age.

Sung relocated to Ohio State University, where he completed a master's degree in chemistry in just nine months, receiving the Science Society's medal and gold key for topping his class. Next, he studied for a doctorate between 1924 and 1926. To qualify, he had to be proficient in both French and German, so he attacked those languages and passed with flying colors, even translating a thick German chemistry text into English.

John Sung received his doctorate at a lavish ceremony on March 19, 1926. He was given cash prizes for his achievements in physics and chemistry and was invited to join the faculty of Harvard and other prestigious universities around the world.

While he had achieved all his academic goals, Sung was now deeply unhappy in his heart and mind. Someone suggested he should study theology, so he enrolled at the Union Theological Seminary in New York City.

The seminary boasted a long list of famous Christian alumni, with the German martyr Dietrich Bonhoeffer attending the seminary a few years later. Sung looked forward to learning all he could about God, but he was soon shocked and disgusted to discover that he had enrolled at a liberal institution, where most of the professors and students did not consider the Bible to be the inspired Word of God and foundational beliefs such as the virgin birth and the bodily resurrection of Jesus Christ were openly mocked or considered mere allegories.

Conversion

Sung became so depressed and disillusioned with his spiritual condition and inner turmoil that he wrote a confidential letter to the one man he felt he could confide in—his good friend at Ohio Wesleyan College, Dr. Rollin Walker, whom he described as "my American father."

In his letter to Walker, Sung said he felt overwhelmed by his tormented conscience and that he sometimes despaired of life. Walker was deeply concerned and forwarded the letter to Dr. Henry Coffin, the president of the seminary where Sung was studying. The letter set off a chain of events that almost destroyed John Sung, as Satan did all he could to derail the young man and stop his future ministry for God.

One day, at his lowest point, Sung attended an evangelistic meeting at the Calvary Baptist Church in New York. He was shocked when a 14-year-old girl named Uldine Utley, dressed all in white, was the main speaker that night. At first Sung was taken aback, but as soon as the girl opened her mouth, the tangible presence of God filled the room as she spoke on the cross of Christ.

Sung was deeply convicted of his sins as the Holy Spirit reminded him of the pure and simple faith he once had in Fujian. For the next four nights he attended the meetings, "awed by the presence of God and vowing that he would entreat the Almighty until he was empowered to preach even as this young woman was."[9]

On February 10, 1927, Sung reached a crisis point in his life. He recalled,

> My spiritual burden was so heavy I could not bear it. I had no peace. My heart was filled with darkness and conflict. I prayed earnestly and tears of repentance ran down my cheeks. I asked the Lord to cover me with His blood and to make me live not

for myself or for the vain glory of this world. I opened my heart, asking God to take pity on me and deliver me from the iron heel of the devil and set me free.[10]

After his dramatic cry for God's mercy, waves of forgiveness and joy flooded John Sung's soul! He felt his sins roll away, and the heavy burden he had carried was gone. He searched for the Bible he had brought with him from China, finding it at the bottom of a bag beneath many science and theological books. He threw the other books in the trash and focused on reading God's Word, which struck him with a freshness and vibrancy he had never experienced before. As he meditated on the trial and crucifixion of Jesus, a vision appeared to him in his room. A friend later described this life-changing event:

> Suddenly the Lord with pierced hands and wearing a crown appeared to him in a vision, standing before him and speaking in a compassionate voice, "My son, your sins are forgiven!" . . . As the vision receded, John felt a wonderful relief in the sudden rolling away of his sin-burden. . . . Leaping to his feet with a shout of "Hallelujah," he sang loud praises to God. His songs of praise rang through the corridors, rousing some early sleepers in the dorms of the fourth floor.[11]

Confined in a Mental Asylum

Unable to contain his excitement for Jesus, Sung didn't care that it was after midnight. As he exuberantly exhorted his fellow students to repent and surrender their lives to God, he received abuse from the blurry-eyed young men.

The next morning saw Sung's zeal continue to overflow. He openly rebuked his liberal professors, warning that they would be thrown into hell if they didn't repent. He even told Harry Fosdick, a leading proponent of the social gospel, "You are of the devil. You made me lose my faith, and you are causing other

John Sung — "China's John the Baptist"

young men to lose their faith."[12] Sung also took direct aim at Henry Coffin with a humorous play on words, telling his classmates they had been duped into attending a "cemetery whose president is a coffin."

Reports of Sung's behavior soon reached the president's desk, and he was not amused. Coupled with the warning letter he had received from Rollin Walker which said Sung "appeared incoherent as the product of an overstrained brain," Henry Coffin decided the young Chinese student had become mentally unbalanced, and a plan was hatched to "help" him. Sung's diary recorded the events that unfolded when he returned to the seminary the next day:

> I reached the gates, which closed behind me as soon as I had entered them, and the seminary president greeted me. He told me that I was getting overly stressed lately and gently insisted that I go to a quiet place to rest and recuperate. I thought his offer over and deemed it reasonable because a week at a tranquil setting would be an excellent opportunity to devour the Word of God. The "quiet place" turned out to be Bloomingdale Hospital, an institution for the mentally sick.[13]

Rarely has a man forged such a diverse reputation in two parts of the world as Dr. Henry Coffin. In America he was viewed as one of the greatest gospel ministers of his generation, and he had been honored on the cover of *Time* magazine just a few months earlier in November 1926. In the eyes of many American Christians, Coffin was a great man of God and one of the cowriters of the famous hymn "O Come, O Come Emmanuel."

To multitudes of Chinese Christians around the world who are familiar with John Sung's testimony, Coffin is remembered as a villain who promoted the "God is dead" theology of his era and as the man who nearly destroyed the life of God's chosen vessel who brought revival to the Chinese world.

John Sung — "China's John the Baptist"

After being admitted to the mental asylum, Sung tried to convince the psychiatrists he was not insane, but they would not listen. He told them, "I am not crazy! I have just been reborn. My soul, which was in misery, is now filled with the joy of the Lord and I cannot stop praising Him!"[14]

The hospital took full control of his life, with all correspondence coming to him censored by the doctor in charge, who wrote back to John's relatives and friends, telling them he was too ill to reply and that they should not write again. When he realized the doctors were reading his Bible notes to evaluate his state of mind, Sung stopped writing in English and used Chinese to frustrate their plans.

Sung was told he was being evaluated for six weeks, but when the period concluded, John asked for his discharge but was refused. The seriousness of his situation dawned on him, and he realized he had been tricked by Henry Coffin and was now imprisoned against his will in a mental asylum. He attempted to escape, but police with flashlights and dogs soon found him hiding in a wheat field, and he was returned to a more secure ward for violent patients.

Finally, God gave favor, and with the help of a friendly nurse, Sung managed to write a letter to the Chinese consulate, explaining he had been locked up against his will.

Rollin Walker, meanwhile, had been away on a trip to Europe and only discovered what had happened to his friend John Sung after returning to America. He immediately realized the gravity of the situation, and he hurried to New York and met the Chinese consul general, who had just received Sung's letter. They secured his release on August 30, 1927, with Walker acting as a guarantor of Sung's behavior. Sung was discharged on condition that he would leave the United States and return to China.

After visiting the asylum, the consul general said that John Sung "was no more crazy than you or I, but he had such a good case of real, old-fashioned religion, and it was so unusual there that they thought he was crazy."[15]

Looking back on his time in the asylum, the man who was to become the greatest evangelist in China during the twentieth century said, "I was kept in the asylum for 193 days. While there, I read the Bible through 40 times. I was led by the Holy Spirit, and I could understand the mystery of truth. The asylum was my theological seminary. The day I left was the day I received my 'diploma.'"[16]

A Watery Grave

Before catching his ship back to China, Sung visited a pastor in Cincinnati, Ohio, where he was asked to play a tune on the piano. Before he started, a blind, deaf, and mute girl was seated at his side, and her hand was placed on the piano to feel the music as he played. When he finished the girl was asked to play, and she reproduced his entire tune from memory without missing a note. This encounter left a deep impression on John, who said,

> God wants me to serve Him in these end times like this girl. To be a servant of the Lord one must not look to the world and its riches, nor listen to man's ridicule and criticism. Unless one remains silent to taunts around him, he cannot carry the cross to follow Him. But these two hands are to do His work daily to fulfill His will.[17]

As he made his way across the vast Pacific Ocean, John Sung had a vivid dream in which he saw himself lying in a coffin with his academic degrees and gown. In the dream the old John Sung was dead, but the new man was alive in Christ and called to preach the gospel.

Although the world now considered Sung a success with a highly valued doctorate, God began to deal with his pride during the long voyage. One afternoon he overheard a group of American passengers vehemently denouncing Chinese people and culture. Sung was shocked and realized there was much work to do in his homeland and that the gospel of Jesus Christ was the only effective answer to China's problems.

As a result, he knelt in his cabin and rededicated himself to God's service and determined in his heart to place no limits on his zeal and consecration to reach his fellow Chinese. He renounced all of his worldly achievements, went up to the deck as the ship neared the Fujian coast, and hurled most of his diplomas, medals, and golden doctoral keys overboard into a watery grave. The only diploma he retained was his PhD, which he gave to his parents as a mark of respect for the effort and expense they had borne to help his career.

After reaching to his home in Putian, Sung reflected on seven dramatic years in America, in which he had lost his faith and plunged to the depths of despair, only to be rescued from the pit by the Lord Jesus, who revived his life and gave him a clear direction for the rest of his days.

John gave all his money to his father and his books and clothes to his brother. From that time forward he donned a simple cotton gown like many Chinese peasants of the time, and he lived as a poor itinerant evangelist.

His parents had been greatly concerned when they heard he had been declared insane and locked up in New York, but after carefully observing him for a week, they were convinced that he had been truly born again and transformed through a direct encounter with the living God.

John was asked to teach chemistry at a local Methodist high school. He worked there for a year, but science was now far down the list of priorities in his life, and he took every opportunity to indulge his real passion—the salvation of souls. He wrote,

The first lesson I gave taught them a great lesson on chemistry, how five loaves and two fishes provided food for 5,000 people. Boys and girls were brought to repentance. Here I spent half of my time teaching and half preaching. Every day I took students out to preach in the villages, and I spoke up to eight times per day.[18]

Discipleship

John Sung was appointed "evangelist at large" for the Methodist Church, and although other contemporary Chinese church leaders like Watchman Nee encouraged people to leave their denominations, Sung remained part of the Methodists for the rest of his life.

For the next three years he traveled around Fujian preaching in small rural churches, and his ministry began to resemble that of John the Baptist. He was uncompromising in his denunciation of sin and did not hesitate to publicly rebuke church leaders and missionaries whose lives failed to glorify Christ. He taught regularly on heaven and hell and the need for people to fully surrender to God and be filled with the Holy Spirit. Multitudes responded with weeping and open confession of sin.

Unlike some evangelists, Sung realized it wasn't enough to only preach salvation, so he established an extensive discipleship program to help new converts gain a strong foundation in God's Word. He grouped more than 100 churches into ten districts for training purposes and arranged several Bible conferences lasting up to a month each during which each book of the Bible was expounded. A co-worker later said, "What drew Dr. Sung's converts to him again and again was the rich, graduated biblical content, not only of his sermons but also of his ever-refreshing Bible studies."[19]

Sung also resembled John the Baptist in his physical appearance and mannerisms, which held the attention of thousands of enthralled people. He often used props to illustrate a point, with a colleague noting, "Sung often pantomimed his messages, jumping from the platform into the assembly, rooting up plants—a modern version of a Hebrew prophet."[20]

On other occasions Sung would call for volunteers to come up on the platform and, to illustrate his message would hang signs around their necks labeling specific sins such as "adultery," "lying," and "stealing."

Once, when asked to summarize the main themes of his teaching, Sung replied, "Repentance, heaven and hell, and the cross and blood of Christ . . . hating of sin and complete consecration; being filled with the Holy Spirit; and the life of faith as well as love. . . . In addition, one must live a life of hope."[21]

Family Life

In December 1927 John Sung married Yu Jinhua, who also used the English name Jean. It was an arranged marriage, having been agreed to by their parents when they were children.

For the first several years their family life was a struggle, as Jean did not yet share the faith of her husband. A wonderful breakthrough occurred in December 1932, which John recorded in his diary:

> I went home after conducting a service, and Jean asked me to repeat my sermon to her. I used this opportunity to give her my testimony. She acknowledged her own sins, like harboring hatred against people who treated her badly and pride. We prayed together and she was born again. I was joyful beyond description. Now that I have led my wife to be born again, there will be no more fear as I help others as well.[22]

The scene was set, and God was ready to launch His servant John Sung out into the spiritual darkness of China. Extraordinary things would happen that would shake every area where he

John Sung's family.

preached. Tens of thousands of supernatural healings and conversions to Jesus Christ took place amid a background of constant attacks, death threats, and intense demonic opposition.

Sung expressed regret that his nonstop preaching schedule caused him to rarely see his family, and he tried to make up for it near the end of his life. He was often away from home eleven months of the year and was not present at the birth of any of his children, who were named after the first four books of the Bible (Genesis, Exodus, Leviticus, Numbers), followed by a son, whom they named Joshua.[23] Jean was largely left to raise the children by herself, while John wrote and occasionally visited.

One of the heaviest personal blows John Sung experienced was when his little son, Joshua, died after a sudden illness. The evangelist was away in another part of China at the time, and during prayer he recorded that the Lord had spoken to his heart from Ezekiel 24:16–17: "Son of man, with one blow I am about to take away from you the delight of your eyes. Yet do not lament or weep or shed any tears. Groan quietly; do not mourn for the dead."

John Sung with his family in 1941. His son Joshua died soon after this photo was taken.

Straight away, Sung knew that God was telling him his son was dead, and he discreetly shared it with his co-workers. Eighteen days later a letter arrived from his wife, announcing their little son had passed away. She had delayed telling him the news because she didn't want it to interfere with his evangelistic campaigns.

Although she undoubtedly felt deep loneliness, Jean never criticized her husband for his absences. She recognized he had a unique call from God and was willing to endure hardship for the sake of the thousands of people being touched and transformed by the gospel.

John Sung — "China's Greatest Evangelist"

Unrelenting Attacks

John Sung's life had been intense—full of great victories and slumps—but after he joined the Bethel Evangelistic Band in 1931, he entered a new realm of spiritual warfare, the type of which few Christians have ever experienced.

Opposition to his preaching was overwhelming, and attacks came from every quarter, including from the government, religious leaders, academics, church leaders, and missionaries. All found some part of John Sung's ministry to be a threat or offensive to them, and they didn't hold back their vitriol.

The ruling Guomindang (Nationalist) government was furious with Sung after he refused to allow his students to bow down before a picture of "the father of modern China," Sun Yat-sen (Mandarin name: Sun Zhongshan). The Nationalists were so incensed by Sung's uncompromising stance that they initiated a smear campaign of lies, slanders, and threats against him, the effects of which lasted for the rest of his life.

One slanderous nickname that many used to revile the evangelist was "Sung the madman," which was used by people who had heard about his experiences in New York and by those who were put off by his obsession for the Lord and for winning lost souls to Christ.

The Bethel Band in 1931. Left to right (Back): John Sung (Song Shangjie), Philip Lee (Li Daorong), Frank Lin (Lin Jingkang); (Front): Lincoln Nieh (Nie Ziying), Andrew Gih (Ji Zhiwen).

When a casino in Fuzhou was forced to close its doors due to the effect of Sung's revival meetings, the owners threatened to beat him.[1] The evangelist recalled,

> The *Fujian People's News* charged that I was a magician, a charlatan, and a deranged person, and that I was out to make money. Between 80 and 90 men came to one meeting to yell and cause a disturbance. Two policemen threatened to arrest me if I persisted in preaching. Thanks be to God that amid such circumstances I had perfect peace and tranquillity.[2]

The rabid opposition did not thwart the gospel however, and Sung continued to see the Lord do great things and transform thousands of broken lives. As a result of those same meetings in Fuzhou, "111 evangelistic teams were set up after the meetings, and 300–400 people gave their lives to preach full time."[3]

In the southern Fujian city of Xiamen, the local newspaper accused John Sung of "deceiving the crowds with hypnosis and magic," and the Xiamen police ordered the meetings to stop due to the unprecedented traffic congestion caused by the large crowds of people trying to attend. The meetings were cancelled, but not before God had performed many mighty miracles. Sung wrote,

> Altogether I prayed for 1,710 patients that day. Before I prayed for them, I told them the principles of divine healing and I helped them confess their sins. A crippled and blind man could instantly see and walk. Another person was carried in on a bed and walked home. A hunchbacked woman instantly straightened up.
>
> Just before I left Xiamen, I prayed for 400 patients. One woman, who had been crippled for many years, cried aloud when she came to see me. I commanded her to walk by faith, and she immediately obeyed. She walked all the way home, testifying to many people along the way.
>
> The dailies in Xiamen lambasted me in their editorials. But despite these, 700–800 waved their evangelistic team banners when seeing me off.[4]

John Sung's diary entries recorded many other serious incidents and threats against his life, which he described in a matter-of-fact manner as if they were regular occurrences that didn't concern him at all. For example, he wrote,

> The leader of a 50-strong Atheist Party wanted me to promote science to save the country. But I only talked about Jesus, and they wanted to kill me. They later realized their folly and confessed their sins. Someone called Li brought a pistol to church on three

occasions. He wanted to raise the weapon but lacked the courage. In a dream from God, Li was advised not to kill me. . . . No one can harm me without God's approval.[5]

On another occasion, during meetings in Hui'an, Sung noted, "A dozen people plotted to sabotage streetlights, blow up the congregation, and assassinate me. These treacheries were foiled by the police in time, and pistols and explosives were uncovered. The Good Lord has been preserving me ever so miraculously!"[6]

As the opposition to his ministry grew more intense, Sung spent more time in prayer and communion with God. At each place he preached, he invited people to fill out prayer cards with their names and details and to list special prayer needs they had. Although some ministers might use such cards as gimmicks, Sung took the responsibility seriously and carried two suitcases of the cards with him wherever he traveled, daily interceding for each person by name.

Missionary William Schubert remembered, "In Nanjing I heard him weeping and praying for these people in places where he had held meetings previously. . . . This is one secret of his success and of the lasting results of his ministry."[7]

The reasons for Satan wanting to destroy John Sung was not difficult to comprehend. In their first year together, the Bethel Band traveled 55,000 miles (89,100 km) together across 13 provinces of China, preached the gospel to more than 400,000 people in 1,200 meetings, and recorded 18,000 decisions for Christ.[8] Moreover, at least 700 new evangelistic teams were formed as a result of the meetings, shining the light of the gospel across the nation.

Despite the earlier fierce opposition in Fuzhou, Sung boldly returned to the city for a series of meetings. It was as if a spiritual dam burst, and God's presence was so strong that thousands of university and government school students cancelled their classes to attend. According to the British missionary Leslie Lyall,

The break came in the second week when hundreds of people were born again, confessing their sins to God. Students made restitution to their teachers, reconciliations were a daily occurrence, and joy overflowed into the streets as the students returned home in groups singing.

Towards the end of the time in Fuzhou, Dr. Sung received threatening letters to the effect: "Leave Fuzhou or we will put you in jail!" The walls of the city were plastered with anti-Sung slogans! The daily newspapers attacked him. But during the month, over 1,000 young people were won for Christ, many of whom formerly followed a materialist philosophy and were open enemies of Christianity.[9]

Setting Out Alone

In 1933, the foreign leaders of the Bethel Band, who were based in Shanghai, received negative reports about John Sung. Instead of confronting him about the charges, it appears they decided that so many criticisms could not be wrong and demanded his resignation from the Band, even though he was recognized as the most fruitful of the evangelists and was the editor of the mission's magazine.

One of the accusations was that Sung had been secretly diverting funds for his personal use, which he vehemently denied. In the end, no evidence was cited to substantiate that claim. It appears to have been no more than a vicious rumor which the missionaries foolishly accepted as fact. In reality, Sung was well-known for his frugal lifestyle, and he preferred to travel third class on trains even when he could afford a better compartment, reasoning that as Jesus had often preferred the company of common people, he should do the same.

Indeed, rather than trying to accumulate money for himself, much evidence exists that Sung's overriding passion was to accumulate souls in heaven! In his diary entry of January 1, 1931, he wrote, "I am neither after money nor name. I plead with you, O Lord, to let me lead 100,000 people to the Lord." At the end of 1932 he requested another 200,000 souls.[10]

There is no doubt that John Sung's strong denunciations of sin and compromise by church leaders and missionaries angered many, and those who preferred a more toned-down type of Christianity were anxious to see the evangelist muted.

Tensions also existed between Sung and the other evangelists on the Bethel team, who were all men with strong personalities. The greatest tension appears to have been between Sung and Andrew Gih, although they held many meetings to try to smooth over their differences in a spirit of meekness. A co-worker of John Sung even said, "His fearlessness of utterance became a severity in denunciation of persons—several of his closest friends of revival times said that he was the rudest Chinese known to them."[11]

In the end, the differences proved too great to iron out, and Sung left the Bethel Band. J. Edwin Orr, a noted documenter of revivals around the world, knew Sung and the other Bethel members and had traveled with them in parts of China. He described Sung's departure from his colleagues as "sad rather than bitter."[12]

Although the Bethel Band continued under the leadership of Andrew Gih until 1947, it could be said they were never again as effective as during the few years that John Sung was part of the team.

Smelly Feet and Big Shots

Some Christians have the type of personality that makes it very difficult for them to be part of a team. John Sung was one of those probably better suited to working independently.

Two stories from Sung's ministry reveal the utter disdain he felt for formality and pretense. He cared nothing for a man's reputation and did not hesitate to openly rebuke people whenever it was necessary.

Once, while traveling in Henan Province, Sung and his co-worker reached a town late at night. Feeling exhausted, they sought out the local mission headquarters to see if they could stay the night before traveling on the next morning. Sung spoke with a security guard through the locked gate and told him that two evangelists were passing through and would appreciate lodging for the night.

The guard went inside and informed the missionary of the unexpected visitors. Even though they had spare rooms in the house, the guard was ordered to tell Sung and his friend they could stay the night in an outdoor barn.

Sung was unable to sleep all night due to the cold and because his face was right next to the smelly feet of another man. Before they left in the morning, Sung wrote a note in English to the missionary, rebuking him for his lack of loving hospitality toward two servants of the Lord, strongly advising him to examine his heart and repent.

The missionary and his wife were enjoying their breakfast when the note was handed to them. Their faces dropped when they realized one of the guests they had treated so poorly was none other than Dr. John Sung, "China's greatest evangelist"!

They quickly rode their bicycles along the road and caught up with the evangelists some distance out of town. They apologized profusely for mistreating Sung, saying they had no idea it was him, and begged them to come back and eat breakfast with them. Sung refused their offer, saying, "No, we are not going back. You are showing your hospitality to a PhD rather than an evangelist. You must thoroughly repent of your behavior!"[13]

John Sung — "China's Greatest Evangelist"

On Christmas Day, 1937, Sung was at Xuchang in Henan Province, where the Chinese Lutheran pastor had prepared a banquet to welcome the famous evangelist to the town. Sung was asked to sit at the main table with leading dignitaries and officials, while his 18-year-old traveling companion, Chu Huaian, was placed at a second table with the church elders and deacons.

When the pastor introduced all the guests, Sung discovered that he was seated between the mayor of Xuchang and the chief justice of the court. Across from him were the police commissioner and the editor of the local newspaper. According to Chu, when the church leaders at the second table were introduced,

> Dr. Sung stood up immediately and commanded me to switch seats with him. He said, "I am a servant of the Lord. I came to lead evangelistic meetings. I should be seated with brothers and sisters from the church. You go and mingle with those officials."
>
> Dr. Sung was always vehemently against churches holding any unnecessary social gatherings during revival meetings. He said, "We are one family as brothers and sisters; we should have the joy of eating together as a family. Why do we invite these big shots? It would be fine to invite them to come for the message. But to solicit their flattery and to have them for show, that is wrong."[14]

After severing his ties to the Bethel Band, Sung continued in the work God had called him to do, and for the remainder of his life he served as an independent evangelist, accepting invitations to preach all over China and Southeast Asia. Miraculous healings continued to be a feature of his ministry. Once, after holding a series of meetings at Gutian in northern Fujian, Sung recalled,

> One crippled woman had a diseased foot that was partially necrotized and very foul smelling. After prayer the lesion instantly dried up, leaving only a scar. Three deaf people recovered their hearing completely. A woman with a deformed spine was instantly healed. One student, after witnessing these miracles, went home and burned all his trashy novels.

John Sung — "China's Greatest Evangelist"

> This time in Gutian, 1,172 persons were saved, and 214 young people consecrated their lives to preach the gospel. Six to seven hundred people sent me off with tears and singing. How hard it was to say goodbye to those who love Jesus![15]

In 1934, John was traveling on a ship to a different part of China when he had a vivid dream in which his father stood by him and said, "Son, I have gone to heaven. But you have seven more years in which to work. So labor hard for the Lord!"[16]

A few days later a Christian woman casually asked Sung how his father was doing. He responded by shining his flashlight up into the sky and said, "He's up there." The sister was deeply offended and considered his comment flippant and disrespectful to his father.

Several days later the news arrived from Fujian that Song Xuelian had died. John took the message in the dream to heart and served Jesus Christ with an even greater determination and zeal. The dream proved wholly accurate, and seven short years later the window of opportunity for John Sung to proclaim the gospel closed.

Between 1935 and 1940, Sung's influence expanded into Southeast Asia. He made five earth-shaking trips there, including at least one visit to each of the countries of Singapore, Malaysia, Indonesia, Thailand, Vietnam, Myanmar, and the Philippines. When he left Singapore in December 1936, the *Straits Times* reported, "He was seen off by more than 1,000 excited Chinese, who paraded at the wharf waving flags and invaded the decks and saloons of the liner. Dr. Sung addressed his followers briefly; they sang hymns and smiled cheerfully, but fully half of them were weeping, some silently and some emotionally."[17]

Sung also crossed the strait from Fujian and preached in Taiwan to crowds of spiritually hungry people. At each place, revival fell upon the churches, and multitudes of sinners repented and received Jesus Christ. It was even said of the fiery evangelist,

"In several countries the Chinese churches survived the war with Japan solely because of the work of John Sung, to whom most of the spiritual life which flows in them can be traced."[18]

After another memorable visit to Singapore in October 1938, the *Straits Times* reported Sung's departure beneath the headline, "700 Chinese Weep on Wharf: Dynamic Evangelist Goes Home."

Sung promised to return to Singapore in 1940, but his health deteriorated to such an extent that he was never able to visit again. The multitude of well-wishers waved goodbye to him at the wharf, not realizing it was the last time they would ever see the beloved revivalist.

The Gift of Healing

Although he was not Pentecostal or Charismatic by today's usual definitions,[19] John Sung exercised a gift of healing that astounded audiences and resulted in countless people surrendering their

A John Sung open-air meeting at Xiamen, 1934.

lives to Christ. He was always quick to emphasize that each person had to repent of his sins lest he end up in hell. Sung carefully explained that he possessed no healing ability whatsoever, but it was the resurrected Lord Jesus Christ who did the miracles. Timothy Tow noted, "Sung was careful not to usurp any of God's glory and would sharply rebuke any who mentioned his name or gave credit to him."[20]

It was noted in one summary of Sung's ministry,

> Beginning in December 1931, John Sung exercised a truly stunning ministry of physical healing through prayer. Thousands of people—perhaps tens of thousands—were delivered from all sorts of illnesses, infirmities, and addictions after he prayed for them.
>
> Most of these miracles were witnessed by countless people, many of them originally skeptical of this aspect of John Sung's ministry. Opium addicts received instant deliverance. Smokers kicked the habit "cold-turkey." Those possessed by evil spirits were delivered. Blind people received their sight, the lame walked, disabled limbs were healed, and leprosy was cured instantly.[21]

At first, Sung seemed as surprised as anyone when a person was healed as a result of prayer. During a visit to the city of Hui'an, he wrote in his diary,

> During the healing service many patients received instant healing. One child, unable to walk for six years, could walk instantly. A woman who had not been able to lift her arm could lift it instantly after prayer. Another person could hear after being deaf for six years.
>
> There were quite a few Party officials and political leaders there ready to dispute with me concerning divine healing, but they were rendered speechless when confronted with this array of God's supernatural works. Twelve Western physicians were in the meeting to observe, and they were so flabbergasted by the signs and wonders that they urged me to go with them to a side room so they could confess their sins and repent of them.[22]

John Sung — "China's Greatest Evangelist"

The gift of healing that was so evident at John Sung's meetings attracted thousands to consider the claims of Christ on their lives. Recalling a meeting he attended in 1937 when he was just 13 years old, Brother Lin provides an eyewitness account:

> It was the first time I had ever been to a city. In a large church that seated 3,000, every hall, aisle, step, and seat was packed with people. There was no PA system, yet his voice was clearly audible. He walked from one end of the platform to the other, and the heads, necks, and eyes of the audience would follow his every move.
>
> The sounds of the audience in praying, crying, and praising came like waves, shaking the rafters. . . . I saw people leading the blind and carrying the paralyzed. The crippled were hobbling forward on their crutches. I heard people say that some were completely healed, some half-healed, and some not healed. However, with my own eyes I saw a pile of crutches and sticks in front of the changing rooms.[23]

When Sung returned to his hometown of Putian in 1937, thousands of people attended the meetings. His voice went hoarse, but he continued to preach and pray for the sick, and countless evangelistic teams were formed to take the message of eternal life into the districts surrounding the city. His diary records,

> 2,576 people attended the morning healing service on April 14, and I prayed for 774 patients. 171 evangelistic teams were sent out to preach. In the afternoon testimony meeting, 576 patients mounted the platform to testify of being healed, among them a hunchback who was straightened. There were blind people who could now see, the paralyzed now able to walk, and the deaf now able to hear. . . . One leper had planned to kill himself, but God healed him, and he opened his shirt to show the audience his now unblemished skin.[24]

Missionary nurse Serene Loland—one of the first Norwegian missionaries to China—was one of many whose future course was deeply impacted by Sung's ministry. She invited the evangelist to hold meetings in Gutian in 1934. Despite opposition from some of the local churches, after two days Loland reported,

> The meetings were filled with great heartbreak and unspeakable joy and caused a tremendous stir in the city. There were between 800 and 1,000 people who reached out for salvation during this campaign. Among theological and other students, tremendous changes took place. Many of the lives of the Christian leadership of the city were totally changed.[25]

Loland was filled with the Holy Spirit after Sung's visit, and she went on to have 50 effective years of ministry in China and Hong Kong. The humble nurse became a firebrand for Christ, and many healings and other miracles flowed through her consecrated life.

A Thorn in the Flesh

Curiously, throughout church history many servants of God who have been greatly endowed with a gift of healing have themselves been afflicted with serious diseases and infirmities they were not healed from.

John Sung was one such preacher, and he saw the irony, once calling himself a "wounded healer." The anal fistulas that first plagued him in the United States flared up whenever he was exhausted or under intense stress. Conflict with other Christians seemed particularly harmful to his health, as his rough exterior concealed a soft heart that was crushed by any disunity he had with other members of the body of Christ.

For years Sung maintained a gruelling travel schedule, sometimes holding as many as eight meetings in a day. For much of that time he was in terrible physical pain, which sometimes necessitated that he preach while sitting down or lying on a cot on the platform. Although still a young man in his thirties, he

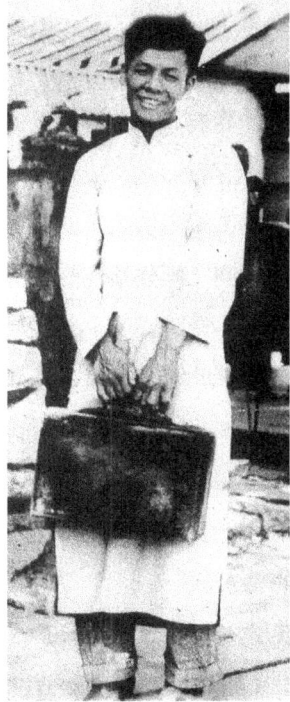

John Sung with his well-used briefcase.

often suffered debilitating fatigue, and his entire body ached from head to toe.

Instead of complaining, the evangelist tried to keep his condition hidden from the public. When he was hosted in a believer's home, he always insisted on washing his own clothes, for his underwear was often full of blood and pus from his horrible affliction. He described it as his "thorn in the flesh," designed by God to humble him.

When his condition flared, people in close proximity to Sung were often aware of an awful, offensive odor. John was aware of people's reactions, but there was little he could do about it, so he concentrated on preaching God's Word with all his heart, and he thanked the Lord for humbling his flesh to keep him from being conceited.

The evangelist also insisted that families who hosted him slaughter one chicken per day for his food, which he often prepared himself as chicken soup. A co-worker explained,

> If you have ever attended his meetings and seen how he preaches, often three times a day and as long as two hours a time, exerting every ounce of his physical and nervous energy from beginning to end, you could not blame him for asking for chicken soup to sustain him. Without such nourishment, he could never have kept up his strenuous work.[26]

Few people among the thousands who came to hear John Sung preach had any idea of the excruciating pain and sacrifice he was enduring both during and between services. When he visited the Malaysian island of Penang, he wrote,

> The doctor found that five serious anal fistulas had developed, and one was very bad. He gave me seven injections. I did not feel anything, but the subsequent pain almost blew me apart. I pleaded with the Lord to take pity on the people of Penang by taking pity on me, and so preached at the pulpit through His blessings. On December 6, Brother Chen Maju helped me put on my clothes and carried me up and down the stairs, and in and out of the vehicle. A sleeping cot was put on standby near the pulpit.
>
> The power of God was still with me as I spoke, and people came forward to confess their sins. Brother Yan sent me back and helped me disrobe after the service. The agony went on all night when the fistulas erupted, resulting in massive discharges of blood and pus. I still carried on with afternoon and evening services although I had hardly slept.[27]

As his condition deteriorated, six surgeries were performed at different hospitals throughout China, but none was able to fix the problem, possibly because he never stayed in one place long enough to recover completely from the operations.

Preaching from Bed

Sung's family, meanwhile, had been based in Shanghai for many years, but when John's condition worsened, doctors advised him to relocate from the humidity of Shanghai to the dry climate of Beijing, where his wounds would heal better. After reaching the nation's capital he was given a thorough checkup, where it was revealed that he was suffering from both cancer and a recurrence of tuberculosis.

As the sun started to set on his whirlwind life, Sung expressed regret that he had spent so little time with his children, and he tried to make up for it by reading them Bible stories and sharing testimonies of God's goodness with them during the final months of his life.

Wang Mingdao, the Beijing house church leader who became a key figure in Chinese church history by standing up to the Communists with an uncompromising faith, visited his good friend John Sung on March 20, 1943, and advised him to have an operation as soon as possible. Sung checked into the hospital the same day, but "medically the operations came six months too late. Dr. Sung had refused earlier advice to have an operation on the ground that he could not leave his work."[28]

After he awoke from the operation, Sung spoke with the surgeons and wrote in his diary,

> I tearfully prayed to God, telling Him I would like to do more work for Him after I am healed, and asking that my brothers and children would join me in the work for the Lord. I prayed that the Lord's will be done in my body. . . . When the incisions were made, two large bowls of blood exuded from my wounds, filling the operation room with a putrid odor.[29]

Although John Sung was forced to remain in bed due to his illness, many Christians traveled from all over China to see him. He counseled and prayed with them, and often conducted three meetings per day from his bed.

On July 1, 1944, John Sung's condition worsened. It was reported,

> The tubercular fistula grew to the size of an adult's closed fist, and the wound was a foot deep. It was so painful that he could not turn over. Many doctors and nurses, all devoted followers of Christ, came to attend to him. He told his wife, "This body of mine is rotting. It's decaying fast.... But my lips are not and can still pray to God!" And pray he did, even as pus, blood, and tears flowed.[30]

After weeks of attempted recovery—which left John feeling increasingly frustrated because he wasn't out preaching—he continued to suffer intense pain. Some of his final diary entries in 1944 reveal his journey through the valley of the shadow of death:

> July 25: "I have turned myself over several times. The pain has been so searing that my wounds feel like they're on fire. I pleaded with God to take me home to heaven soon."

> July 28: "I begged God to give me some proof that He still loves me. Jean is too weak to turn me over, so a man is needed. Dr. Lee examined my wounds and said I need to take opium to stop the pain."

> July 30: "I confessed my sins to God. I feel utterly drained of strength."

> July 31: "I returned the tin of opium to the doctor. The pain is the worst ever. If this continues, I don't know how I could take it anymore."

August 11: "Now I can't hold anything with my hands. I feel a little discouraged. I asked God to open a way out for me."

Finally, on the morning of August 16, 1944, John's limbs began to swell. He told his wife that God had shown him he was going to die soon. He fell into a coma that night but rallied again and sang three hymns, while vomiting continually into a bucket. Jean was overcome with grief as she saw her husband fade away before her eyes, and at about midnight his last words to her were, "Don't be afraid! The Lord Jesus is at the door. What is there to fear?"

Jean later shared the holy moment when her beloved husband began his journey to God at the age of 43:

> At the time the room was very dark, but his face suddenly shone with a brilliant radiance. When I saw this strange light, my heart was greatly comforted. At five in the morning on August 18, his pulse weakened, and at 7:07 that morning, the Lord's servant was peacefully taken away. He had a smile on his face.[31]

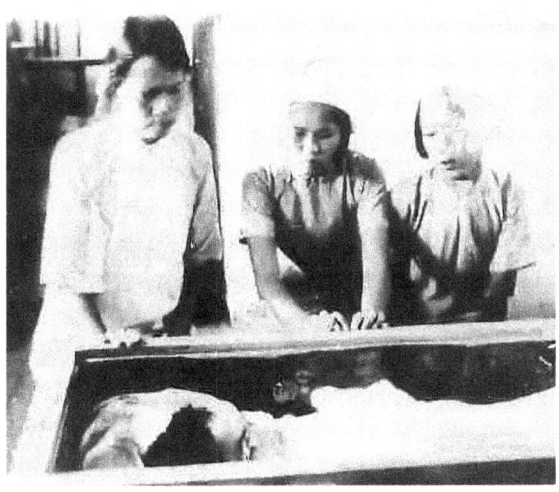

Jean and two of John Sung's daughters grieving over the casket.

After Sung's death, numerous tributes and memorials flowed in. Some estimated that at least 100,000 people had been directly and solidly converted through his preaching, which was about one-tenth of all Evangelical Christians in China at the time. More than three decades after the evangelist's death, his close friend William Schubert wrote, "John Sung was probably the greatest preacher of this century. I have heard almost all the great preachers from 1910 until now, including R. A. Torrey, Billy Sunday . . . and finally Billy Graham. Yet John Sung surpassed them all in pulpit power, attested by amazing and enduring results."[32]

Although the span of his life and ministry was relatively short, a fellow house church pastor who had been influenced by Sung's ministry—Allen Yuan of Beijing—later offered this insight during a time of intense persecution in the late 1950s:

> Many people did not understand why God did not give him a longer life so he could serve Him more. Now many of them have realized that it was the grace of God, so that Dr. Sung wouldn't have to suffer. If he were alive today, he would surely be in prison right now.[33]

The quality of John Sung's ministry can be seen eight decades later by the lasting fruit of his life. Tens of thousands of Christians throughout Asia still call him blessed and are the direct or indirect result of his preaching. Perhaps the greatest impact he had was in preparing the Chinese church for the onslaught that was to come against them during decades of Communist persecution.

Many Chinese believers who had been deeply impacted by John Sung went on to enjoy years of effective ministry, including Lin Pei Xuan (Hokkien: Lim Puay Hian), who continued in the late evangelist's footsteps with powerful meetings across Fujian, south China, and in every country in Southeast Asia.[34]

John Sung — "China's Greatest Evangelist"

On a number of occasions before he died, Sung prophesied that God would soon remove all foreign missionaries from China, and the church would have to learn to trust Him alone for their spiritual sustenance. After that, a mighty revival would take place that would sweep millions into the kingdom of God.

The last word on the life and ministry of this complex and contradictory man is best left to his biographer, Leslie Lyall:

> A flaming evangelist, but a man uncouth in appearance and seeming to lack in ordinary social graces. A scholar and a scientist of the highest academic attainments, but a man whose simple gospel sermons never bore a trace of erudition or display of learning. . . . Noisy and acrobatic and full of humor on the platform, but silent and almost morose off it.
>
> Denouncing sin vehemently wherever he found it, but able as no one else to move audiences with the message of God's love. A born organizer and leader who resisted the temptation to found a new organization of his own. A man greatly beloved, yet greatly hated; bitterly criticized, yet utterly careless of criticism. Such was the greatest evangelist China has ever known.[35]

Friends and family at the funeral of John Sung.

John Sung — "China's Greatest Evangelist"

The death of John Sung did not signal the end of suffering for this family. The Communists swept into power in 1949, and even though the evangelist had died five years earlier, the fanatical atheists were determined to stamp out every vestige of his influence that they could find.

Jean was always a silent hero in the background of the John Sung story, quietly offering her support and raising the children while her husband blazed a pathway of salvation for the multitudes. She also suffered much but continued to follow the Lord until her death in January 1980.

In 1958, during a brutal persecution of Christians throughout China, Sung's oldest daughter, Tianying (Genesis) was sentenced to 20 years in a prison labor camp after being found to have been "poisoned by an imperialist religion," while daughter Leviticus (better known as Levi) shared the extreme struggle she was forced to endure:

> The Red Guards confiscated everything after giving my mother 10 yuan, a few pieces of clothing, and some food. The Bibles and my father's diaries were taken away too. The Red Guards also asked me to surrender the entire collection of photographs tracing my father's trips to America and all over the world, including all the testimonies from believers who had been blessed. I suffered a mental breakdown after that and was on the brink of death.[36]

A great miracle took place in 1970. Levi had asked for her father's books to be returned, but her efforts had been constantly rebuffed by government officials.

One day she ran into an official on the street, who remembered her and directed her to a warehouse where items confiscated from "criminals" were stored in a huge pile. She walked around the small mountain of boxes and bags, wondering how she would ever be able to find her father's precious books, which he had guarded so closely during his life.

Finally, feeling completely overwhelmed by the impossible task, she stopped and called on the Lord for help. When she finished praying, she looked down at the ground, and through her tears she saw her father's invaluable diaries at her feet!

Levi was instrumental in having the diaries carried to Singapore and published in both Chinese and English.[37] God, as always, had the last word, and hundreds of thousands of Christians in China and around the world have been greatly blessed and strengthened by reading the gripping accounts and spiritual insights of John Sung, China's greatest evangelist.

Watchman Nee — The Early Years

Watchman Nee in his teenage years.

In 1920, when John Sung was in the United States gathering degrees, which he would later throw into the ocean, another young native of Fujian Province—a man just two years Sung's junior—was touched by God and called to a unique and far-reaching ministry that would ultimately impact millions of people across China and around the world.

Ni Tuosheng, who was known outside China as Watchman Nee, was born in November 1903, the third of nine children, to God-fearing parents who faithfully attended a Methodist church in Fuzhou City.

Growing up, Nee attended an Anglican school from the age of 13 but did not have a personal relationship with Christ until he was 17, when evangelist Dora Yu (Chinese name: Yu Cidu) visited Fuzhou.

Although Nee's mother identified as a Christian, she also did not have a personal relationship with the Lord. After attending several of Dora Yu's meetings, she accepted Jesus as her Savior. Her life was radically transformed, and she started daily family prayer times and Bible studies. Watchman observed his mother's conversion and found it curious but was not interested in following in her footsteps.

A short time later, Watchman's mother was playing the piano and about to sing a hymn, when the conviction of the Holy Spirit stopped her in her tracks. She could not sing a word as God reminded her of an earlier incident when a vase had been broken in the house, and she assumed Watchman had been the culprit. She had severely punished him, but even though she later discovered he was completely innocent in the matter, her pride prevented her from apologizing to him.

Now that she had been born again, the Spirit of God convicted her of her sin. She admitted her wrongdoing and asked her teenage son for forgiveness. As a result,

> [t]he young man was greatly moved by his mother's sincerity ... and decided to attend a gospel meeting with her. Thanks be to God, the Holy Spirit worked in a sweeping way at that meeting. He saw his own sins, and simultaneously realized the salvation of the cross. Watchman received Christ and so was saved through grace. He not only believed in God but dedicated his whole life to His service. After this, his life underwent a great change.[1]

Nee, who at six feet (1.8 meters) was comfortably taller than most of his contemporaries, was a serious-minded young man, fully committed in everything he did. After coming under the influence of Margaret Barber, he realized that his "baptism" by sprinkling as a child in the Methodist church was meaningless, and he was baptized again in the Min River, this time upon confession of repentance and faith in Jesus Christ.

Watchman was a brilliant student, with one of his teachers at Trinity College saying that he never saw him take notes because he was able to retain everything he read and heard. Missionary Charles Barlow recognized great potential in the young man, saying, "Some of these dear brethren are very sincere and thirsting for truth. Watchman Nee is undoubtedly the outstanding man among them. He is far beyond all the rest. He . . . has had a good education and is possessed of marked ability. He is a hard worker and reads much."[2]

When news of his academic prowess spread, Nee was offered the chance to go to the United States to further his education. Although he was aware that great material benefit could result if he studied overseas, he prayerfully sought God's will, and unlike John Sung who experienced seven years of distress in America, Nee decided to remain and serve the Lord in China. His parents were furious when he broke the news to them, for they hoped he would enjoy a lucrative career and provide for their needs in their old age.

Trinity College in Fuzhou where Watchman Nee went to school.

The Fall of the King God

In 1923, Nee joined other young believers, including Wang Zai (Leland Wang) and his younger brother Wang Zhi (Wilson Wang), John Wang from Taiwan, Lu Zhongxing (Faithful Luke)[3] from Gutian, and Miao Shaoxun (Simon Meek) from Lianjiang.[4] The group, dubbed the "Fuzhou Six" by other Christians, established a fellowship, and the fresh touch of God's Spirit was on their work.

Because of fervent evangelism by the Fuzhou Six, many students at Trinity College were saved, and the gospel spread to the suburbs surrounding the campus. They also traveled to rural areas where salvation had never been proclaimed.

On one occasion they visited Meihua ("Plum Flower") Village. They held an open-air meeting as soon as they arrived but encountered a surprisingly cold reception. People seemed completely uninterested, and few remained to listen to their message.

The next morning, one of the team members, an 18-year-old new convert named Wu, asked a local why people were not interested. The man replied, "We have many gods here and cannot accept another. We worship the great King god and we hold a festival in his honor every year."

The young evangelist discovered that the festival was due to take place a few days later, on January 11, and people claimed that for more than 200 years every procession in honor of the King god had been held in perfect weather under cloudless skies.

As soon as he heard this, Wu declared that it would surely rain on the day of the procession to show the villagers that Jesus Christ is the true and all-powerful God. This bold prediction spread like wildfire among the community, and people were eager to see who was more powerful: the King god or Jesus.

When Watchman Nee was informed about the challenge laid down by his zealous co-worker, he immediately recognized the potential danger of a showdown and that the reputation of the gospel in that place would be seriously undermined if the day of the idolatrous procession took place in fine weather. He called the team together for concentrated prayer, and they believed the Lord assured them by reminding them, "I am the God of Elijah."

Two days before the festival, the team went into the community again, telling people that it would rain on the eleventh to prove that Jesus Christ is the Living God. Many locals sneered at them, but most were curious onlookers keen to see what would transpire.

On the morning of January 11, a beautiful day dawned without a cloud in the sky, and the faith of the evangelists was tested. With the procession due to start at nine o'clock, the team members fell on their knees and cried out to God, asking Him to intervene. Then, just as the procession was about to begin,

> [t]he sky suddenly changed and the rain pelted down. It showed no sign of stopping even at eleven o'clock, and the streets were flooded with two to three feet of water.... No sooner had the great King god left the temple than all the carriers tumbled into the water lying on the street. Three of the idol's fingers and one of its arms were broken, and even its head was twisted. The rain then became a torrent, and it was impossible to proceed with the parade. The great King god was expediently left in an ancestral hall.[5]

After lunch, Nee and the team prayed again, asking God for fine weather so they could preach the gospel. Within minutes the rain stopped, the sun appeared, and they spent all afternoon testifying to the power and grace of Jesus Christ. The people now gave their full attention, and the evangelists sold all their Gospel literature. Many villagers openly declared, "The King god is not true. Only Jesus is God."

Embarrassed by what had occurred, the temple priests consulted the spirits and announced that a mistake had been made, and that the procession should have taken place on the evening of January 14. The sky was clear for the next three days, and then just before the rescheduled procession began, the heavens again opened and flooded the streets. As a result, more people were convinced of the gospel and believed in Christ.

A Contentious Stance

After only about a year of fruitful outreach together the Fuzhou Six split up after Nee stated that the ordination of believers into Christian ministry was wrong and a stumbling block to the gospel. In his opinion, all titles such as "pastor," "reverend," etc. were to be shunned, as all believers were equal in God's sight.

Some of Watchman's colleagues strongly disagreed, and the evangelists went their own ways, with some refusing to fellowship with Nee.

Later, some of the workers focused their anger on the brother who had demanded Nee's excommunication. The debate became so heated that some of the men threatened physical violence against the brother and gathered around to beat him. At that moment, Nee stepped in and protected his antagonist with his own body, crying out in a loud voice,

> "Don't touch him! If you want to beat him, beat me first! He is loved by God and loved by me too. He is our brother! I have forgiven him. You should also do the same. At any rate, you must not lay your hands on him." . . . The man was deeply moved and shed tears on the spot. . . . This agitation subsided.[6]

After this incident, Watchman Nee felt he should move away from Fuzhou, and in 1924 he left for Shanghai where he focused on producing Christian publications and edited *The Christian Message* magazine. He also founded the Gospel Book Room in the city and held regular conferences which helped revive God's people.

Nee also began to receive invitations from Christians around the world, and he ministered in Southeast Asia, Japan, North America, and Europe.

While in the United Kingdom, Nee met with key figures such as T. Austin Sparks, whom he later regarded as his spiritual authority, and with Jessie Penn-Lewis, who was closely associated with Evan Roberts of the Welsh Revival. It was there that he also encountered the Plymouth Brethren for the first time. Watchman was deeply impressed by their lives and practices and later sought to incorporate many of their ways into the churches in China.

Despite his name becoming increasingly known throughout the Christian world Nee did not forget his roots, and he regularly returned to Fujian to hold revival meetings. The following report of a 1926 meeting at a school in Xiamen provides a rare glimpse into the man and his message. One of the students at the meeting, James Chen, recalled,

> Brother Nee, wearing a blue cotton long gown, walked up the school platform, sat down, and prayed silently; he did not look at anything or anybody.
>
> I, like others, at once despised him. Then when he stood up and prayed aloud, all the students were tittering for we never heard anybody praying in such a peculiar way as he did. But after he had spoken five minutes, the atmosphere of the whole place changed dramatically! The audience was listening attentively, and everybody was astounded because he preached—just as the Bible says—"as one who had authority."
>
> Many people began to deal with their sins. Even the man in charge of the school kitchen was amazed, for the number of bowls and plates, etc. in the kitchen suddenly increased. Formerly many students took kitchen utensils to their own rooms to use, but now they knew it was unrighteousness, so they returned all of them to the school. The Holy Spirit was working everywhere, and everybody praised God![7]

In church life Nee often appeared stern toward others, and he appeared to handle the Word of God with great sobriety. Those who knew him best, however, told how he spoke in a warm and loving manner that attracted people to Christ. One church member recalled,

> Watchman Nee's preaching style was gentle. There was no pulpit, and he made those around him feel that he was listening and not judging. Standing before a crowd, dressed in the dark blue cotton gown of a traditional Chinese man, he prayed slowly, letting the words out deliberately, and he distilled his thoughts in language that anyone could understand. Never referring to notes, he relied on stories or anecdotes to convey his message.[8]

The Local Church

Of all the controversial positions promoted by Watchman Nee over the years, the one that caused the greatest outcry in China was his insistence that denominations were unbiblical and that God only recognizes one fellowship of believers in each city or location. He supported his teaching by pointing out that in the New Testament writers only referred to the church in each location, such as "the church at Corinth," or "the church at Ephesus."

Nee further noted that the apostle Paul had appointed elders in every city he visited. This, he claimed, showed that the elders of a church had the spiritual authority in each city and that the boundary was the city or town where the church was located.

Reflecting this belief, Nee's movement came to be called the Local Church, although it was also referred to as Local Assemblies or Assembly Hall. Outsiders often referred to it as the Little Flock after the title of a hymnal they used. Nee himself despised the name Little Flock, saying that it gave the impression they had started a new denomination—the very thing he sought to avoid.

Unsurprisingly, when other church leaders and missionaries heard about Watchman Nee's "new doctrine" they strongly pushed back, seeing it as an attempt to steal their sheep by creating confusion among God's people. Nee's strong, uncompromising stance on this and many other issues created barriers within the body of Christ.

Nee's fellow Fujian native, John Sung, returned to China in 1927, and the ministries of the two revivalists flourished at the same time. However, it appears there was little contact between the two strong-willed men. One of the few accounts that link the duo includes the following:

> The work of Watchman Nee was against the established churches, substituting for them his own brand of the Little Flock, whose practice was castigated by John Sung, though he did not mention Nee by name. Nor did John Sung agree with Watchman Nee's stress on unleavened bread for the Lord's Supper and his requirement of women to cover their heads in church.[9]

A rare photo of John Sung, Leland Wang, and Watchman Nee together in Shanghai.

The Spiritual Man

Whereas John Sung focused on revival preaching, Watchman Nee knew the power of the written word, and after contracting tuberculosis in 1927 he took an extended break from preaching and focused on writing. A German doctor who treated Nee compared X-rays of his condition with that of another patient who had died and found the evangelist's disease was at least as bad as that of the man who had already passed away.

Battling the debilitating illness, Watchman commenced work on a book titled *The Spiritual Man*, which he completed in July 1928. It was described as "the first and last book he ever sat down and wrote, the rest of his publications all being transcriptions of his preaching and teaching."[10] At the end of the book, Nee wrote,

> It has been 16 months since I started writing this book. During this period, it can be said that my concern was always about this task. Naturally the enemy, seeing the truth of God being proclaimed this way, would not leave me alone, and therefore the fierce attacks aimed at me were quite overwhelming.
>
> Since 1926 my physical condition has been getting worse and worse. I have too many responsibilities and there is not enough time to rest. Upon finishing *The Spiritual Man*, I was completely exhausted both mentally and physically. This poor condition is still with me.[11]

The Spiritual Man went on to sell more than one million copies around the world and was translated into 35 languages, encouraging believers to a more wholehearted commitment to Christ. However, critics claimed that he had plagiarized much of the teaching directly from the writings of his Welsh friend, Jessie Penn-Lewis, and that parts of the book were word-for-word translations of Mrs. Penn-Lewis' articles in her magazine *The Overcomer*.

It was around this time that additional concerns were raised about Nee's theology, especially his teaching on the tripartite nature of man, the nature of God, and his subtle slant on the Scriptures, which many saw as containing an underlying current of Gnosticism. Critics were concerned that Nee and his fellow leaders

> believed that they had a special insight into spiritual knowledge and saw their insight (intuition) as more important than the Bible's specific teaching. They were very prideful and looked down on those who just simply clung to the specifics of the Bible. They had the idea that despite what the Bible seemed to say on certain points, they had been given the illumination of the true will of God. They could read between the lines to get the *real* meaning God intended.[12]

A Controversial Marriage

In keeping with the theme of his life, Watchman Nee's 1934 marriage to Zhang Pinhui (Charity Zhang) proved highly controversial and divided opinion among Chinese Christians.

The Nee and Zhang families had known each other for three generations, and when he was in his early twenties Watchman fell deeply in love with the bright young lady, whose academic achievements paralleled his.

After he committed his life to Christ, Watchman was anxious for Charity to become his wife and partner in the ministry, but she showed no inclination toward the gospel and even openly mocked Jesus in front of him. This deeply grieved the young preacher, but he continued to pray hoping she would change so they could marry.

One day as he was reading the Bible, Watchman realized Charity had captured his heart to such a degree that she had become an idol to him. He realized that if he wanted to serve

Christ, he would have to surrender Charity to God and walk away from pursuing a relationship with her.

A decade passed, during which Watchman Nee threw himself into the work of the kingdom of God. By 1932 more than 20 fellowships had been formed under his leadership, and "over 4,000 people had been saved and revived."[13]

Then one day Nee heard that Charity had placed her trust in the Lord Jesus. He immediately went to see her so he could find out if it was true. When she gave a clear testimony of how she had repented of her sins and believed in Christ, he was thrilled!

Soon Watchman saw that marrying Charity would be no simple task. Her aunt vehemently opposed their relationship, considering the preacher too low on the socio-economic scale for her niece who had graduated with a degree in literature from the prestigious Yanjing University in Beijing. Charity was old enough to make her own decisions, but Watchman delayed proposing not wanting to offend her aunt and cause a rupture in the family.

Watchman's mother, however, was not put off by the aunt's opposition. Her son was already in his early thirties and it was time for him to marry! She decided to act quickly, so while he was conducting a 10-day conference in the city of Hangzhou, his mother arranged a secret wedding for him in Shanghai.

Nee continued to preach blissfully unaware of his mother's plan, but somehow before the end of the conference, a rumor began to circulate among the attendees that their pastor was about to marry. He brushed it off, knowing that any wedding without the approval of Charity's aunt would lead to major turmoil.

When he discovered that the rumors were true, Watchman decided to escape from the conference and hide in a remote location until the wedding date passed. When he shared his plans with some of his co-workers, they admonished him saying, "It would be nothing to you if you should escape, but you should consider the bride, our sister. What ignominy she would have to suffer on her wedding day if the bridegroom was nowhere to be found! If you escape, we will not be your co-workers!"[14]

Nee submitted himself to his mother's plans. The day after the conference concluded he traveled to Shanghai and, still wearing the same clothes he had preached in all week, Watchman and Charity were united in marriage on October 19, 1934.

Watchman and Charity on their wedding day.

The fear of Charity's aunt was not unfounded. When she received news of the secret wedding she exploded in fury, even taking out ads in multiple newspapers to slander Watchman Nee's reputation and to condemn the "illegitimate" marriage. A number of believers in the Local Church joined in denouncing him, but Nee refused to respond or defend himself.

Watchman was a sensitive man at heart, and the brutal slanders deeply affected him. Instead of enjoying life with his new bride he felt totally depressed, and for a period he withdrew into the background and rarely spoke in meetings. A co-worker recalled this dark season: "Brother Nee was assailed by Satan in many respects, and for over a year he was utterly disillusioned and dejected. He could hardly lift up his head because reputation, virtues, and everything seemed to have been annihilated."[15]

Watchman Nee — The Latter Years

Author's Note: While most Western Christians hold only a favorable impression of Watchman Nee, Chinese believers both in China and around the world are deeply divided in their views of his legacy. The Bible never whitewashes the mistakes made by men of God, whether Abraham, Moses, David, Peter, or Paul. All had their faults, and at times their faith failed or they let their flesh take over. These are valuable lessons we can all learn from.

For many readers, some of the events and claims documented in this chapter will be shocking and unwelcome. My first indication that the story of Watchman Nee had more to it than meets the eye came over 20 years ago, when I would mention his name to Chinese house church leaders and they would immediately look down at the floor. Their reluctance to talk about Nee revealed a deep sadness in their hearts.

Sidetracked

The year 1938 was a pivotal one in the life and ministry of Watchman Nee. Early in the year he published a book in Chinese titled *Rethinking Missions*, which reportedly "hit the Chinese churches and the mission-orientated denominations like a bombshell. A storm of criticism broke over Watchman's head as churches closed their doors and Christians left their denominations and united with the Little Flock."[1]

Under constant pressure both from within the church and from the world, Nee continued to steadfastly follow the course he believed God had laid out for his life until a momentous

Watchman Nee in England in 1938.

decision took place which appears to have been a turning point for the worse.

As the influence of the Local Church spread, with hundreds of new fellowships springing up throughout China, Nee discovered that many of the pastors and evangelists that had been sent to pioneer new work were struggling to survive, and some were even starving due to a total lack of support from the movement's leaders who had a policy of sending workers to live solely by faith.

At the time, Watchman's younger brother Ni Huaizu (who went by the English name George) had established a small pharmaceutical factory in the Portuguese colony of Macau. A research chemist, he had produced some patented medicines that were as effective as those produced in the West, but for a fraction of the price. The company was not growing due to Huaizu's lack of business *nous*, however.

Watchman, responding to a request from his parents, agreed to help his little brother in the business, thinking that if successful it would provide funds to support the workers and help the movement expand even more.

Their company, China Biological and Chemical Laboratories, soon grew and became well known throughout China. By the second year, personnel problems meant that Watchman devoted most of his time to running the business and little time obeying God's call to preach the gospel and establish churches.

This new emphasis deeply concerned many of Nee's closest co-workers. They pleaded with him to put God's kingdom first, but he ignored their advice. Ruth Lee, who had been a key worker in the literature ministry for many years and had transcribed into shorthand hundreds of Watchman's sermons which were later used as the basis for some of his best-selling books, was so disappointed that she resigned. Others followed.

Nee's new focus on business incited widespread ridicule and rumors from other Christians. The Local Church elders in Shanghai, who had been carefully selected and trained by Nee, now turned against him. After pronouncing him unfit to minister the Word of God, they excommunicated the founder of their movement. A church member recalled this difficult time: "Those were days of darkness! Many people felt the heaviness of spirit and were exceedingly sad. Those pure in spirit could only shed tears, suffer pain, sustain grief, and pray."[2]

Norman Cliff, a veteran British missionary to China and a prolific author, noted, "Nee later admitted this decision was a serious misjudgement. It set in motion a chain of events that would cast a dark shadow over his public ministry as a preacher."[3]

After several years, Nee finally came to his senses and realized he had neglected the gifts God had given him. Using some of the profits from the then highly successful company, he purchased several houses in the Guling mountains outside Fuzhou which he used to train workers.

Although he was again preaching and teaching, in many ways the damage to Watchman Nee's reputation had been done by his long absence and expulsion from the Shanghai church, where many members had become disillusioned and moved on. Some recalled his teaching before 1938—the year he decided to engage in business—when he had often said, "Fear money just as you should fear the fire of hell."[4]

Slide into Error

In 1948, a decade after being excommunicated by the elders in Shanghai, Nee was allowed to speak there again. The atmosphere was tense as he began his message, with many believers considering him a traitor to the faith and to their church movement.

After sharing a story about himself in the third person, Nee expressed contrition for the many mistakes he had made. He then broke down in a genuine torrent of tears, and the atmosphere changed. Those who harbored resentment against him confessed their sins, and mutual forgiveness was asked for and given. He was once again welcomed into the Shanghai fellowship.

In the early years after the Local Church was established, Nee had always gone out of his way to encourage believers to develop their own relationship with Jesus Christ and to be careful not to allow men to become mediators between them and the Lord. He learned those lessons from observing the weaknesses of the missionary movement in Fujian, and he strongly emphasized the priesthood and equality of all believers.

By the late 1940s, Nee was struggling on numerous fronts, and his position as leader of the movement was under threat. He began to teach the exact opposite of what he had first taught, demanding unquestioning obedience from every church member. In one message reminiscent of the control typically exhibited by cults, he said,

> Living the church life demands our very life. The first thing we have to do is not to think, but to submit. The saints should present all the problems to the elders, and the elders should present the problems before God. In this way the saints can come to God through the elders, and God's authority can be realized among the saints.
>
> The only solution is for man to listen and obey. If you think that something is right, you should obey. If you think that something is not right, you should nevertheless obey. Everyone should rise up, and everyone should learn obedience.[5]

Another area that brought great concern to many Christians was Nee's launch of what he called "handing over." He started by handing the pharmaceutical company over to the control of the Local Church, and then church members were instructed to hand over their property to Nee and the apostles of the movement. By twisting the Scriptures, he taught that members must surrender their possessions to the "Jerusalem Mother Church," and if someone refused to cooperate,

> [t]hey were seen as unwilling to come under the assembly leadership and lost the right to represent God on earth. This was interpreted as a power struggle. From then on, it evolved into asking for the unquestioning obedience of the members, deeming it as obedience to the Holy Spirit. It was a change from freedom in the Spirit to arrangement by the church, and from local assembly independence to central control.[6]

Despite all the troubles and Nee's slide into error, the Local Church continued to expand across China due to the influence of its hundreds of evangelists and pastors. By 1951, the movement numbered almost 1,000 churches in China, containing approximately 90,000 Christians.[7]

Watchman Nee in the prime of his life.

The Three-Self Deception

In 1950, with China now firmly under Communist control, the Three-Self Patriotic Movement (TSPM) increased its pressure on all Christians, threatening and seducing them to come under its umbrella. Harsh penalties awaited those who refused. In Fujian, the local TSPM succeeded in convincing many hundreds of churches to join it, but Watchman Nee and his fellowships had stubbornly refused to budge.

When he visited Hong Kong in 1950, the believers there strongly encouraged Nee not to return to Mainland China, but to continue his ministry in Southeast Asia. After much thought and prayer, he decided to return to China and sacrifice everything for the Lord's work there. He explained,

> If a mother discovered that her house was on fire, and she herself was outside the house doing the laundry, what would she do? Although she realized the danger, would she not rush into the house? Although I know that my return is fraught with dangers, I know that many brothers and sisters are still inside. How can I not return?[8]

Ever-increasing pressure and accusations were brought against Nee and other leaders of the Local Church, and one by one they defected and joined the government-approved religious movement. Nee knew there was now no way to escape severe persecution.

Author Randy Alcorn detailed an incident during one of Nee's final sermons:

> He knew in the crowd there were many authorities waiting to arrest him as soon as he spoke about Jesus or the church. When he stood, there was a glass of water by him. Suddenly he threw it down, then crushed it with his heel. But the more violently he crushed it, the more the glass spread. Everywhere he put his foot down, glass spread farther. The unbelievers thought he had gone mad. But the believers understood. It was a sermon without words. . . . In attempting to destroy the church, the government would spread it.[9]

Then, in December 1950, another bombshell moment occurred that shocked the members of the Local Church throughout China, which is still felt today. Apparently without consulting any of the other church leaders—and without the permission of the believers themselves—Watchman Nee submitted a list, containing the signatures of 32,782 members of 475 churches, to the head of the TSPM in Fujian Province, effectively signing them up as members of the Three-Self Church.

When news circulated that Nee had done this, many refused to believe it, thinking it was false news or a lie created by the government. The signatures had been collected for an earlier petition during the "handing over" policy, when many church members gave their land and property to the Local Church.

After realizing they faced a massive tax liability as legal owners of all the newly acquired real estate, Nee and the other church leaders had members sign a petition asking the government to exempt church properties from having to pay land tax.[10] The petition was rejected, but it was those same signatures that Watchman Nee later fraudulently used to sign his members up with the TSPM.

Later, when the full fury of Communist persecution broke upon the church in Fujian, all the property that had been willingly given by Local Church members was confiscated by the authorities. Many Christians struggled to survive, having lost their homes as part of the manipulative "handing over" campaign.

To compound the terrible fallout from Nee's betrayal, the government later used the extensive list of believers' names to brutally suppress them, with one source saying, "The Communists captured nearly all of their local leaders and sentenced them to 15 to 20 years in prison."[11]

Decades later, former church members were still angered by Nee's deceptive and underhanded act. One believer wrote,

> The submission was the sole decision of Nee. He did not notify the Local Church leaders. The congregation did not know anything about his manipulation of the believers' signatures. . . . Nee's action was cunning, dishonest, and against our will. With this, the Communist government gained a name list and information

of the distribution of Local Churches and the church members throughout the country at no cost.[12]

Further compromises followed as Watchman Nee sought to protect his flock from persecution by pandering to the Communist Party's demands. Other Chinese Christian leaders not connected to the Local Church were grieved by the developments, with the great patriarch of the house church movement, Wang Mingdao, writing in his diary, "Two pastors visited today to ask which way today's churches should go [to register with the TSPM or remain unregistered]. I pointed out the mistake of the Local Church. They had to repent with humiliation and ask for God's mercy. Do not go down to Egypt for help."[13]

Imprisonment

The storm clouds were now hovering menacingly over Watchman Nee's head and were about to burst. In 1951 *Tianfeng*, the official magazine of the Three-Self Church in China and a mouthpiece for the Communist Party, launched a sinister campaign against Nee and his church movement.

In April 1952, the 49-year-old church planter was on his way to northeast China when he was seized by the authorities and charged with being a "lawless capitalist tiger." For months, nobody knew where Nee was or if he was still alive. Just before his arrest, Nee had been diagnosed with a serious heart ailment, and conditions in prison were so harsh that many assumed he had not survived.

After many months, Charity was told where her husband was being held, and she was allowed to visit him for 30 minutes once a month. The first time she saw him was difficult, as she scarcely recognized the gaunt figure as the tall, healthy, and handsome man she had married.

The visits were full of anguish for the couple, who were not allowed to face each other. Watchman was required to sit sideways so the guards could observe him and listen to every word he said.

A Nine-Volume Indictment

Although Nee's voice had been silenced, outside the prison walls he was constantly in the news, as the government brought serious criminal and moral charges against him.

In keeping with their usual mode of operation, the Communists waited until they had their target locked away and unable to defend himself before launching a relentless campaign of character assassination against him. In Watchman Nee's case, it wasn't enough for them to destroy his name. They also sought to destroy the faith of his church members, while shredding his reputation so thoroughly that future generations would view him as a charlatan who got his deserved punishment.

On January 30, 1956, a large crowd of 2,500 people attended an accusation meeting at the Nanyang Road Church in Shanghai. All the city's pastors were required to attend, and many of Nee's former church members were also present.

Numerous charges were laid against Nee, outlined in a massive nine-volume, 2,292-page criminal indictment. The charges included ludicrous claims that he was a spy and the leader of a counter-revolutionary movement that stockpiled guns and grenades, while accusations included testimony from two female co-workers who claimed he had affairs with them, claims that he had slept with numerous prostitutes in Shanghai, and even that he had in his possession a pornographic film that he had shot on a camera he purchased in England.

While overseas Christians who heard about the accusations generally dismissed them as fabrications, the renowned revivalist and author J. Edwin Orr, who had ministered with Nee, shocked many readers when he later casually mentioned in one of his books, "Nee was accused of having seduced a hundred girls."[14]

In China, many Christians believed the charges against Nee. Many believers had witnessed his moral decline and manipulations, and they felt thoroughly devastated.[15] As an example of how many thousands of Chinese Christians felt at the time, one young female church member recalled,

> The piercing pain in my heart was intolerable. My mind and body were totally paralyzed. It was even difficult for me to take a step. I was in such a weak stupor as if in a vegetative state. I felt like I could not live on because I always highly honored Watchman Nee.... As I walked, I looked down at the ground with a deep, heartfelt shame. I did not want people to look at me. I was speechless for several days with bitterness in my heart.[16]

Finally, on June 21, 1956, Nee appeared in the Shanghai High Court to face trial. He remained calm throughout, and when evidence was shown to him and the judge asked if he had committed the immoral acts as charged, he simply replied, "Yes."

Nee was sentenced to 20 years in prison for "crimes against the people," including the four years he had already spent behind bars. He was handcuffed and returned to the Shanghai First Municipal Prison and locked in his tiny cell, which measured 9 x 4.5 feet (2.7 x 1.3 meters).

The Gospel Continues to Spread

Ironically with Watchman Nee still firmly behind bars, his teaching continued to impact millions of believers around the world. In 1957, *The Normal Christian Life* was published, a collection of his teachings on the book of Romans over the span of his ministry.[17] Nee's book became a bestseller, selling over one million copies and was translated into more than 30 languages.

Later, his exposition of Ephesians was published under the title *Sit, Walk, Stand*.[18] It also blazed a path through the Christian world, selling almost a million copies and being translated into 22 languages.

Unbeknownst to Nee at the time, he had become like the apostle Paul in that his message was being widely spread while he was in chains. In total, more than 50 books have been written either by or about Watchman Nee.

The years passed and in 1962 the 59-year-old Nee was diagnosed with coronary ischemia. Inmates reported that he had become frail and weighed less than 100 pounds (45 kg).

During his long incarceration, numerous false reports spread around the world about this man who had influenced millions for Christ. Some of these rumors are still believed to the present day. For example, one false claim in *The New Foxe's Book of Martyrs* stated, "For refusing to stop preaching about Christ, Watchman Nee had his eyes gouged out, and his tongue and both hands cut off."[19]

Death

For many years after his conviction, monthly visits by his wife and sister afforded a chance for Nee to have brief contact with people who loved him. For years he was sustained by the hope that one day he would return home and live a quiet life with Charity. She had walked through many storms with her husband and had also suffered much for the gospel. At the start of the Cultural Revolution in 1966, Charity was arrested and severely tortured. While her relatives waited outside the police station for her,

> [t]hey could hear the lashings of a leather whip amid sounds of threats and abuse. When she emerged from the torture chamber her face was scarred and her eyes swollen. . . . The Red Guards

then proceeded to throw shoes and other objects at her and called out, "Your obstinacy will send you to God sooner than you expect."[20]

In the summer of 1971 Charity suffered a heavy fall, which fractured several ribs and caused her to have a stroke. Her condition quickly deteriorated, and she died a few days later. News of his beloved wife's death deeply affected Nee. Now all hope in this world was extinguished, and all he had left was Jesus Christ and the hope of eternal life.

Charity's death also deeply affected Nee's sister, Ni Guizhen. Now that there was no one to visit or to bring him food and encouragement, his health quickly deteriorated. He was transferred to a prison in Anhui Province. In the last letter he was allowed to send to his sister dated April 22, 1972, he wrote,

> You know my physical condition. It is a chronic illness—it is always with me. When it strikes, it causes pain. Even if it should be dormant, it is nonetheless there. The difference is whether it strikes or not. Recovery is out of the question. In summer, the sun can add some color to my skin, but it cannot cure my illness. But I maintain the joy in me. Please don't be anxious. I hope you will take good care of yourself and be filled with joy! All the best to you.[21]

The prison authorities finally realized that Nee's heart condition needed urgent medical attention, so he was "placed on a tractor to go to the prison hospital some 12 miles (19 km) away. The prisoner was too weak to travel along the rough and bumpy mountain road, and as the tractor jolted to the discomfort of the frail and dying passenger, Watchman Nee died en route."[22]

After more than 20 years in prison, the 69-year-old preacher's death certificate listed heart failure combined with tuberculosis as the cause of death. His shattered soul had also played a major role in his demise, as the Communists had cruelly and systematically stripped him of his dignity, reputation, and ministry.

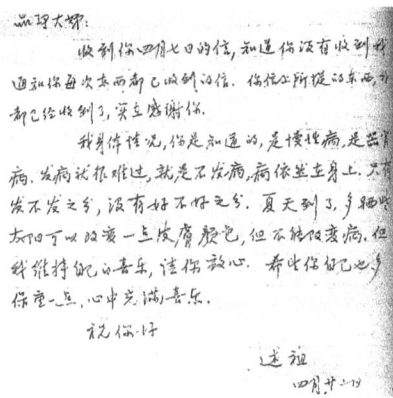

Watchman Nee's final letter from prison.

Divisive even in Death

Even after his death, the authorities continued to attack Watchman Nee, with rumors circulated by the Three-Self Church that he had renounced his faith while in prison. This lie was dispelled when Nee's niece collected her uncle's few belongings after his funeral. She found a crumpled note which read, "Christ is the Son of God. He died as the Redeemer for the sins of mankind and was raised up from the dead after three days. This is the most important fact in the world. I shall die believing in Christ."[23]

Long after his death, details emerged of the impact Nee had on some of his fellow prisoners, whom he led to faith in Jesus. Wu Youqi, who spent years in prison with him, said, "It was the way he lived that had a great influence on me.... I didn't become a believer because of what he spoke, but because of how he lived. Watchman Nee's character was different."[24]

Because of his uncompromising stance and unwavering convictions, Nee had long been a divisive figure in the Chinese church. More than 50 years after his death, Chinese Christians remain divided on his legacy. Many refuse to believe the allegations against him, while others, including many respected church leaders, have publicly denounced him. For example, in 2013 Elder Shi Peichu of the Chinese Christian Family Church in Alhambra, California, wrote, "The teachings of Watchman Nee have cultivated some dedicated and respectable servants of God, yet, in the meantime, they have also produced a number of arrogant, diehard separatists! In my judgment, Nee did more damage than up-building to the church of Jesus Christ."[25]

Watchman Nee was an explosive figure whom God used greatly to launch a movement across China, which continues to this day. Many books were written by him or about him that have greatly blessed and strengthened the faith of Christians around the world.

It is also clear that from the time he made his ill-fated decision to go into business in 1938 until his death in prison in 1972, he was a highly controversial figure who accumulated large numbers of both adoring supporters and harsh critics.

The final word on Watchman Nee's life and work, as with every person, will be decided by the Judge of all Mankind.

1940s to 1960s

The Christian Lin family in 1942.

Apart from Fuzhou, Xiamen, and other main cities, Fujian was still a largely undeveloped province in the 1940s, with one mission society noting, "The mountains cut off Fujian from the rest of China politically and socially as well as geographically. Even as late as 1942, many of the province's 67 counties were without roads, electricity, telephone, or modern industry, and there were no railways."[1]

As the People's Liberation Army under Mao Zedong gradually took over the country, culminating in the establishment of the People's Republic of China in 1949, Christians in Fujian were divided in their opinions of how they should view the new regime. On one hand, Mao promised religious freedom and equality, and the people had grown tired of the rampant corruption of the Guomindang (Nationalist) government.

Some Fujian church leaders saw how the Communists had brutally persecuted Christians in other parts of the country, so they warned believers to prepare for great hardship. Some bluntly stated that the Communists were wolves in sheep's clothing and that they posed a far greater threat to the church than any of the previous forms of government.

Revival in the Taiwan Hills

Meanwhile, God was moving among the tribal groups across the Taiwan Strait. The Ami today number just 2,000 people in Fujian but they have grown to 200,000 in Taiwan. The small number of Ami on the Mainland had their genesis when about 100 Ami men in Taiwan were forcibly enlisted in the Guomindang army between 1946 and 1949 and taken to Fujian to fight in the civil war. After the Communists triumphed, they remained in Fujian and formed a small Ami community.

In Taiwan, there were only 100 Ami believers in 1945, but the situation changed so dramatically that just a decade later the tribe had 80 flourishing churches, and by the late 1990s the Presbyterians alone boasted 20,989 Ami believers in 138 churches.[2] The Ami churches had sent missionaries to a number of countries, including Malaysia, the Philippines, Indonesia, and Papua New Guinea.

Similarly, the Bunun tribe today boasts a population of 58,000 in the mountains of central Taiwan, but only 1,500 in Fujian Province. In 1946 there were no known Christians among the Bunun at all, but by 1959 they numbered 8,881 in Taiwan and 14,990 in 76 churches by the late 1990s.[3]

The Ami, Bunun, and Paiwan tribes each had the Bible translated into their languages in the 1990s, but those Bibles are not available in Mainland China. Christians from these three tribes in Taiwan have crossed the strait to share the gospel with their cousins in Fujian—where the Chinese government has lumped them together under the label of the Gaoshan ("high mountain") ethnic nationality—but it is not known what level of response they encountered.

Into the Furnace

As predicted by many church leaders, Christians in Fujian experienced a gradual erosion of their freedoms during the 1950s, with many pastors and evangelists arrested in 1958. Those who were identified as key leaders were sentenced to long prison terms of 15 to 20 years with hard labor. Most died from the stress of the ordeal. A generation of church leadership was wiped out, and few shepherds remained to lead God's flock.

All foreign missionaries had been expelled from China by this time, and the body of Christ went deeply underground, like a seed in hibernation. Almost all communications from Fujian ceased, as a thick bamboo curtain descended on God's people, cutting them off from the rest of the world for the next two decades.

The long season of suffering also afflicted the Catholic churches in Fujian. A survey completed in 1950, just after the Communists took control of China, found there were 94,776 Catholics in the province.[4] As Catholics were generally more visible than Evangelicals, with cathedrals and distinctive clothing, persecution of the Catholics was severe, and many thousands suffered terribly for their faith.

As the persecution intensified, doctrinal differences that had created barriers among denominations and believers in Fujian suddenly faded in importance. As Christians ran for their lives, all that mattered was whether a person belonged to Jesus or not. In the furnace of affliction, religious labels meant nothing, and those man-made bonds were burned away like the cords that had bound Shadrach, Meshach, and Abednego in a fiery furnace long ago.[5]

At the outbreak of the Cultural Revolution, Mao's Red Guards combed every home, confiscating and destroying Bibles and other Christian material. Only a small number of Bibles that had been carefully concealed escaped the destruction. One source said, "Some had one or two Bibles which were used for worship meetings and stored in secret hiding places. Many divided their Bible into separate parts so that members of the congregation could each take home a portion to be returned the following meeting—almost like a public library."[6]

Because of the large number of believers in Fujian, the purging of the church in the province occurred in several stages. The most severe period commenced in 1966, when thousands of Christians were arrested. One veteran missionary who was still able to communicate with his contacts in Fujian summarized the frenzied situation in the city of Xiamen at the time:

> All church windows were smashed, the pews burned, and the cross taken down. Every pastor was made to "walk the street" with a dunce hat on his head and a placard around his neck announcing his crimes (a common practice in humiliating intellectuals). One woman was beaten to death.
>
> They then gathered over 20 YMCA and YWCA leaders and forced them to kneel in front of the pile of burning books while a large crowd stood around observing the great spectacle. As the flames intensified and radiated their heat towards them, the victims cried out in excruciating pain. It was a pitiful sight.
>
> Tormented by their excessive burns, most of them, including the general secretary of the YMCA, committed suicide by jumping

from high buildings.... After this terrible ordeal, all church meetings in Xiamen ceased.... By Easter 1967, the liquidation of the entire organized church was complete, and believers were forced to go underground and to gather in semi-secret family groups.

Violent attacks on the churches continued. 1968 was the darkest and most difficult period of all, with persecutions intensifying, vile tortures being perpetrated, and even the household meetings had to be suspended.[7]

By the end of the 1960s the church in Fujian remained in crisis, and only the Lord knew how many Christians existed. There were no networks of fellowships at that stage, just individual pockets of believers who had survived by the supernatural protection of God.

An accused criminal forced to wear a dunce hat on the streets in 1967.

1940s to 1960s

Another decade passed full of excruciating experiences, yet the church in Fujian continued to endure the suffering, and a remnant of refined believers emerged from the furnace of affliction. When the dark curtain that had fallen on Fujian finally began to lift many years later, two Christians from Southeast Asia visited a pastor's home after being given an address. When the door was opened, they found themselves standing in front of a small group of vibrant believers who were holding a Bible study.

After the meeting, the pastor Zhai shared some of his experiences during the worst times of the 1960s. The wide-eyed visitors took notes and reported,

> On one occasion, he had been arrested at gunpoint and called upon to deny Christ. The Red Guards assured him that if he would simply deny Christ, he would be freed. He refused. For several hours, they continued to harangue him, but he would not meet their demands. The fanatics produced a large color picture of Chairman Mao and began to chant over and over, "Kneel before our great and wise leader."
>
> When he would not comply, they roughly grabbed him by his shoulders and tried to force him to his knees. After that failed, they decided to "encourage" him by savagely beating him on his legs with sticks. The attack was so brutal that he collapsed on the floor.[8]

Zhai was asked if he would move to Hong Kong to escape the afflictions if the opportunity arose. He explained that he had already been offered the chance to leave China but had turned it down, as he believed God wanted him to remain in Fujian to serve the flock entrusted to his care.

1970s

A Lonely Life of Suffering

The brutal and mindless violence of the Cultural Revolution devastated millions of families throughout China, and countless Christians were killed or lost their faith as the turmoil spread.

Ni Guizhen, the older sister of Watchman Nee, was deeply affected by her brother's arrest and trial in 1956. The toll of the "evidence" presented against him was so great that she suffered a complete physical and nervous breakdown. For years she lived in isolation, battling memory loss and poor eyesight, and she often stayed indoors due to light intolerance. Because of her brother's status as a despised counter-revolutionary, almost all of Guizhen's friends turned against her, and her own children

Ni Guizhen, the faithful sister of Watchman Nee.

scattered to different parts of the world. One of the few people Ni interacted with was her sister-in-law, Charity, with whom she would quietly sing hymns and recite Scriptures.

Despite her massive challenges, Ni retained her faith in Christ, and for several years she managed to join Charity on her monthly visits to Nee in prison. The rest of the time Ni rarely ventured outside but calmed her nerves by knitting and reading the Bible.

The Public Security Bureau frequently interrogated the ailing woman, and if they weren't happy with her answers they would savagely beat her. The cowardly Communists often made fun of the suffering saint, forcing her to kneel on the floor for long periods while repeating out loud, "I come from a bad family. My son-in-law is a capitalist and my brother is a counter-revolutionary. My sons are running dogs in America."[1]

One day her dear friend Charity was placed under house arrest which ended the rich fellowship the two suffering women enjoyed together.

Ni's miserable life in this world was compounded when all three of her granddaughters, under pressure from the authorities, publicly denounced her. One of them, Terri, screamed, "I hate being born into this family! You have done so many wrong things. The church is bad. And Watchman Nee is the cause of all our troubles."[2]

That night, Ni Guizhen suffered a stroke and lost the use of the left side of her body. Subsequent visits by the brutal Red Guards ground her down. She suffered from heart disease, insomnia, and a host of other ailments, and her mind began to falter when she learned that some of her grandchildren had been arrested and sent to prison solely because they were related to the hated preacher Watchman Nee.

The final straw for Guizhen was the death of her beloved friend and sister-in-law, Charity, in November 1971. It devastated her, and for the next month she sat alone in her bedroom, repeatedly mumbling, "I've done nothing wrong."

Ni Guizhen died on December 14, 1971, about six months before her brother Nee perished in prison. Her family was not allowed to give her a proper burial or a headstone. Because she, too, had been labelled a counter-revolutionary, the mortician refused to fix her face for the funeral. None of her family members were allowed to grieve at the service or to send flowers, as such actions would be seen as supporting an enemy of the great Chinese Communist Party.

To an outsider looking through mere human eyes, Ni's life was a disaster. The success of the Local Church, which numbered tens of thousands of members across China, had struck fear into the hearts of the maniacal atheistic government who showed their weakness by taking their anger out on this partially blind and enfeebled old lady and her offspring.

Thrilling News from Fuzhou

For many years little news had emerged about the state of Christianity in Fujian Province. It was well known that the entire leadership of the body of Christ had been removed, killed, or sent to prison, but it was uncertain how the remaining believers had coped. Some former missionaries feared the worst and expected that if the door to China ever reopened, the entire missionary enterprise would have to start again from scratch.

The first solid news about the church in Fujian appeared in 1973, exciting all who heard it. While official churches had been closed at the start of the Cultural Revolution in 1966, small meetings had continued secretly in people's homes, until they were suspended in 1971 due to another wave of arrests and harsh persecution.

1970s

When that wave passed, a move of the Holy Spirit swept across many parts of the province. The unbearable pressure created by Mao and his cohorts caused many to cry out to God for mercy, and thousands of mostly young people embraced the gospel including hundreds in the provincial capital, Fuzhou.

In response to this awakening, the Communists launched another crackdown with the veteran missionary Leslie Lyall reporting,

> By 1973 a Christian community numbering over 1,000 in Fuzhou had grown up, and it was this thrilling news that cheered all who had been praying for China and her Christians. The authorities, alarmed by the large number of Christians, then ordered the meetings to cease. In 1974, five leaders were arrested, paraded in dunce caps, and imprisoned. On their release these men and women continued their pastoral visiting, and the number of believers multiplied dramatically.[3]

A painter, Brother Wu, turned his home into a Christian counseling center, and discreetly used it to share the gospel with many artists in Fuzhou. Despite not having any Bibles, the group met regularly to worship God, and their numbers grew as they shared the gospel in the workplace. Some of these courageous believers were said to include a

> young woman named Meimei, an apprentice in a factory, secretly witnesses for Christ while working on her electric meters. She approaches her fellow workers on the assembly line individually, sharing the good news of Jesus Christ by her life and her words.
>
> Occasionally there are larger groups, at most a dozen people, who meet in open areas like parks and forests, but no Bibles or hymnbooks are brought to the meetings. The preacher has his text memorized and delivers his message in a modulated tone.[4]

The Spirit of God continued to blow wherever He pleased, untroubled by human barriers or the policies of evil men.

1970s

The Blessed Old Man

In one village in southeast Fujian near the Guangdong border, Chinese believers told a remarkable story of God's provision and power. An elderly brother had believed in the Lord for many years when the Communists took control of the area in 1949. The Blessed Old Man, as other believers affectionately dubbed him, came from an impoverished family and had never learned to read or write properly. Despite these impediments, after he received the Lord Jesus he proved to be a powerful evangelist, leading hundreds of people to faith in Christ throughout the district.

Hatching a plan to give Christianity a blackeye and to show the supremacy of Marxism, the government decided to make an example of the old preacher by giving him the best house in the village and a generous supply of food. They also appointed him chairman of the village's Communist committee, thinking that when he abandoned his religion they would display him as a shining example of the goodness of Communism and the futility of Christianity.

The Blessed Old Man, however, belonged to Jesus Christ. Instead of being seduced by the Communists,

[h]e used the large house he had been provided to hold house church meetings and distributed the food he was given to those believers in need. After some time, the government saw that their plan was badly backfiring, so they issued an ultimatum to the "chairman." He had to choose between his faith and the new lifestyle and status he had been afforded by the authorities. Although he knew that he would return to a life of extreme poverty and hardship, the old brother did not hesitate for a moment. "I choose Jesus!" he boldly declared.

The enraged officials threw him out of the house. He had nowhere to go, but another believer provided him with a small room on the side of a shack. China at the time was suffering terribly from Mao's disastrous economic experiments, and millions of people were starving to death. Even though the old man now had somewhere to stay, there was no food available to eat. All the meager crops were taken by the government, and the other Christians were too poor to help him.

For some days the old man wasted away in his tiny room, with no food passing his lips. He grew weak and ill and knew that his life would soon be snuffed out. Then one morning he awoke to find a hole in the bottom of the wall. He didn't know what had caused it and repaired the damage. A few hours later he found another hole and started to wonder if these strange occurrences were from the Lord. While he was still pondering it, a large rat came through the hole with some food in its mouth. After entering the room, the rat dropped the food on the floor and then left. A short time later it returned and did the same again. A small collection of nuts and vegetables lay on the dirt floor!

Each morning the rat paid a visit to the elderly brother. In response to his commitment, God had saved the old man from starvation by instructing a rat to feed him! This miraculous provision continued for several months. On some days the rat brought more food than usual. Those were the days when the old man was expecting a visitor![5]

Salvation Everywhere

The excesses of the Cultural Revolution—when tens of millions of people throughout China were slaughtered in Mao's pursuit of ideological purity—created a void in people's hearts. Their lives were empty and meaningless, and a hunger developed for spiritual truth that didn't exist prior to the advent of Communism. Across Fujian, even in the smallest villages, God's salvation came to families that had long lived in spiritual darkness.

The progress of the gospel in Fujian did not come easily with thousands of Christians suffering terrible injustices so that others would hear of Christ's salvation.

Among the hundreds of church leaders who suffered terribly for the gospel was Xu Daoheng, who was arrested and hurled into prison on January 24, 1974. Xu was born in 1928, and even though he grew up in a Christian family he did not serve God wholeheartedly until he was challenged by the perils of the Cultural Revolution.

Xu decided to publicly preach the gospel in 1969, though the situation in China was dire at the time. For five years the Lord supernaturally protected him, and Xu was used by the Holy Spirit to bring a great revival to Fuzhou, which spread to surrounding counties. Many miracles took place when he preached, and thousands of new believers were baptized.

The authorities finally caught up with Xu, and he was imprisoned for five years. These were difficult times for the evangelist, and he nearly died when an illness swept through the prison.

After gaining his freedom, Xu Daoheng was shocked to discover that many of the churches he had started had been decimated by the "Shouters" sect, led by Watchman Nee's successor, Witness Li. Xu was furious when he saw the damage being done to God's people, and he spent the rest of his life teaching the truth of God's Word and combatting Li's extreme views.

The lack of Bibles and church leaders because of persecution had created some absurd situations, with many believers lacking a basic knowledge of the Scriptures. For example, in one part of Fujian a preacher shared that Jesus warned that people must "enter through the narrow gate" to be saved. Taking the admonition literally, one woman returned home and greatly reduced the size of her front door so that visitors could hardly squeeze through it to enter her home.

1970s

The Smiling Widow

In 1951, a Christian couple teaching at a remote inland school had been arrested, and their own daughter falsely accused them of crimes against society. Though heartbroken, the couple kept their eyes on Jesus remembering His warning that "a man's enemies will be the members of his own household" (Matt. 10:36).

After a year in prison they were released, but being surrounded by thousands of lost and hopeless people they could not remain silent, and in 1958 they were rearrested for preaching the gospel. After a while they were again set free, only to continue their ministry and be captured for the third time in 1965.

On this occasion the persecution had again originated from their own home. They discovered their son was dating an unbeliever, and when they voiced their disapproval, he reported them to the authorities, disclosing that they had never renounced their faith and had been secretly leading others to Jesus. This time each received a five-year prison sentence to be served in separate facilities.

While her husband (who by now was in his early seventies) was incarcerated in an unknown location, the wife sensed the Lord tell her that he was about to be taken home to heaven. She was so convinced that she woke up early, worshipped God, and her face brimmed with joy at the thought that her dear partner was going to meet Jesus and be with Him forever.

Other prisoners were confused and asked why she was so happy. When she told them it was because God had shown her that her husband was about to die and go to heaven, they thought she had lost her mind and reported it to the prison authorities.

Before they could decide what to do with her, news arrived that her husband had died and she needed to collect his body for burial. She went to the men's prison, singing and smiling all the way. The staff there were confused and assumed she must have had a terrible relationship with her husband, but she told them,

> "When a hen gathers her newly hatched chicks, she certainly won't cry over the broken eggshells; she can only be happy for the chicks. Now my husband has left the shell of his body and has gone to the most beautiful place there is. Why shouldn't I be happy?" The others acknowledged that she was right.

After she left prison, she continued to testify and preach the gospel. Brothers and sisters in many places wrote to her and received much encouragement and uplifting. All felt she was filled with the strength of the Holy Spirit. It was truly the grace of God.[6]

An Army Captain Meets Jesus

In 1974, two overseas Chinese believers visited Fujian, where they discreetly met with Christians and gathered information about the state of the church. When they reached the large city of Fuzhou, Brother Joseph—a Chinese Filipino—and Uncle Liu found that a revival had recently broken out there and hundreds of people had come to faith in Jesus. They reported,

> The revival in Fuzhou started after two little old ladies started to meet for prayer, asking Jesus Christ to visit their city in power and might. One day they prayed for a young girl who was deaf and mute. The Lord healed her instantly, and news spread quickly that Jesus was still alive in China. Soon their little meeting of two grew until more than 200 people met in their home.[7]

Sharing more details of the miracle, the women said that when they first attempted to help the girl, she cowered fearfully in a corner. They knelt beside her and lovingly hugged her as they prayed for deliverance. Then suddenly,

> [t]he girl let forth an unearthly shriek, despite her inability to speak. Then she became calm and looked up in interest as

the women spoke to her. From that day on, she could not only hear, but also began learning how to speak. News of her healing spread through the area and soon others came to their home to present their needs for prayer. Each of their requests was met and increasing numbers began to attend.[8]

Once, while a worship meeting was in progress, a captain in the Chinese army was walking down the street and heard people praying and singing to God. He knocked on the door and demanded to know what was going on. "Oh," one of the old ladies replied, "These people here all have needs and God is meeting them." In response, the soldier

> mockingly asked what kinds of needs were being met by God. "Well, some are sick and have no coupons for medicine. So, we have been praying to our God and He has been touching and healing them. Others have no food or clothes, so we have been praying to our God and He has been providing for them."
>
> The captain pointed at his nose, which had a cancerous growth protruding from it, and asked, "Do you think your God might be able to help me too?" The Christians invited the captain in, laid their hands on him, and earnestly asked God to heal him. The man felt no different and went home.
>
> That night, as he lay on his bed, his nose began to tingle. When he woke up the next morning the cancer had disappeared, and he was completely healed. He excitedly returned to the house and told the ladies what had happened. He asked, "Who is this God of yours?" They shared Jesus Christ, and the man opened his heart and received the King of Glory.
>
> The army captain immediately started to spread the gospel throughout the city, and dozens more people found the Lord in Fuzhou. By February 1974, there were already 1,200 people worshipping the Lord in those house meetings.[9]

Revival Touches the Catholics

The Catholics, meanwhile, had also survived the two decades of intense persecution. During the darkest times, many of the doctrines and practices that had long divided Catholics and Evangelicals faded. Many abandoned the worship of Mary and other traditional Catholic practices during those years. All that mattered was Jesus Christ and His truth. By the end of the 1970s the Bishop of Fuzhou, whose predecessor had been tortured to death,

> reported a community of 20,000 Christians in this single city [Fuzhou] of a million people! On one of his pastoral journeys the bishop had found 7,000 new Christians in seven remote mountain villages being taught by two elderly workers. The churches in Fujian were clearly growing much faster than in the days when the missionaries had been present.
>
> Two congregations of 2,000 each were worshipping every Sunday at the Flower Lane Church in Fuzhou, half of them young people. "They are thirsty for something spiritual," the bishop reported, "and they appreciate long sermons!"[10]

Letters From Fujian

I conclude this chapter by reprinting a selection of letters that were received from Fujian by various Christian ministries during the 1970s. These precious communications reveal both the strengths and weaknesses of Christianity in Fujian and provide insights into believers' daily lives and personal struggles. Their letters also offer a fascinating snapshot of the ever-changing conditions experienced by the body of Christ at the time.

1970s

1974

"Christmas is here. May we adore Him with our hearts, like the shepherds in the wilderness during the cold night. They were alert and went to worship the Lord. At the same time in the town of Bethlehem, all the Pharisees and the scribes were asleep. They could not see the birth of Jesus. Only the alert shepherds were able to hear the good news proclaimed by the angels, and they were directed to go and see the baby Jesus. We who are awake will see the second coming of Jesus. May the Lord be with you."[11]

1975

"Although Christians in the Mainland now are not able to go to church and worship God, we can only gather about ten people to worship in our homes and have fellowship and prayer. Please pray for us. May God call His own people to work for Him and to proclaim the gospel.

I have asthma and am physically very weak. I am already 68 years old and my remaining days on the earth are not many. I am waiting for Him to take me home. Please pray I will not be found empty-handed when I meet my Lord. May our Heavenly Father save sinners and give faith and love to all people."[12]

1976

"Time flows like water. I always remember all Christians in prayer. Yesterday, I received your gift. Thank you. May our Heavenly Father take care of your family and give you peace and happiness. God loves mankind. The most important thing is that all believers learn to trust Him, and thereby enjoy Him now and forevermore."[13]

1980s

A Baptism of Fire

The Holy Spirit continued to move among the people of Fujian in the 1980s. As the dust began to settle on the harsh years of Mao's fanatical rule, it became clear that God had done a mighty work throughout the province, with one source saying,

> In 1980, Christians throughout the whole province were known to number at least 600,000, and in that same year, in one area alone, 6,000 new believers were baptized. One lady, who had been traveling around the province preaching God's Word, was arrested and put into jail. There she went on a hunger strike, and when moved to hospital she led another patient, the wife of a Communist cadre, to Christ. Christians were appearing in the most unlikely places—even within Communist Party ranks and in the Youth League.[1]

In 1973 at the remote village of Luyao, 25 miles (42 km) from the nearest town, a boy was born paralyzed from the waist down. His parents hoped the best for their only son, so they named him Ping Kang ("peace and health").

Although he was mostly consigned to bed for the first eight years of his life, Ping's father was determined to give him an education, so every day he bundled the boy onto his back and carried him two hours to the nearest school. By the time he was 12, Ping had learned to speak and write Chinese, but he had grown too big for his father to carry him, so he had to stay home and study.

One day, Ping Kang's older brother surprised him by giving him a radio. It became his constant companion, and one evening

1980s

A crowded house church meeting in 1980.
VOM Canada

he came across a shortwave Christian radio broadcast from overseas, with a presenter talking about someone called "God." He had never heard that word before but was attracted to the strange message and began to tune in with his family.

Gradually, the light of the gospel dawned on Ping and his family, and they accepted Jesus as Lord and Savior. Two years later, ten more families in their village believed in Christ, so they "met together regularly to worship, sing, and testify to answered prayers. They had no Bible. The only Scripture verses they knew were what they heard on the radio."[2]

Across Fujian, the Living God was saving and transforming people who had long lived in the valley of the shadow of death.

True peace and health was granted to Ping Kang and countless thousands of others like him. Reports emerged of mass conversions, such as this one in 1982: "All the people of the village of Shenghu, numbering 250, were converted following an unusual case of exorcism. Churches in Quanzhou City have experienced steady growth over a 20-year period. One house church that numbered 100 to 200 people in 1975 had grown to 1,000 members."[3]

The Anti-Spiritual Pollution Campaign

After failing to extinguish God's people during the previous three decades, the Communist authorities appeared to have been infuriated, and 1983 saw the launch of a massive crackdown against Christians in Fujian and throughout the nation, as believers were targeted in an "anti-spiritual pollution and crime" campaign.

A Christian from Taiwan who visited Fujian in January 1984 reported on the dire conditions for believers as the campaign was implemented. He wrote,

> From what I experienced personally and heard about the suffering and bravery of the Christians there, my life was totally changed and could never be the same again. My love for the Chinese church and my burden for the mission field began to burn like a fire.
>
> As a foreigner, I was followed everywhere I went by at least two spies. They also sent devious agents to us, pretending to be Christians, in a bid to befriend us and reveal our true reasons for coming and then to discover our contacts in the underground churches. Previously, I thought these kinds of things only happened in fictional spy movies.
>
> Gunfire was often heard at night in the city of Xiamen, and some Christians were shot dead as soon as they opened their doors. Many believers who had received Bibles from Hong Kong were rounded up, put in police vans, and never seen again. As a

warning to others, hundreds of villagers were loaded onto buses and taken to public squares to watch Christians being shot in the head.

> Each province was given a quota of criminals the government wanted to be executed. Naturally, those provinces with a high percentage of Christians, including Fujian, did not have so many criminals, so the authorities had trouble meeting their quota and so began executing Christians.[4]

After several months the government's campaign of terror—which had threatened to plunge the country back into the dark days of the Cultural Revolution—subsided, and life slowly returned to normal.

The Three-Self Dilemma

During the 1980s, as the Three-Self Church grew in profile throughout China, its leaders tried to smooth over the concerns of many Christians by putting on their best face and appearing more conciliatory toward the house churches than in previous years.

Thousands of fellowships in Fujian from various denominations and Chinese networks were faced with the difficult decision of whether to register with the TSPM and receive certain benefits and freedoms, or to remain in the shadows as illegal, unregistered house churches and face the likelihood of many more years of persecution and hardship.

Thousands of churches chose to register, and a marked increase of TSPM members in the province was seen throughout the decade. In 1986, the TSPM listed 400,000 adult baptized church members in Fujian,[5] but in the next three years that figure jumped 50 percent to 600,000.[6]

Although reliable house church statistics in Fujian were not available in the 1980s, most observers believe a similar number of believers chose to spurn the Three-Self and remain independent.

Christians around the world were aware of the apparent thaw in relations between the state and religious bodies, and many overseas church leaders freely advised the Chinese churches to "obey the laws of the land" and register with the government. Having never had to practice their faith under a totalitarian regime, their advice was often misguided.

For many house churches, the decision to remain independent was simple. They had already faced three decades of harsh persecution, and they would never consider submitting their faith to an atheist authority. Jesus Christ was the Head of the church, and to substitute Him with another authority was a compromise they were unwilling to make even though they fully realized their stance would result in continuing hardship.

The decision of many Christians not to register with the Three-Self was galvanized by the ungodly lives and threats of many of the senior leaders of the movement. Remarkably, the first leader of the TSPM, Wu Yaozong, went as far as to declare, "God has taken the key of salvation away from the church and given it to the Communist Party."[7]

It's little wonder, then, that great multitudes of Christians in Fujian and throughout the country refused to submit to such an organization. In the early 1980s, one house church leader issued the following extremely strong statement when asked about the Three-Self Patriotic Movement:

> We try to expose the TSPM to those brothers and sisters who still don't understand. We're trying to pull them away from the TSPM, and we think we can do it. We're praying with all we've got, and we tell those brothers not to unite.

So we call them—the TSPM and the China Christian Council—whores and partners with Judas. They are the church of Baal. We must kill that whore so that all will know they're not of the Spirit. Last year we held prayer meetings, praying that the Spirit's power would come to burn that whore to death.[8]

Another house church leader, whose movement grew to one of the largest in China, tried to help overseas Christians understand why millions of believers refuse to register with the TSPM by reversing the argument and asking what they would do if faced with the same choices in their countries:

Some people in the West have said we should be good citizens of China and obey our nation's laws by registering our churches with the government. To that, I ask you to place yourself in our position and see if you would be willing to do this.

Imagine if your church leaders were appointed by an atheistic government. You could not preach the gospel to anyone outside the scheduled church services, and you could not instruct or baptize your children until they were 18 years old.

Imagine if your pastor was forbidden to teach certain parts of the Bible such as the book of Revelation, the Second Coming of Christ, casting out demons, and other key passages. If your pastor did so, he could be arrested, tortured, and spend years in prison.

Imagine if songs and messages were frequently required in your church that reinforced submission to the government and its political system.

And finally, imagine that the leaders at the top of this religious structure were avowed atheists who did not even believe in God!

If you enjoy your freedom in Christ in America, Europe, Singapore, Australia, or wherever you may live, consider the above questions and ask yourself if you would still be keen to register your church with the government if you were in our shoes.

The choice was quite simple for us. We are the Bride of Christ, purchased by the precious Blood of the Lamb. How could we ever submit to an organization that proudly advocates atheism?

1980s

The Three-Self is not a church, even though people often call it the "Three-Self Church." The official name, "Three-Self Patriotic Movement," reveals that it is not a church, but a political movement carefully designed to control the spread of Christianity.[9]

Today, the dichotomy between the TSPM and unregistered house churches continues to be strong in Fujian Province. Yet remarkably, it has become clear that in recent decades the Holy Spirit has powerfully responded to all believers who call out to Him with a repentant heart and a child-like faith. As a result, revival has come even to many TSPM churches in the province.

An Innocent Faith

During the 1980s, it was clear that a lack of Bibles was the major hindrance and gravest threat to the growth of the house church movement in Fujian. While TSPM churches enjoyed access to Bibles officially printed by the Amity Press, the house churches were deliberately starved of God's Word and had to rely on a few crumbs that fell from the table of the Three-Self and from the supply of Bibles that Christians from around the world smuggled across the border from Hong Kong.

The exponential growth of Christianity meant that the quantity of Bibles they received was a tiny fraction of what was needed just to provide a copy to the hundreds of thousands of new believers coming to Jesus in Fujian each year.

Chinese Christians had learned to rely on God and hear His voice during the decades of harsh persecution, and their innocent faith and desire to obey the Lord gave birth to many remarkable testimonies. One of them was of a house church leader in Fujian who took the Bible literally. One day, as he read the story of Noah, he said the Lord illuminated to him the words, "cover it inside and out with pitch" (Gen. 6:14).

The pastor decided God wanted him to coat the walls both inside and outside his home with pitch. His neighbors were greatly amused and mocked him when they saw what he was doing, but he replied, "This is my ark, and God told me to cover it with pitch." He neglected his work in the fields for a time and lost most of his crops, which added to the derision of his neighbors. Then just after he completed the task of covering his home with pitch,

> the most torrential rains and floods came to his area. For the first time in hundreds of years entire villages were swept away and houses collapsed, except his home. The extra coats had strengthened his house so that it was the only one left standing in the village of 200 homes. The neighbors were so impressed that they donated some of their harvest, and he and his family ate better than ever throughout the following winter.[10]

Letters From Fujian

1982

> *"Now we have God's peace, for His glory. If we are persecuted, it is also for His glory. Satan always wants to kill, steal, and destroy, but we have God's glorious peace. He has granted us great success so that we now have more Bibles to send to various districts and mountain areas."*[11]

1984

"During my long recovery from illness I realized I have been too focused on external things. Now I draw closer to God in real fellowship. Truly, the Chinese church is not free. Our freedom is controlled by the Three-Self, and the Three-Self is controlled by the Communist Party. As a result, for many years spiritual brothers and sisters have chosen to separate from the Three-Self. They just want to serve the Lord without any human control. . . . Consequently, some Christians here have been arrested and labelled 'cult members.' I do not understand these things, but they will be clear when the Lord comes in final judgment."[12]

"On the train we had the chance to share the gospel with a dozen people and the response was very good. After returning home we found many church members had brought enquirers to our meeting. After hearing the gospel, many immediately received Jesus as their Savior. Hallelujah! There are over 200 believers in our fellowship. We were originally a house church, and although the church is now under the control of the Three-Self, we have not lost our spiritual fervor and there are many young people serving the Lord here."[13]

1986

"Thank you for your prayers for the reconstruction of our church building. This is God's love and a great encouragement to us. We are deeply grateful. To begin with, many of our farmers offered their labor for free to construct the church. Every day about 60 people gathered for work. The standard of their work was high, and we just had to give them rice gruel for their midday meal. These dedicated believers were not afraid of hard work, and together the project has progressed with great joy and cheerfulness. We are confident the work will soon be completed."[14]

1987

"All is well here with our big family of believers. The churches are flourishing 100 times better than in the days of the old society when there were only four churches in the whole county. The Cultural Revolution came, which wiped everything out, but now there is a church in every village and our county has been divided into seven areas. In my area there are many believers in each village. A large village may have 200 or more families, while the smallest may have five or six families. We have seen the great work of God! By His power the gospel is being preached to the ends of the earth!"[15]

1988

"Thank God that I came to know Him when I was young, and I was baptized in January 1937. My family also came to know the Lord. By God's grace, He has sustained my faith and has protected me all these years. I believe the Lord's return is near and there is an urgent need for us to unite and spread the gospel. I have opportunities to speak in four registered churches and two home meetings. The believers have some Bibles, but they are insufficient to meet the needs. The only available Bibles are in the traditional script, but the younger generation generally only know the simplified text."[16]

The Local Church Today

Witness Li

Witness Li

Born in Shandong Province in 1905, Witness Li (Mandarin name: Li Changshou) converted to Christ at the age of 20 and became a full-time co-worker of Watchman Nee in 1933. The two traveled extensively throughout China together, and over time Li emerged as Nee's likely successor as the leader of the Local Church. Witness Li was a gifted and influential teacher, and he shared the same radical views on the church as those developed by Nee.

In November 1948, Nee realized the Communists would soon gain a complete victory in the civil war, and he knew that perilous

The Local Church Today

times awaited the followers of Jesus once the new regime assumed control. He sent an urgent message to all of his leaders, urging them to consider moving to Taiwan, Hong Kong, or Southeast Asia so they could carry on the work of the Local Church.

One of the leaders Nee strongly urged to migrate to Taiwan was Witness Li, but he was unconvinced and didn't want to leave China. When Li hesitated, Watchman admonished him, "Brother, you must realize that although in this desperate situation we trust in the Lord, it is possible that the enemy will one day wipe us out. If this happens, you will be out of China, and we will still have something left. So, you must go."[1]

Li finally submitted and moved to Taiwan, where several Local Church congregations composed of 350 believers had already been established. The work in Taiwan grew exponentially, and by 1952, just a few years later, the movement on the island boasted more than 20,000 members in 65 churches. From there, the Local Church spread across Southeast Asia to the United States and many other Western nations.

Li moved to California in 1962, and from there he preached unceasingly for the next 35 years until his death in 1997. His speaking ministry was complemented by a publishing arm, Living Stream Ministry, which produced more than 400 books and commentaries.

The controversies and divisions that had marked the ministry of the Local Church not only continued after Watchman Nee's death in 1972, but it could be said they greatly intensified under Li's leadership.

Some of the accusations of heresy against Witness Li included the teaching of aberrations on the nature of God, the nature of man, and many other fundamental Christian doctrines.

Li's claims to be a "revealer of hidden truth" prompted many Christians to closely examine his teachings. Some of his beliefs alarmed many Christians, such as, "To be a Christian simply means to be mingled with God, to be a God-man. It is not enough to be a good man; we have to be a God-man."[2]

On the matter of salvation, Witness Li had this to say:

> We have seen that to reach the unbelievers, no preaching is necessary. If we help them to say, "O Lord," three times, they will be saved. If they open the window, the air will get in. All they have to do is open their mouth and say, "O Lord, O Lord." Even if they have no intention of believing, still they will be caught.[3]

The Shouters

During the 1980s, the teachings of the then California-based Witness Li re-entered China and found their way to churches formerly associated with Watchman Nee. Tons of special Bibles were smuggled into China. These contained extensive notes by Li in the margins of each page, giving commentary and interpreting passages to readers.

Most of the elderly believers in Fujian immediately recognized that the new teachings were different from those passed down to them, and they rejected them.

Many younger believers embraced the teachings and literature from Witness Li. They enthusiastically adopted the practice of shouting passages of Scripture or "Jesus is Lord!" in unison at the top of their voices, sometimes for hours. The believers were nicknamed "Shouters," "Yellers," or "Screamers" by people who lived near them.

Inevitably, the division between the older and younger believers caused a split, which brought great pain to hundreds of thousands of Christians in Fujian and throughout China. According to the respected Chinese church researcher Jonathan Chao, the older group generally consisted of orthodox, Bible-believing Christians, but the younger group opposed their elders, saying,

"They cannot be saved, cannot enter into the kingdom of heaven, and cannot receive eternal life!"

The younger group insists on shouting out the Name of the Lord, believing a person can shout his way into heaven. They shout very loudly early in the morning, waking up their neighbors. They boast, "We will shout from the top of the hills, from the top of the trees, from the top of the train, and from the top of our bicycles."

One day, as they were riding their bikes, they shouted so loudly that cyclists in front of them were frightened and fell. Each time they meet, they shout. The non-believers have protested against the shouting by beating drums even louder.[4]

This practice of shouting made the younger group stand out, and the authorities launched a series of extensive crackdowns in a bid to eradicate them. The entire Local Church was officially labeled an "evil cult" by the government, and many Christian groups were quick to distance themselves from them.

Tragically, the authorities in China failed to distinguish between the newer extremist part of the Local Church and the older believers who had rejected the heretical teachings. Both were targeted as cult members and have experienced much brutal persecution to this day.

Furthermore, over the years many Chinese Christians who have nothing to do with the Local Church have also been arrested and imprisoned after being labeled "Shouters" by the police.

One man, Shi Yunchao, was arrested in 1983 and falsely charged with being a member of the Shouters. When Shi protested that his church was not part of the sect, an official from the Religious Affairs Bureau replied, "You are part of the Shouter sect if you shout loud; you are also part of it if you lower your voice. We think you are still a Shouter even if you mumble words in your mouth! The Shouter sect is counter-revolutionary."[5]

Shi was eventually martyred for his faith in 1996.

The Local Church Today

Lawsuits

Beginning in the 1970s, concerns were raised by Christian leaders in America about the doctrines and practices of Witness Li and the churches under his leadership. When some condemned the Local Church as a dangerous cult, the denomination denied all accusations of heresy and strongly fought back. In the late 1970s two books, *The God Men*[6] and *The Mindbenders*,[7] declared the Local Church to be a cult. Feeling their backs were up against the wall, the church sued the publishers of those books for defamation.

More recently, Harvest House Publishers in the United States faced a long and debilitating $136 million lawsuit brought against them by the Local Church after it was included in the book *Encyclopaedia of Cults and New Religions*.[8]

It appears the strategy of the Local Church in America was to litigate and appeal continually until the defendant ran out of money and was unable to continue, while the lawyers representing the Local Church were often members who offered their services for free.

This propensity for litigation fueled new suspicions about the biblical orthodoxy of the Local Church, but many Christians were confused after hearing mixed messages about the movement by some who were considered experts on cults. In 1996, Hank Hanegraaff—who was well known for his *Bible Answer Man* radio shows in the United States and as president of the Christian Research Institute—strongly denounced the Local Church with a detailed analysis of their key doctrinal errors. He concluded,

> Some of the basic teachings of Witness Li and the Local Church are heretical and dangerous. We urge Christians to pray for those in the Local Church, help them see Li's errors, and return to the

truth as it is in Jesus and the Word of God. . . . A number of the basic teachings of the Local Church are false."⁹

In January 2007, an open letter signed by 70 Evangelical scholars and ministry leaders from seven countries rebuked Witness Li and the Local Church, detailing their doctrinal errors and urging them to "discontinue their use of lawsuits and threats of litigation against Christian individuals and organizations to answer criticisms or resolve disputes."¹⁰

By late 2009, however, Hanegraaff and other leaders of the Christian Research Institute shocked many of their supporters and lost much credibility when they performed a dramatic U-turn and published an article on the Local Church titled, "We Were Wrong!"¹¹

Other Christian scholars rebuked CRI's new stance, and insinuations were made that Hanegraaff had accepted bribes from the Local Church before declaring his new position. One researcher, David Lister, sarcastically asked Hanegraaff, "What does it profit you to gain all the world's golf courses and country clubs and forfeit your soul?"¹²

Many Christian leaders were astounded to learn that Hanegraaff had not only radically changed his position on the Local Church but had even joined in filing the legal brief in their lawsuit against Harvest House Publishers.¹³

A Complex Riddle

While the Local Church outside China had become a lightning rod for controversy, inside China the situation was even more complex because of the government's involvement and the need for members to stay in the shadows to avoid persecution.

Presenting a chapter on the Local Church in Fujian today is like trying to unravel a ball of string. It is a highly complex tangle of separate components, with no single structure or recognizable

The Local Church Today

A Local Church congregation in the 1990s. Women wear head coverings, a practice that was adopted by Watchman Nee after he visited the Plymouth Brethren in England in the 1920s.

leaders of the movement. Nor does it appear to hold to a cohesive set of doctrines. Each fellowship seems to have largely been left to develop individually.

Gaining access to Local Church leaders in Fujian today is problematic, as they tend to keep to themselves and spurn contact with outsiders. Furthermore, they have generally been isolated from other parts of the body of Christ in China, who shun them due to their questionable doctrines and practices.

In 2001 and 2002, the author was able to form a friendship with Enoch Wang (Chinese name: Wang Xincai), a Local Church leader from Henan Province. His responses to many searching questions about the movement helped clarify some of the complex controversies surrounding the movement today.

An Interview with Enoch Wang

Enoch Wang in 2002.
Paul Hattaway

Hattaway: Many Christians around the world are confused about the Local Church. Can you share some background information to help us better understand the movement?

Wang: Thank you for giving me the opportunity to share about our churches. May the Lord Jesus be glorified!

The first thing to know is that the thousands of fellowships associated with the Local Church in China today are not part of one unified movement. There are many churches that decided to join the Three-Self Patriotic Movement and multitudes of other congregations that decided to remain as unregistered house fellowships.

Hattaway: Did you know Witness Li, and what do you think about claims that he promotes a false gospel and that parts of the Local Church have become a cult?

Wang: Witness Li left China long before I became a Christian, so I never met him. Among believers who meet in house churches, there is a major division between those who follow the teachings of Witness Li and those who do not. I would estimate that in China today, 40 percent of Local Church fellowships are associated with Witness Li and 60 percent are not.

The Chinese government, Three-Self Church, and some overseas organizations have labeled those associated with Witness Li as cult members. Stories and rumors about their strange teachings and practices have been portrayed as typical of a cult, but in my experience those accusations are confined to a small minority of churches.

I know hundreds of Local Church pastors in China, and in my experience, the great majority of them love God and earnestly seek to follow His truth according to the Bible. They know little about the controversies that have clouded Witness Li and his ministry overseas.

It has therefore been my conviction not to create a barrier between those parts of the Local Church who follow Witness Li's teaching and those who do not. I have spent years trying, by God's power, to teach the Scriptures and bring true unity between all those who love the Lord Jesus Christ and who trust in His blood to cleanse them from sin.

Hattaway: What about the Shouters? Can you please explain what influence they have on the Local Church movement?

Wang: The government and the TSPM have cast all members of the Local Church as cult members. They have deliberately shut their ears and have no interest in hearing the truth about our doctrines and practices. Instead, they have eagerly seized the opportunity to mercilessly crush us.

Subsequently, all Local Church believers have been labeled Shouters regardless of what they believe or practice, or even whether they "shout" in their meetings or not! Thousands of pastors have been arrested, imprisoned, and tortured because the Local Church is on the government's list of cults.

Nevertheless, God has been good to us! While we have suffered heavy losses and endured many setbacks, we know we shall win the overall war because our Commander in Chief has already defeated the enemy, and He has called us to conquer the hosts of hell!

The Local Church in China today is not a unified group by any stretch of the imagination, but there are millions of believers who walk humbly with God and who zealously live for the evangelization of their fellow countrymen. May the Lord be glorified!

Hattaway: You also have suffered much for your faith. Can you share some of your testimony, and what the Lord has taught you through it all?

Wang: I have spent 16 years of my life in prison for my faith in the Lord. My only "crimes" were that I followed Jesus Christ and refused to accept the control of an atheist government in church affairs.

I first became a Christian in 1969—during the Cultural Revolution—when I was part of the Red Guards. My faith in God was shallow for the first year and I kept it a secret. I was promoted to a leadership position in the Communist Youth League, and in 1972 I was assigned to work at a People's Liberation Army weapons factory. It wasn't until the following year that I really got serious about serving the Lord Jesus.

Hattaway: How did you survive being a Christian while serving in the Communist regime?

Wang: I was first sent to prison from 1982 to 1994 because of my faith in God. They hated the fact that a Red Guard and a leader of the Communist Youth League was now a Christian pastor! In all those years they tried to break me and make me turn away from the Lord, but by God's grace they could not remove the deposit of the Holy Spirit in my heart.

After I was transferred to a prison labor camp in a different town, my wife and daughter also moved so they could continue to visit me. I was sentenced as a counter-revolutionary and a traitor—the very worst crime in China. Anyone found trying to help the family of a counter-revolutionary is accused of the same crime, so fear of punishment resulted in other Christians being unwilling to help my family.

Consequently, for years my dear wife raised our daughter all by herself, with no Christian fellowship, husband, or money. Sometimes they scavenged through garbage cans looking for scraps of food to eat or for some item they could sell at the market for a few cents.

Many Christians around the world pray for pastors in China when they are sent to prison, and for this we are deeply grateful. However, please remember to also pray for the families of those pastors, as often their ordeal is worse than those in prison. At least I got to eat a couple of coarse meals each day.

Visits from my family were bittersweet experiences. They never complained about their lives, but their malnourished bodies revealed their desperate struggle. I longed to see them and was encouraged when they came, but the pain of knowing what they were going through was the worst form of persecution the authorities could give me.

When I was finally released in 1994, I ignorantly thought I would have a joyous reunion with my family. I didn't understand what my wife and daughter had been through all those years, and a lot of raw emotions that had built up over 13 years came flooding out.

My wife and I had to start our relationship all over again. Only by the gracious help of our Lord Jesus did we survive. Now everything is fine, and I am deeply grateful to the Lord for having given me such a wonderful helpmate. Without her I couldn't do anything. God has always been very good to us!

1990s

The 1990s dawned with the gospel continuing its steady ascent in Fujian. Although white-hot revival like that seen during the 1970s and 1980s had tempered slightly, God's children continued to flourish, and steady growth was seen all over the province.

Although statistics by the Three-Self Church typically only count adult, baptized church members, the official count for Fujian Province rose from 400,000 in 1986[1] to 600,000 in 1989,[2] and then to 900,000 by 1997.[3]

House church Christians worshipping God in the 1990s.

While the TSPM numbers were impressive, unregistered Evangelical house churches in the province contained at least as many members as the registered churches.

The Catholics, meanwhile, also experienced strong growth during these years. In 1950, just after the Communists took control of China, there were 94,776 Catholics in Fujian.[4] After decades of hardship and severe trials, according to one source there were an estimated 200,000 Catholics in the province in 1986,[5] and by 1992 the number had increased to 300,000.[6]

The expansion of God's kingdom among the 35 million people of Fujian did not go unchallenged in the spiritual realm, and in 1990 the government arrested hundreds of believers in northern Fujian and vowed to execute two sisters, claiming they had been complicit in the murder of a sick woman for whom they had prayed, but who later died. The executions did not take place, but large numbers of Christians were brutally beaten and tortured in prison, all on the pretense of belonging to the Shouters cult, with which they had no connection.

One Christian, Brother Yin, was so severely beaten in prison that when he appeared before the judge and threatened with further punishment if he didn't confess his crimes, he calmly opened his shirt and showed the judge his battered body, saying, "I have nothing to confess. There is not much left of this body. Come with your electric cattle prods and your bayonets."[7]

After the believers were released, they returned home and conducted revival meetings, hastening a mighty outpouring of the Holy Spirit in northern Fujian.

Jesus Visits Tade Village

Among the numerous stories of God's love transforming whole communities in Fujian during the 1990s, came one from Tade Village in the south of the province. The story begins with a woman named Wu Shining. She was raised in a Christian family but was later influenced by the atheistic education system and abandoned her childhood faith. As the manager of a bus station she earned a good salary, and she lived to accumulate wealth and possessions.

One day, Wu fell seriously ill and was confined to bed for an extended period. Many doctors examined her but could offer no explanation or medicine to relieve her condition. As she lay there in agony, the Holy Spirit revealed to her that she was being punished because she worshipped money and had wandered far from the faith. When she saw the hopelessness of her condition, Wu cried out for God's mercy and repented of her sins.

The next morning, Wu awoke to find that she was completely healed. Shocked by the dramatic transformation, she dedicated the rest of her life to serving Jesus Christ. Never again would she allow herself to be sidetracked by greed and the lure of the world. In 1990, Wu Shining began sharing the gospel in the Fujian countryside. God's hand was so strongly on her ministry that in 1996 alone, Wu and her co-workers led more than 60 families to abandon their traditional folk religions and embrace a living faith in Christ. She described a few of the conversions that took place that year:

> Four members of the Wei family lived in remote Tade Village, where nobody had ever heard the gospel before. Like many who live in the dark, the Weis were in turmoil from Satan's evil power. The son, Mulin, was 25 years old and had suffered from a severe stomach disorder for years. . . . The father, Pushi, aged 63, had to slave in the fields to earn money to pay all the medical bills. Yet, despite all his efforts, he was in debt. One day, while tending his ox, the animal suddenly knocked him down and stepped on him, breaking three of his ribs.[8]

God's mercy was about to come to the Wei family. After Mulin was admitted to hospital when he was close to death, the doctors told his parents there was nothing they could do to save him. At their lowest point, they walked from the hospital to the place they were staying, passing by the home of Dr. Tu Yili, whose family had followed Jesus for several generations. The Holy Spirit stirred Tu's wife to share the gospel with the distraught family. She took them to a meeting that night, where the believers prayed and asked God to heal their son.

A few days later, after further prayer and discussions with the family, the church sent a dozen of its members to Tade Village to the Wei family's home, where they proceeded to destroy all the idols. The Weis repented of their sins and believed in the Lord, and from that day forward, the spiritual darkness lifted from their lives. Mulin began to recover, and a year later he was a healthy young man, his life having been completely transformed by Jesus.

Amazed by the dramatic change others saw in the Wei family, "within a year they led three families of relatives, a total of 14 people, to Christ. Six more families from their village came to Christ, bringing the total to ten families, including the Weis."[9]

Many miracles of healing and deliverance took place at Tade, with even sick animals belonging to the villagers recovering after the Christians knelt and asked God to heal them. The church in this small community, which had never previously heard the gospel, grew by leaps and bounds as Tade forged a reputation as a place of great peace and joy.

God's Powerful Word

In 1993, a team of Christians from Hong Kong preached during a lunch break to more than 1,000 factory workers in a coastal city. Many believed in the Lord for the first time and were given Bibles. One young man was so overcome with joy that he decided to immediately return home to tell his family and relatives the good news of Jesus.

As a brand-new believer just one day old in his faith, he boarded a bus for the three-day journey home and began the trip by reading the Bible for the first time in his life. When he randomly opened the book, the first thing he read was how Jesus stopped a funeral procession and a little girl was raised from the dead. He was greatly touched and impressed by the power and authority of Jesus.

By the time he got off the bus he had been a Christian for four days. Walking toward his village, he encountered a funeral procession for a 13-year-old boy who had tragically died in an accident. When the young man lifted his hands and started to pray in Jesus' Name, about 70 people in the procession were incensed and began to beat him. Nevertheless, he continued to pray out loud and repeated the words he had read in the Gospel. "Get up in Jesus Name!" he commanded.

As the crowd tried to seize him, they heard a noise behind them and turned around to see the boy sitting upright in his coffin. He said, "Mother, I'm very hungry and thirsty," so they helped him out of the coffin and gave him some food and drink.

Unsurprisingly, all 70 of the mourners who had witnessed the event immediately knelt down on the ground and received Jesus as Lord, declaring that God was real and His Son Jesus held all power and authority, even over death.

Raised from the Dead

Enoch Wang—who shared in the previous chapter about the Local Church in China today—experienced a remarkable miracle after a tragic accident killed his baby daughter. He shared the following testimony of this extraordinary event:

> In late 1995 my wife and I had another little girl, whom we named Sheng Ling ("spiritual blessing"). I was 45 years old and not expecting to be a father again.

1990s

On New Year's Day 1997, a combined house church leaders' meeting was held near my hometown. The leaders of various house church networks came to fellowship with one another, to pray together, and to break down the barriers that existed between us.

At the time my family was being hunted by the police, so we were living in a fourth-floor apartment that was still being constructed. We couldn't get a normal residence because registering with the authorities would have led to our immediate arrest.

On the morning that I was to travel to the unity meeting, I was talking on the telephone when my wife burst into the bedroom shouting hysterically. My teenage daughter had been holding her baby sister, 15 months old at the time, on the unfinished balcony overlooking the street. Somehow, Sheng Ling managed to slip out of her sister's grasp. She fell four stories and landed, headfirst, on a pile of bricks on the street below.

My wife was holding our daughter in her arms and shouting, "Hurry, we must take her to the hospital at once!" I immediately saw that Sheng Ling was dead. Her head was smashed, and a small piece of white brain tissue was protruding through the front of her skull. I told my wife, "There's no point going to the hospital. She's already dead, and there's nothing anyone can do to make her better."

An array of emotions swept over me. I knew that if we went to the hospital the authorities would soon discover we were on their wanted list, and I would be sent back to prison, probably on charges of murdering my own baby. We would be in trouble for living illegally in an unfinished building, and the family who had given us permission to live there would also be in deep trouble.

I knelt and prayed, "Lord, if it is your will for the church in China to be unified, then I ask you to bring my daughter back to life. I pray that today you will put the breath of life back in her body, tomorrow you will allow her to speak, and the day after tomorrow she will be able to walk. But if it is not your will for the church to be unified, I will remove myself from the frontlines and never preach again."

1990s

Some people might say I had no right to speak to God like that, but I was in deep shock, and I knew this accident was a targeted demonic attack designed to stop me attending the meeting.

My wife continued to hold Sheng Ling in her arms and rock her lifeless body back and forth. She had completely stopped breathing, had no pulse, and had turned pale.

Deciding to put my grief aside, I went to the meeting in defiance of Satan, and as an act of faith in God. I wanted to show the devil that he could never intimidate or stop me.

I left home with my anguished wife still holding our daughter in her arms. The piece of brain was still exposed, sticking out of a crack in her skull. My teenage daughter was devastated, blaming herself for the accident.

I arrived at the meeting to find it already underway, and I sat down and didn't tell anyone what had happened. After the first day's meeting concluded, I returned home to find my wife and elder daughter still weeping. Their eyes were red and swollen, and my distraught wife was still holding our dead baby in her arms.

When I leaned forward and prayed over her in the Name of Jesus Christ, I suddenly heard a noise come from Sheng Ling's mouth, like a small burp. I realized she must be breathing, and I cried out, "Praise be to God!"

All four of us slept in the same bedroom, but that night none of us got any rest. Emotionally drained, we just lay there praying quietly. At five o'clock I got up and went back to the meeting and spent the whole day with the other house church leaders, who were still ignorant of what had happened. The meeting concluded after dark and I again returned to my family.

I entered the front door to find a dramatically different atmosphere. Despair had been replaced by joy, and my wife was breastfeeding our little daughter. She was breathing normally, the color had returned to her cheeks, and she was hungry!

God had miraculously healed her skull, and skin now covered the part of her brain that had been exposed. No medical help had been provided except that of the great physician, Jesus. To remind us of His grace, the Lord kept a small scar in the middle of her forehead.

Despite these remarkable improvements, our baby was still far from normal. She couldn't walk or move, her eyes were closed, and she just lay motionless except for breathing and sucking.

When I called out her name, "Sheng Ling," she stopped drinking her milk and a small sound came from her mouth, as if she was greeting me. That night I was able to sleep soundly, knowing the Lord was doing a great miracle.

The next morning, I again woke early and made my way to the third day of the meetings. Many years of bitterness and division came tumbling down at the foot of the cross, and tears flowed as we embraced and accepted one another as true brothers and sisters in Christ.

When I returned home on the third night, my wife was again breastfeeding our daughter. I held out my arms and said, "Sheng Ling, come and let your daddy hold you." She took one step toward me and toppled over, but we all rejoiced that she had taken that first step. Just days earlier she had been dead with her brain sticking out of her smashed skull.

On the fourth morning I went to the meeting with overwhelming joy in my heart. My enthusiasm was soon dampened, however, when a number of house church leaders pointed at me and said, "Those attending this important meeting are expected to stay here. What kind of commitment to unity do you have if you can't even stay with us, but go scurrying home as soon as the meeting ends each night?"

In the final session of the meeting, the leaders intended to pray together one last time before everyone dispersed. My teenage daughter came into the room and whispered excitedly in my ear, telling me that Sheng Ling was now walking and talking normally!

It was then that I stood up and declared to everyone: "Now I know that it is God's will for the church in China to be unified!" Before more than 100 leaders, I testified about what had happened to my baby daughter. Everyone praised God, and those who had criticized me for going home each night asked my forgiveness.

Not only did the Lord heal Sheng Ling from the fall, but he has blessed her in a very special way. When she was eight, she was so smart that her school made her skip a year ahead of her classmates! She has suffered no long-term brain damage as a result of the fall. The only thing that remains is the small scar on her forehead.[10]

Later in 1997, just when his family life was becoming more settled, Enoch Wang was rearrested and sentenced to three more years in prison.[11]

Letters From Fujian

1993

> "I am not a Christian and I don't believe in anything at the moment. I think a person's belief will follow them for the rest of their lives, so I'm hesitant to commit to one particular belief. As I grow older, I've come to realize how empty and evil the world is, but I'm too weak and powerless to do anything about it. I think what I need most is a strong faith. My understanding of Christianity is limited to novels and magazines. Now it seems rather fashionable to believe in Christ in Fuzhou. I find this rather disgusting."[12]

> "I am an evangelist from a mountainous region. I have not received any seminary training and therefore I don't know much about the truth. I preach by faith. There are now more than 200 believers in my church, and we have several fellowships. I am afraid I cannot lead them properly, so I'm writing to ask for your help and for some books."[13]

1994

"I am a non-believer and have argued with Christians concerning their faith on many occasions. Though I listened to their sermons and the Christians were very friendly to me, this has not changed my mind concerning Christianity. It was for the sake of my blind brother that I started to reluctantly attend church meetings. . . . Now I am pleading on behalf of my brother that God would give him peace. If he is healed from his blindness, I will seek and follow Him."[14]

"I am an evangelist working in a remote area. The believers are weak in their faith and spiritual lives. Not having had much training, I have difficulty preparing sermons. Whenever I preach, I feel nervous and inadequate and struggle to feed God's flock. This makes me sad."[15]

1995

"In the place where I live there is a population of 60,000 people with 1,000 believers. The non-Christians always persecute us. They expect us to share in the cost of the offerings they make to idols, but they object whenever we Christians want to build a church."[16]

"Am I a preacher? Even I am not sure! I dedicated my life to the Lord in 1981 and I became a full-time church worker, but I cannot satisfy the needs of all the brothers and sisters during Sunday services. I applied to study at the seminary several times but was unsuccessful. Now I am too old to enroll, yet I lead church meetings four or five nights per week. It is so hard to get equipped for service. What should I do?"[17]

1990s

"I am an evangelist responsible for 13 meeting points. I should encourage the believers, but I find it hard to do when I'm feeling discouraged. I try to be faithful in serving and would like to study the Bible for a year, but I don't know how to finance this."[18]

"My wife died three years ago and I have since lived with my son and daughter. My son is disobedient and does not believe in God, while my married daughter also does not accept Christ as her Savior even though I have often urged her to do so. I am the only Christian in our family. My health is poor, and I always feel lonely and in pain. I can only leave it to the Lord in prayer."[19]

1996

"There are many believers here, but not many who are willing to serve the Lord full-time. The young pastors who have recently graduated from college are not concerned about their flocks, and they only do the bare minimum that they have to. They are more interested in comparing their income levels and boasting about how large their congregations are."[20]

1998

"I am an evangelist who graduated in 1995. I am responsible for five fellowships, but I only have a high school education and my time in seminary was very difficult. I struggle with public speaking, but every week there are many meetings I have to lead, including services for the youth, the elderly, prayer meetings, and choir practice. It is an enormous burden for me, but I know I cannot give up as the people are so hungry."[21]

"In 1988 I started on the path of serving God, and His call was very clear to me. Old habits like smoking, gambling, and fits of rage left me, and my heart was filled with joy. I became sensitive to other people's needs, and God gave me a gentle heart that loved to pray and commune with Him.

In those days I was often filled with the Holy Spirit and had great faith. His power was evident in my preaching and prayers. However, I did not embrace or practice holiness or humility, and I had little discipline in my life. I had a fragile biblical foundation and I just went around casting out demons and healing the sick. After I preached to others, I myself was disqualified. Pride took root in my heart, and later I was controlled by the lust of my eyes. Joy and peace left me, and I became spiritually weak.

Now I am still a minister, but I have little interest in studying God's Word and I receive no light from the Holy Spirit. I feel I am bound, but if I don't preach there is no one to take my place. When I preach there is no power anymore. I hope you can help me."[22]

"There are few members of our church who want to serve God. We have only one preacher, but when she shares there are too many wild children disrupting the meetings. She asked me to be the Sunday school teacher, but the children are very naughty. When I try to tell a story, they are so noisy that I have to stop. How can I deal with this situation?"[23]

1990s

1999

"I was functionally illiterate when I became a Christian 12 years ago, but I learned to read the Bible and write sermons, and I started serving in a house church. Later, I came across your gospel broadcasts and was able to share them with other brothers and sisters. Now we have six co-workers and our church has grown to 40 members!"[24]

"Several years ago my husband had an affair and also became addicted to gambling. Every day there were arguments in our family, but praise God, for He lavished His grace on me when I was in deep despair. I heard the gospel and believed, and by the Lord's mighty power my husband and I have reconciled. The harmony in our family has been restored! Whenever people ask me how this change occurred, I witness for Christ. In the past two years more than 200 people have turned to the Lord!"[25]

2000s

Lin Mingying — The First Martyr of the New Millennium

Lin Mingying, who was killed for Christ in 2000.

The start of the twenty-first century saw China entering a new era of economic prosperity, but the persecution of Christians continued. A house church pastor in Fujian, Lin Mingying, was beaten to death by Chinese police because of his refusal to register with the Three-Self Church.

When his family was allowed to see the body, they found Lin's head had been smashed open and his entire torso was covered with deep bruises. Local officials, concerned that news of their murder would reach the outside world, offered Lin's wife 20,000 Yuan (approximately US$3,000) in an attempt to cover up their

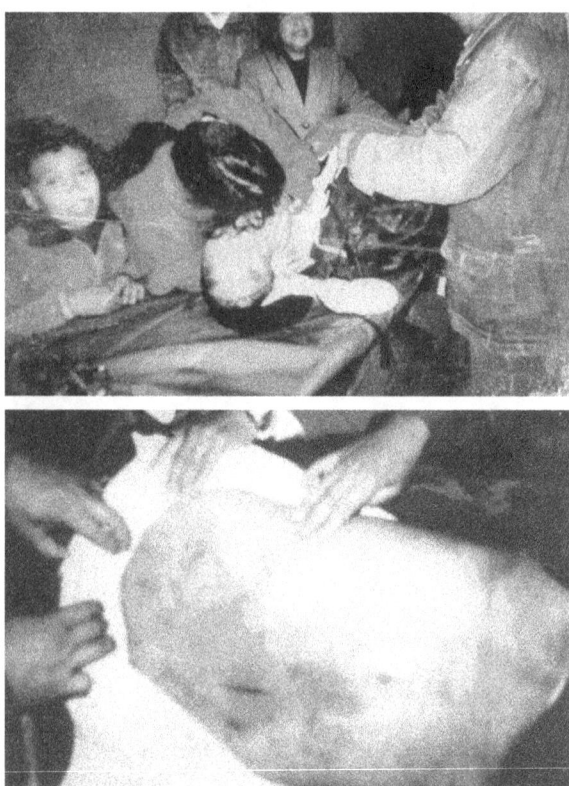

The battered and bruised body of Lin Mingying.
VOM Canada

actions. Their efforts failed, and pictures of Lin Mingying's body were published around the world by Christian ministries.

A Long Way to See a Corpse

While many Christians continued to suffer severe persecution throughout Fujian, the Spirit of God continued to blaze a path across the province, delivering thousands of people from Satan's grip and bringing them into the glorious kingdom of Jesus Christ.

A small fellowship had formed in a village outside Fuzhou City, but they lacked a leader and struggled to access solid Bible teaching. Desperate to know more of God's Word, they called a pastor named Liu in neighboring Guangdong Province, inviting him to come to their village to teach the Scriptures.

Liu accepted the invitation, but a series of bizarre events postponed his trip, and a further year passed before he was able to reschedule his visit.

When he finally reached the village, Liu expected to find a room full of excited believers, but instead, the gathered Christians were dejected and weeping. The man who had invited him lamented, "Teacher Liu, our sister has passed away. We invited you last year, but you didn't come. Even now, if you had come a day earlier, she might still be with us. Now she has left us, and there's no more hope. Let's forget about the meeting. You may as well go home."[1]

A co-worker who had accompanied Liu on the trip entered the room where the woman's body was laid, only to come out reeling moments later, shouting, "She's dead. How horrible!"

Pastor Liu then mustered the courage to enter, and he saw the corpse with a greyish face and sunken cheeks, lying on a bed. It was obvious that she had been dead for some time. Feeling terrible because of what the leader of the meeting had said to him, Liu asked God, "Why did you send me such a long way just to see a corpse?" At that moment,

> [h]e felt a tremendous sense of faith rising from within. The next moment, he found himself leading the people in worship and singing praises to the Almighty God. As Pastor Liu was worshipping God with his eyes closed, someone forcefully pulled on his hand and shouted, "Our sister has awakened! Her eyes are open!"

In a moment of quietness, the husband of the resurrected sister led their children to the bedside and asked his wife is she could tell him their names. The next moment, the sister's complexion began to turn from gray to white and from white to pink.

All the people who witnessed the miracle shouted praises to God and rejoiced with the resurrected sister! In no time, news of the miracle spread like wildfire, and God's Name was greatly feared and honored.[2]

Grace Zheng — A Vessel of Love

Grace Zheng Huiduan

The new millennium dawned with churches across Fujian experiencing unprecedented growth, while it also witnessed the graduation to heaven of many key church leaders who had suffered terribly through the decades of Communist persecution. One of them, Grace Zheng Huiduan, was born near Gutian in 1914.

After being abandoned by her parents soon after birth, she was found on the side of the road and adopted by a Chinese pastor. He died when she was just two, and her adoptive mother passed away when Grace was still a teenager. By then, she had developed her own relationship with God, and He called and enabled her to have a powerful evangelistic ministry throughout Fujian and other parts of China for almost two decades.

In 1949 after the Communists came to power, Zheng had an opportunity to move to safety in Hong Kong or Taiwan, but she decided to remain in Fujian and be with God's suffering children than to enjoy life outside the furnace of affliction.

After her arrest in March 1958, Grace was sentenced to seven years in prison with hard labor. Upon reaching the labor camp, the guards threatened to permanently handcuff her if she refused to write a confession denying Christ. Not willing to sacrifice her faith for temporary gain, she was handcuffed for three months, initially with her hands in front, and then with them behind her back.

Grace clung to Jesus as her dearest Friend and Master, and He helped her survive the worst that evil people could throw at her, including many brutal tortures and beatings as the authorities did everything possible to break her and destroy her faith.

When her seven years were completed, Zheng faced a further devastating blow when her sentence was extended another 14 years and she was transferred to a labor camp in Anhui Province.

Finally, after being released from prison in 1979 after 21 years behind bars, Grace Zheng's application to return home to Fujian was denied, and she spent the rest of her life at Yantai in Shandong Province where she was a much beloved figure in the house churches. Grace lived up to her name and was recognized as someone without any hint of bitterness in her. She had learned the power of forgiveness and was able to genuinely love her enemies.

For the final decades of her life, countless young Christians visited her tiny room to be counseled and to pray with her, and when Grace Zheng Huiduan went to be with the Lord on July 20,

2003, there was an outpouring of grief by thousands of people who had been influenced by her life.

A year after her death, an autobiography of her life—which she had been discreetly writing for years—was published in both Chinese and English,[3] ensuring that the memory of this precious woman, who had been abandoned by her parents as a toddler but adopted into God's family, would live on to bless and encourage future generations.

The "Jesus Virus" Continues to Spread

In many parts of Fujian, the fame of Jesus Christ continued to spread, and church leaders often found their faith stretched to the limit. While revival had largely been confined to the house church movements during the 1980s and 1990s, in the new millennium greater spiritual freedom also came to many registered Three-Self churches in the province, with hundreds of thousands of people saved and transformed in those government-approved fellowships.

The Chinese Communist Party, baffled as to why all their efforts to crush Christianity had only appeared to make it grow stronger, labeled this threat "the Jesus Virus" and promised to continue their efforts to destroy the church.

At the start of 2004, a house church congregation led by a man named Paul was attended by 60 people who were mostly migrant workers and university students. By the end of that year, the church had grown ten-fold after a great miracle attracted hundreds of people to the gospel.

The Cai family had an 18-year-old son who suffered a traumatic brain injury after he was hit by a van. As he lay in a coma for two months, his parents enlisted Daoist priests, Buddhist monks, and other religious practitioners, hoping they could cure him.

2000s

Scenes from a Three-Self Church meeting in Nanping, 2005.
RCMI

A neighbor of the Cai family, who had recently started attending Paul's church, told them about the healing power of Jesus Christ. They were initially hesitant, thinking that if they sought help from God they would offend their traditional deities and ancestral spirits. However, as time went by without any improvement, they decided to let the Christians come and pray for their son.

The Cai family immediately saw that the Christians were different. They seemed to genuinely love and care for the bedridden teenager. The family was shocked when they asked how much money they should pay for the Christians' prayers and were told it was free because Jesus had already paid the price with His own life.

More times of prayer followed, and Mr. Cai began to attend the church services. He liked being around the Christians as they appeared to possess an inner joy that he longed for.

After the son had been in a vegetative state for more than six months, something remarkable began to occur. As the believers continued to intercede for him, he started to follow the voices of people in the room, and became increasingly aware of his surroundings.

He began to say a few words, and strength returned to his upper body, enabling him to sit up in bed. Then, finally, according to a report,

> [t]he unforgettable day came when he could stand once more! It was a miracle! . . . Everyone in the neighborhood heard the marvelous news and was astonished! At least ten different families ultimately came to know the Lord because of this awe-inspiring healing.
>
> Today, Paul's church has more than 600 members. Because of its size and continual growth, it has unavoidably come to the attention of the local government. As a result, the church has moved location several times over the past few years.[4]

Letters From Fujian

2000

"I first listened to your broadcast in 1991. At first, I had a very critical attitude, but strangely, when arguments against Christianity arose in my mind, your show would answer them almost immediately. It was as if the answers were made just for me, like I had submitted the questions in advance! Because of these miracles I started to read the Bible, and after one year I prayed to the Lord and received Jesus as my Savior. Glory to God!"[5]

2001

"After I requested prayer for people to be saved in a remote mountainous region, over 30 residents of a village of less than 50 people were converted to Christ! At a funeral in another small village, another 48 mourners were saved! I thank God for doing this great work among us. I also thank those who prayed for us. The problem we face is that the harvest is huge, but the workers are so few. May the Lord raise up more workers."[6]

"Recently a typhoon attacked Fujian Province, and the hut of a Christian family collapsed and floated away. The father and 16-year-old son were trapped under the sinking hut and started to drown. Amid the crisis they held on to a piece of driftwood and cried out together, 'Save us, Lord!' After floating in the sea for several hours they reached the shore safely. God saved them from death."[7]

2002

"I have been listening to your broadcasts for a long time, but I need to work long hours on a crew that constructs railways, highways, and tunnels, so I am not usually able to listen to a complete program. My work is very dangerous, and rocks can fall on us at any time, but I trust the Lord is with us. At night I often listen to your programs, and I feel peaceful and happy. May the Lord be glorified!"[8]

"I don't remember when I first heard your program, but I was surprised because I didn't think the radio was allowed to broadcast superstition. When I listened more attentively, however, I realized it was not superstition but love, truth, and joy. I never thought God existed, but I now have a strong desire to know Him. I am lonely and I thank God that your broadcast comforts me so much. I am sure Jesus Christ is part of my life. I don't know Him yet, so please teach me what to do."[9]

"I am a believer who accepted Jesus as a child. Now I am the mother of a 6-year-old and my marriage has been in crisis for years. My husband's family are Buddhists and he is an atheist. Since he began trading shares his mentality has completely changed. He always says I am a burden to him and he wants to divorce me. I feel sad as I love him so much and I am willing to sacrifice anything for him, but he has no feelings toward me, and I don't know what to do. Please pray for my marriage, so I can have a strong faith to fight against Satan's influence in my family."[10]

2003

"I am 14 years old and a student in junior high school. I want to wholeheartedly believe in the Lord, but my faith is weak because of the struggles of living in this filthy world. Sometimes I feel close to the Lord and other times He seems far away. I have been troubled about my mother. She has a very dominant personality and often reduces me to tears. If I try to talk back, she immediately slaps me in the face. I have no idea how to communicate with her, as I fear her response will be to hit me again. What should I do?"[11]

2010s and 2020s

She minority believers with Hong Kong pastor Dennis Balcombe in 2010.
RCMI

The 2010s continued to see the passing of many of God's faithful servants who had survived the hardships of imprisonment and suffering in Fujian from the 1950s to the 1970s.

One beloved Christian was Yang Xinfei, who died in 2011 at the age of 83. Yang was a pastor's daughter and a musical child prodigy. She gave her first public piano performance at the age of just three and later attended the prestigious Shanghai Conservatoire of Music, graduating top of her class in 1953.

In spite of the prospect of a glittering musical career, Yang decided to return to her home city of Xiamen to engage in full-time evangelism, spurning the opportunity.

Because of her refusal to join the Three-Self Church, Yang was arrested in 1958 and sentenced to 15 years in a prison labor camp. She entered at the age of 30 and spent the best years of her life in backbreaking punishment because of her love for Jesus Christ. She later said, "God was always with me, and I experienced His miraculous working in my life. I clearly saw God leading me there, and His love was sweet to my soul."[1]

When Yang was finally released in 1974, China was still in the grips of Mao's mad Cultural Revolution, and every church had been closed. Nevertheless, she began to quietly evangelize. When the religious situation began to thaw in 1979, she still refused to join the registered church, but insisted on meeting in house fellowships outside the control of the Communist regime.

Because her home was near Xiamen University, over the years many students were influenced by Yang Xinfei's ministry and gave their lives to Christ. The years of suffering in prison had

Joyful house church believers worshipping God with all their hearts.
RCMI

crushed her, but only in the way that crushing spices can produce a beautiful scent, and many people were attracted to the aroma of Christ through her life.

The Purging

In the mid-2010s, President Xi Jinping began to consolidate his power in China, removing all leaders he suspected of not being completely committed to his militant Marxist philosophies. In 2018, Xi was able to convince enough Communist Party leaders to change the constitution and appoint him president for life.

Christians in Fujian and throughout the country were deeply alarmed by these developments, for although Xi presented a smiling face to the public, in reality the pressure on Christians had intensified every year, and his stated plans to completely control Christianity and alter the Bible so it had "socialist characteristics" indicated that many difficult years lay ahead.

To prepare for the approaching storm, in 2017 house churches across Fujian began to radically restructure themselves, breaking down into small groups of four or five believers who discreetly met together in apartments and homes for prayer and worship. The Chinese church had done a full circle back to the dark times of the Cultural Revolution as it prepared to again go "underground."

As Xi gradually implemented his God-hating laws, each year the pressure was ramped up against the body of Christ. Throughout the province churches were shut down, and many pastors were arrested, fined, and sentenced to prison. Some simply went missing and were not seen again after being bundled into "death vans" by government agents.[2] Few of those who were taken into China's notorious "black jail" system ever came out alive.

Among the many persecutions inflicted on the Fujian church under Xi Jinping, just a few are documented in the remainder of this chapter.

Pastor Lin Kezhen of the Yongfu Church.
China Aid

On October 21, 2018, a group of officers broke into Yongfu Church in Fuzhou. Refusing to identify themselves, the men shouted for the service to end, but Pastor Lin Kezhen calmly replied he would be willing to speak with the officers later, but worshipping God was their priority.

The men continued to shout and cause a disturbance, and when a mother attempted to leave the service with her 1-year-old baby, a government agent chased after her and pushed them, injuring the child's eye.[3]

The officers then damaged church property before threatening to return the following week if the church didn't stop meeting. They raided the church eight times in the next two months.

It appears the local authorities were furious because Lin had refused to modify the church to comply with the Communist Party's orders. They ordered the church to install facial recognition cameras above the pulpit and the main entrance. They also

2010s and 2020s

made it mandatory for churches to fly the national flag in the sanctuary and, in some cases, to display portraits of President Xi instead of the cross.

The United Front Work Department was responsible for the raids on the Yongfu Church. They cut off the electricity and water to the building and visited church members' homes to intimidate them.[4] By the end of 2018, no more news was heard about the fate of the Yongfu Church or its brave leader Lin Kezhen.

In June 2019, officers attacked a Bible study at the Xinzao Church in Xiamen City. When the bullies demanded to see the believers' identity cards, they refused to comply and calmly continued to worship God, despite a line of officers standing at the front and back of the sanctuary. A short video of this bizarre scene was uploaded to the internet.[5]

The following month saw further raids on the Xinzao Church, but the believers refused to be intimidated. They continued to meet in other locations and hired a lawyer to defend the church against the Communist oppressors.

Firemen and officials during a raid on the Xinzao Church.
China Aid

The anti-Christian crackdown continued, and on August 19, 2019, officers again broke into the Xinzao Church. Once again, the believers calmly and politely refused to submit to their threats. When the officers were asked to identify themselves, they covered their badge numbers with their hands and refused to comply. Firemen who participated in the raid appeared confused and hesitant to carry out the orders of the United Front, which is the unit responsible for implementing the dirty work of the Chinese Communist Party. Ten days later, the firemen were again ordered to break into the building to disrupt a Bible study.

On the other side of the city, the Huoshi Church was one of a group of more than 40 unregistered churches ordered to close in Xiamen.[6] Many congregations that rented the buildings they met in found that their landlords had been pressured to cancel their leases, while many churches that owned their properties had them seized by the government.

Catholic churches throughout Fujian were also affected, with special retribution against those that refused to hoist the Chinese flag above their buildings. In some locations, believers were ordered to sing patriotic songs instead of hymns.[7]

By the end of the 2010s, the harassment of Christians had shifted from church buildings to their private homes with many believers being evicted from their rented apartments. When asked why, one landlord simply said it was because of their faith and that the government had bullied them to act against the followers of Jesus.

The severe crackdown against God's people continued into the 2020s, but the believers in Fujian were flexible and continued to meet in tiny groups across the province, making the government's task of identifying and eliminating them much more difficult.

When the Covid virus struck China in early 2020, many people in Fujian were infected and all public movement was banned. During the ensuing lockdowns, the house churches in Fujian

Officers form a human barrier outside the Xunsiding Church, preventing Christians from worshipping God.
China Aid

once again demonstrated their flexibility by quickly setting up online services until the authorities intervened and closed down their websites and social media channels.

Just days after the virus lockdown restrictions finally eased, the government resumed its severe crackdown on Christians. In Xiamen, which the government seems to have identified as a key hub of Christianity, a huge number of Public Security officers from at least four platoons were mobilized to crush the churches.

On June 11, 2020, hundreds of officers, along with leaders of the province's Religious Affairs Bureau, marched through the streets in an open display of force. According to one report, "Their mission was to go to known locations where Christians meet, drive out any remaining church members, take out desks, chairs, and other furniture, tear down suspended ceilings, paneling, and glass used to subdivide the space, and destroy Bibles, teaching materials, musical instruments, and computers."[8]

In 2021, the waves of suppression against Fujian's Christians continued to intensify, and secret Christian schools were identified and harshly eliminated. One school located in a fishing village near Fuzhou was shut down after someone in the village told the authorities that the school was a cult. The government "dispatched nearly 50 police officers, over 20 of them armed, and 20 teachers and students were interrogated overnight."[9] Students were ordered to return home, books and other equipment owned by the church were confiscated, and the government demolished part of the privately-owned building.

In the last few days of 2021, the authorities in Siming District raided another Christian school. They fined the school's leader, Huang Yuanda, 100,000 Yuan (US$15,000) and closed the facility, depriving children the opportunity to learn about Jesus Christ.[10]

Densely-populated Zhongzhou Island. The church in the bottom right of the picture with a red cross on the roof was built on land donated by Watchman Nee. The authorities demolished it in 2024.
Lin Muli

Political Loyalty Demanded

Meanwhile, registered Three-Self churches in Fujian also continued to feel the brunt of President Xi's anti-Christian wrath. In April 2023, an "annual inspection meeting" was held at which Three-Self pastors were examined to ensure their obedience to the teachings of the Communist Party. Leaders were ordered to

> study Xi Jinping thought, familiarize themselves with his speeches and themes of "love the motherland," "love the Communist Party," and "love socialism...." Political loyalty is above all else, so annual inspections also operate as an excuse to remove the unqualified "dissidents"—religious clergy who are evaluated as being not patriotic enough.[11]

In Fuzhou City, the famous Zhongzhou Church, which was founded after Watchmen Nee donated his ancestral property and converted it into a meeting place for Christians, had grown to contain more than 2,000 members by 1994.

The new "Noah's Ark" Three-Self Church at Julong in Hui'an County.
Zhang Wenbin

The church functioned as part of the Three-Self Patriotic Movement for decades, until the government redeveloped tiny Zhongzhou Island at the start of the twenty-first century as part of their plan to transform the island into a modern international city. The congregation was forced to relocate near the Min River, and the authorities demolished the famous church in 2024.

Meanwhile, a dichotomy emerged in Fujian, with some Christians being harshly persecuted for their faith, while others who agreed to toe the Communist Party line without questioning operated in relative freedom. As an example of the strange inconsistency, while thousands of church buildings were being demolished or shut down throughout Fujian, in 2024 a large new building for a congregation of 1,000 members was constructed in Julong township in Hui'an County. A German architect was contracted to design the new building, which is a towering, four-story "Noah's Ark" design that overlooks the town.[12]

In one of the last snippets of Christian news to emerge from Fujian before this book went to press, Yang Xibo and his wife, Wang Xiaofei, the leaders of the largest house church in Xiamen, were fined 400,000 Yuan (US$55,000) for holding unregistered meetings and were ordered not to leave the country. Their Xunsiding Church was banned after jealous officials from the Religious Affairs Bureau grew incensed that they could not control the unregistered congregation. Officers surrounded the building for 30 days to prevent believers from gathering there.

In response, the fellowship broke into smaller groups of believers and met at various meeting places, although ". . . the government successfully located them at every new venue. Authorities would raid their gatherings, beat and arrest the attending Christians, and force them to send their children to public schools. However, the persecution failed to break up the Xunsiding believers."[13]

Yang Xibo, Wang Xiaofei, and their son.
China Aid

Yang and Wang, who owned no home or significant assets, refused to pay the exorbitant fine. In response, in June 2023 the court doubled the amount. Yang and Wang announced on social media that they would not pay the fine, declaring, "Thank God for allowing us to have a part in His affliction, and we are especially thankful that on earth we have no property for the court-enforced implementation, which is definitely a great grace of God."[14]

The Xunsiding Church has a godly history dating back more than a century. Yang is the fourth generation of men in his family to lead the church. His father and aunt were well-known house church figures who suffered for Christ, spending 15 years and five years in prison respectively, for their refusal to submit to the atheistic government-controlled religious system.

The Future of the Church in Fujian

Despite years of persecution, the body of Christ in Fujian is large, vibrant, and full of youth, promising a bright future for Christianity in the province.
RCMI

As we reach the end of our look at the great things God has done in China's Blessed Province, there is much to thank the Lord Jesus Christ for.

Although evidence points to the presence of Nestorian Christians in Fujian from as early as the eighth century, 600 years passed until Catholics arrived in the province in the 1320s, with many suffering martyrdom as they sought to establish churches.

More than five more centuries elapsed before the first Evangelical arrived in 1842, and a fierce battle ensued as missionaries sought to establish the gospel in Fujian. The graveyard in Fuzhou was soon filled with the bodies of dozens of missionaries who perished in the province.

The Future of the Church in Fujian

Through the efforts of pioneers like Irishman John Wolfe—who served in Fujian for 53 years—and Australian Amy Oxley-Wilkinson, the kingdom of God finally took hold, and within several decades the province emerged as a powerhouse for Christianity in south China.

Many setbacks were encountered as the gospel took root, including the slaughter of 11 missionaries and their children at Gutian in 1895, but God's people persevered, and a strategy focused on aggressive evangelism and Christian education began to produce dividends.

Some of the early missionaries labored for years to produce Bibles in various Fujian dialects, but long before the advent of the Communist rule in 1949—when spoken Mandarin and standard Chinese script were promoted—the early Bible translations in Fujian became obsolete, although audio and video resources continue to be used in many of the unique Chinese vernaculars spoken in Fujian.

Starting with a powerful revival at Putian in 1907, the Holy Spirit moved with such force throughout the province that by 1922, Fujian had more Evangelical Christians than any other province in China, although they have dropped back to seventh on the list today.[1]

The 1920s and 1930s saw the emergence of many gifted Fujian church leaders who were influential not only in the province but throughout China. In the case of John Sung, Watchman Nee, and Leland Wang, their ministries expanded to be a blessing to Christians around the world.

The 1950s, 1960s, and 1970s were times of miserable darkness for the body of Christ in Fujian, with hundreds of Christian leaders dying for their faith or spending many years in prison as Mao and the Communist Party attempted to eradicate Christianity from China.

The Future of the Church in Fujian

When the first signs of spring started to appear in the late 1970s, it became clear that the church in Fujian had not only survived the furnace of affliction but had come through purified and equipped for service by the Spirit of God!

From the 1980s to the present time, the churches in Fujian have continued to experience steady growth, and while a new wave of persecution launched by President Xi Jinping following his rise to power in 2023 has brought many new challenges, God's children in Fujian have continued to share the gospel and are well-positioned to withstand whatever attacks they are called to endure.

As the table and graph in the following pages indicate, the church in Fujian had grown exponentially, and today an estimated 4.4 million Evangelicals in the province are divided evenly between the registered and unregistered churches, while an additional 1.4 million Catholics make a total of 5.8 million professing believers, or nearly 15 percent of Fujian's population.

Fujian, the Blessed Province, has lived up to its name! Today the once obscure region in southeast China is ranked fifth out of China's 31 provinces and regions for the number of all professing Christians (including Catholics), or seventh overall for Evangelical believers.

Throughout its long history, the church in Fujian has experienced great victories tempered by harrowing seasons of persecution. They are going through one such period now. Christians the length and breadth of Fujian are learning the truth of Jesus teaching from the Sermon on the Mount:

> Blessed are those who are persecuted because of righteousness, for theirs is the kingdom of heaven. Blessed are you when people insult you, persecute you and falsely say all kinds of evil against you because of me. Rejoice and be glad, because great is your reward in heaven, for in the same way they persecuted the prophets who were before you. (Matt. 5:10–12)

Appendix

Table 1. Evangelical Christians in Fujian (1842–2024)

(Includes both Three-Self and house churches)

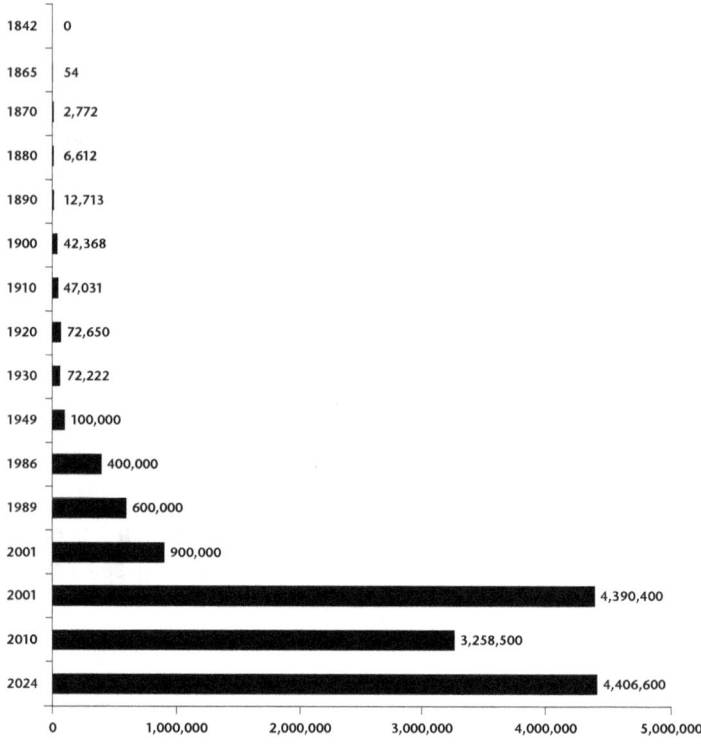

Evangelical Christians in Fujian (1842–2024)

Sources for Table 1.

0	(1842)
54+	(1865 - Fitzgerald & Slater, *JRW*)
2,772	(1870 - Dunch, *Fuzhou Protestants and the Making of a Modern China*)
6,612	(1880 - Dunch, *Fuzhou Protestants*)
12,713	(1890 - Dunch, *Fuzhou Protestants*)
42,368	(1900 - Dunch, *Fuzhou Protestants*)
47,031	(1910 - Dunch, *Fuzhou Protestants*)
72,650	(1920 - Dunch, *Fuzhou Protestants*)
72,222	(1930 - Dunch, *Fuzhou Protestants*)
100,000	(1949 - Lambert, *China's Christian Millions*)
400,000*	(1986 - *Bridge*, January–February 1986)
600,000*	(1989 - Lambert, *The Resurrection of the Chinese church*)
900,000*	(1997 - Amity News Service, September–October 1997)
4,390,400	(2001 - Johnstone & Mandryk, *Operation World*)
1,179,000*	(2004 - Amity News Service, November–December 2004)
3,258,500	(2010 - Mandryk, *Operation World*)
4,406,600	(2024 - Hattaway, *The China Chronicles*)

+ This number represents only the work of The Church Missionary Society.
* These sources may refer to registered church estimates only. TSPM figures typically count only adult baptized members.

Map of All Christians in Fujian

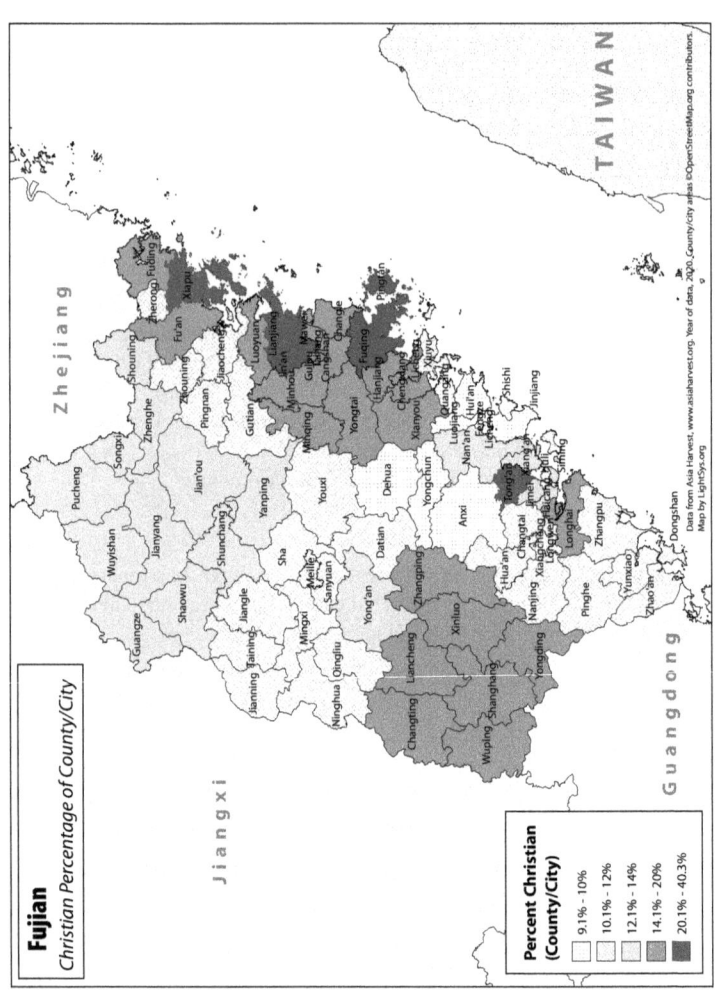

All Christians in Fujian

Table 2. All Christians in Fujian

Fujian 福建		POPULATION						CHRISTIANS							Total Christians	
									Evangelicals			Catholics				
Location		Census 2000	Census 2010	Growth	Growth (percent)	Estimate 2020	TSPM	House church	TOTAL Evangelicals	CPA	House church	TOTAL Catholics	TOTAL	Percent of 2020 population
Fuzhou Prefecture	福州市	6,386,015	7,115,369	729,354	11.42%	7,844,723	955,992	799,209	1,755,201	96,490	106,139	202,629	1,957,830	24.96%
Cangshan District	仓山区	482,039	762,746	280,707	58.23%	1,043,453	93,911	78,509	172,420	12,834	14,118	26,952	199,373	19.11%
Changle City	长乐市	689,815	682,626	-7,189	-1.04%	675,437	43,903	36,703	80,607	8,308	9,139	17,447	98,053	14.52%
Fuqing City	福清市	1,174,540	1,234,838	60,298	5.13%	1,295,136	194,270	162,410	356,680	15,930	17,523	33,453	390,134	30.12%
Gulou District	鼓楼区	559,858	687,705	127,847	22.84%	815,552	73,400	61,362	134,762	10,031	11,034	21,066	155,828	19.11%
Jin'an District	晋安区	510,611	792,491	281,880	55.20%	1,074,371	214,874	179,635	394,509	13,215	14,536	27,751	422,260	39.30%
Lianjiang County	连江县	599,962	561,490	-38,472	-6.41%	523,018	78,453	65,586	144,039	6,433	7,076	13,510	157,549	30.12%
Luoyuan County	罗源县	232,351	207,677	-24,674	-10.62%	183,003	16,470	13,769	30,239	2,251	2,476	4,727	34,966	19.11%
Mawei District	马尾区	203,527	231,929	28,402	13.95%	260,331	23,430	19,587	43,017	3,202	3,522	6,724	49,741	19.11%
Minhou County	闽侯县	580,048	662,118	82,070	14.15%	744,188	66,977	55,993	122,970	9,154	10,069	19,222	142,192	19.11%
Minqing County	闽清县	288,598	237,643	-50,955	-17.66%	186,688	16,802	14,046	30,848	2,296	2,526	4,822	35,670	19.11%
Pingtan County	平潭县	371,922	357,760	-14,162	-3.81%	343,598	70,506	58,943	129,450	4,226	4,649	8,875	138,325	40.26%
Taijiang District	台江区	368,400	446,891	78,491	21.31%	525,382	47,284	39,530	86,814	6,462	7,108	13,571	100,385	19.11%
Yongtai County	永泰县	324,344	249,455	-74,889	-23.09%	174,566	15,711	13,134	28,845	2,147	2,362	4,509	33,354	19.11%
Longyan Prefecture	龙岩市	2,684,310	2,559,545	-124,765	-4.65%	2,434,780	145,885	121,960	267,844	42,122	46,334	88,456	356,300	14.63%
Changting County	长汀县	403,121	393,390	-9,731	-2.41%	383,659	22,444	18,763	41,207	6,637	7,301	13,938	55,146	14.37%
Liancheng County	连城县	297,498	248,645	-48,853	-16.42%	199,792	11,688	9,771	21,459	3,456	3,802	7,258	28,717	14.37%
Shanghang County	上杭县	433,700	374,047	-59,653	-13.75%	314,394	18,392	15,376	33,768	5,439	5,983	11,422	45,190	14.37%
Wuping County	武平县	329,916	278,182	-51,734	-15.68%	226,448	13,247	11,075	24,322	3,918	4,309	8,227	32,549	14.37%
Xinluo District	新罗区	543,731	662,429	118,698	21.83%	781,127	45,696	38,202	83,898	13,513	14,865	28,378	112,276	14.37%
Yongding District	永定区	411,587	362,658	-48,929	-11.89%	313,729	18,353	15,343	33,696	5,970	5,970	11,398	45,094	14.37%
Zhangping City	漳平市	264,757	240,194	-24,563	-9.28%	215,631	16,065	13,430	29,494	3,730	4,103	7,834	37,328	17.31%
Nanping Prefecture	南平市	2,816,581	2,645,548	-171,033	-6.07%	2,474,515	133,795	111,852	245,647	42,809	47,090	89,899	335,546	13.56%
Guangze County	光泽县	142,214	134,113	-8,101	-5.70%	126,012	6,716	5,615	12,331	2,180	2,398	4,578	16,909	13.42%
Jian'ou City	建瓯市	478,651	452,174	-26,477	-5.53%	425,697	24,052	20,107	44,159	7,365	8,101	15,466	59,625	14.01%
Jianyang City	建阳区	317,848	289,362	-28,486	-8.96%	260,876	14,348	11,995	26,343	4,513	4,964	9,478	35,821	13.73%
Pucheng County	浦城县	321,272	304,583	-16,689	-5.19%	287,894	15,345	12,828	28,173	4,981	5,479	10,459	38,632	13.42%
Shaowu City	邵武市	288,401	275,112	-13,289	-4.61%	261,823	13,772	11,513	25,285	4,530	4,982	9,512	34,797	13.29%
Shunchang County	顺昌县	231,599	191,588	-40,011	-17.28%	151,577	8,079	6,754	14,833	2,622	2,885	5,507	20,340	13.42%
Songxi County	松溪县	142,453	125,472	-16,981	-11.92%	108,491	5,783	4,834	10,617	1,877	2,065	3,941	14,558	13.42%
Wuyishan City	武夷山市	212,156	233,554	21,398	10.09%	254,952	13,869	11,595	25,464	4,411	4,852	9,262	34,727	13.62%
Yanping District	延平区	488,818	467,875	-20,943	-4.28%	446,932	23,821	19,915	43,736	7,732	8,505	16,237	59,973	13.42%
Zhenghe County	政和县	193,169	171,715	-21,454	-11.11%	150,261	8,009	6,695	14,704	2,600	2,859	5,459	20,163	13.42%

All Christians in Fujian

Fujian 福建			POPULATION					Evangelicals			Catholics			Total Christians	
Location		Census 2000	Census 2010	Growth	Growth (percent)	Estimate 2020	TSPM	House church	TOTAL Evangelicals	CPA	House church	TOTAL Catholics	TOTAL	Percent of 2020 population
Ningde Prefecture	宁德市													
Fu'an City	福安市	554,057	563,640	9,583	1.73%	573,223	39,667	33,162	72,829	9,917	10,908	20,825	93,654	16.34%
Fuding City	福鼎市	521,070	529,534	8,464	1.62%	537,998	34,862	29,145	64,007	9,307	10,238	19,545	83,553	15.53%
Gutian County	古田县	398,990	323,700	-75,290	-18.87%	248,410	9,067	7,580	16,647	4,297	4,727	9,025	25,672	10.33%
Jiaocheng District	蕉城区	400,293	429,260	28,967	7.24%	458,227	16,725	13,982	30,708	7,927	8,720	16,647	47,355	10.33%
Pingnan County	屏南县	168,482	137,724	-30,758	-18.26%	106,966	3,904	3,264	7,168	1,851	2,036	3,886	11,054	10.33%
Shouning County	寿宁县	230,571	175,874	-54,697	-23.72%	121,177	6,847	5,724	12,570	2,096	2,306	4,402	16,973	14.01%
Xiapu County	霞浦县	456,474	461,176	4,702	1.03%	465,878	47,939	40,077	88,016	8,060	8,866	16,925	104,941	22.53%
Zherong County	柘荣县	92,434	88,387	-4,047	-4.38%	84,340	3,078	2,574	5,652	1,459	1,605	3,064	8,716	10.33%
Zhouning County	周宁县	168,887	112,701	-56,186	-33.27%	56,515	2,063	1,724	3,787	978	1,075	2,053	5,840	10.33%
		2,991,258	2,821,996	-169,262	-5.66%	2,652,734	164,152	137,231	301,384	45,892	50,482	96,374	397,758	14.99%
Putian Prefecture	莆田市													
Chengxiang District	城厢区	413,853	413,853	0	0.00%	413,853	32,901	27,505	60,407	7,160	7,876	15,035	75,442	18.23%
Hanjiang District	涵江区	470,097	470,097	0	0.00%	470,097	37,373	31,244	68,616	8,133	8,946	17,079	85,695	18.23%
Licheng District	荔城区	499,110	499,110	0	0.00%	499,110	39,679	33,172	72,851	8,635	9,498	18,133	90,984	18.23%
Xianyou County	仙游县	855,439	824,707	-30,732	-3.59%	793,975	45,495	38,034	83,528	13,736	15,109	28,845	112,374	14.15%
Xiuyu District	秀屿区	570,741	570,741	0	0.00%	570,741	21,289	17,797	39,086	9,874	10,861	20,735	59,821	10.48%
		2,809,240	2,778,508	-30,732	-1.09%	2,747,776	176,737	147,752	324,489	47,537	52,290	99,827	424,315	15.44%
Quanzhou Prefecture	泉州市													
Anxi County	安溪县	1,011,437	977,435	-34,002	-3.36%	943,433	28,303	23,661	51,964	16,321	17,954	34,275	86,239	9.14%
Dehua County	德化县	301,834	277,867	-23,967	-7.94%	253,900	7,617	6,368	13,985	4,392	4,832	9,224	23,209	9.14%
Fengze District	丰泽区	397,847	529,640	131,793	33.13%	661,433	19,843	16,589	36,432	11,443	12,587	24,030	60,462	9.14%
Hui'an County	惠安县	897,381	944,231	46,850	5.22%	991,081	29,732	24,856	54,589	17,146	18,860	36,006	90,595	9.14%
Jinjiang City	晋江市	1,479,259	1,986,447	507,188	34.29%	2,493,635	83,287	69,628	152,916	43,140	47,454	90,594	243,509	9.77%
Licheng District	鲤城区	292,157	404,817	112,660	38.56%	517,477	15,524	12,978	28,503	8,952	9,848	18,800	47,303	9.14%
Luojiang District	洛江区	160,071	187,189	27,118	16.94%	214,307	6,429	5,375	11,804	3,708	4,078	7,786	19,590	9.14%
Nan'an City	南安市	1,385,276	1,418,451	33,175	2.39%	1,451,626	81,001	67,717	148,717	25,113	27,624	52,738	201,455	13.88%
Quanggang District	泉港区	342,211	313,539	-28,672	-8.38%	284,867	8,546	7,144	15,690	4,928	5,421	10,349	26,040	9.14%
Shishi City	石狮市	498,786	636,700	137,914	27.65%	774,614	23,393	19,557	42,950	13,401	14,741	28,142	71,092	9.18%
Yongchun County	永春县	516,700	452,217	-64,564	-12.49%	387,653	11,630	9,722	21,352	6,706	7,377	14,083	35,435	9.14%
		7,283,040	8,128,533	845,493	11.61%	8,974,026	315,306	263,596	578,902	155,251	170,776	326,026	904,928	10.08%

All Christians in Fujian

Fujian 福建		POPULATION					Evangelicals			CHRISTIANS Catholics			Total Christians	
Location		Census 2000	Census 2010	Growth	Growth (percent)	Estimate 2020	TSPM	House church	TOTAL Evangelicals	CPA	House church	TOTAL Catholics	TOTAL	Percent of 2020 population
Sanming Prefecture	三明市													
Datian County	大田县	331,019	311,631	-19,388	-5.86%	292,243	10,287	8,600	18,887	5,056	5,561	10,617	29,504	10.10%
Jiangle County	将乐县	158,491	148,867	-9,624	-6.07%	139,243	4,901	4,098	8,999	2,409	2,650	5,059	14,058	10.10%
Jianning County	建宁县	133,918	119,979	-13,939	-10.41%	106,040	3,733	3,120	6,853	1,834	2,018	3,852	10,706	10.10%
Meilie District	梅列区	156,874	176,539	19,665	12.54%	196,204	6,906	5,774	12,680	3,394	3,734	7,128	19,808	10.10%
Mingxi County	明溪县	109,102	102,667	-6,435	-5.90%	96,232	3,387	2,832	6,219	1,665	1,831	3,496	9,715	10.10%
Ninghua County	宁化县	298,434	272,443	-25,991	-8.71%	246,452	8,675	7,252	15,928	4,264	4,690	8,954	24,881	10.10%
Qingliu County	清流县	135,660	136,248	588	0.43%	136,836	4,817	4,027	8,843	2,367	2,604	4,971	13,815	10.10%
Sanyuan District	三元区	180,231	198,958	18,727	10.39%	217,685	7,663	6,406	14,068	3,766	4,143	7,908	21,977	10.10%
Sha County	沙县	228,548	226,669	-1,879	-0.82%	224,790	7,913	6,615	14,528	3,889	4,278	8,167	22,694	10.10%
Taining County	泰宁县	114,187	110,278	-3,909	-3.42%	106,369	3,744	3,130	6,874	1,840	2,024	3,864	10,739	10.10%
Yong'an City	永安市	334,852	347,042	12,190	3.64%	359,232	17,890	14,956	32,846	6,215	6,836	13,051	45,896	12.78%
Youxi County	尤溪县	392,759	352,067	-40,692	-10.36%	311,375	10,960	9,163	20,123	5,387	5,925	11,312	31,436	10.10%
		2,574,075	2,503,388	-70,687	-2.75%	2,432,701	90,876	75,972	166,848	42,086	46,294	88,380	255,228	10.49%
Xiamen Prefecture	厦门市													
Haicang District	海沧区	227,007	288,739	61,732	27.19%	350,471	16,682	13,947	30,629	6,063	6,669	12,733	43,362	12.37%
Huli District	湖里区	413,316	931,291	517,975	125.32%	1,449,266	68,985	57,672	126,657	25,072	27,580	12,733	139,389	9.62%
Jimei District	集美区	148,678	580,857	432,179	290.68%	1,013,036	48,221	40,312	88,533	17,526	19,278	36,804	125,336	12.37%
Siming District	思明区	683,256	929,951	246,742	36.11%	1,176,740	56,016	46,827	102,840	20,358	22,393	42,751	145,591	14.14%
Tong'an District	同安区	496,129	496,129	0	0.00%	496,129	23,616	19,743	43,358	8,583	9,441	79,555	122,913	24.77%
Xiang'an District	翔安区	304,333	304,333	0	0.00%	304,333	14,486	12,111	26,597	5,265	5,791	11,056	37,653	12.37%
		2,272,719	3,531,347	1,258,628	55.38%	4,789,975	228,003	190,610	418,613	82,867	91,153	174,020	592,633	12.37%
Zhangzhou Prefecture	漳州市													
Changtai County	长泰县	190,288	206,809	16,521	8.68%	223,330	7,504	6,273	13,777	3,864	5,522	9,385	23,163	10.37%
Dongshan County	东山县	206,152	211,505	5,353	2.60%	216,858	8,241	6,889	15,130	3,752	5,647	9,399	24,529	11.31%
Hua'an County	华安县	159,099	159,152	53	0.03%	159,205	5,349	4,472	9,821	2,754	4,249	7,004	16,825	10.57%
Longhai City	龙海市	816,318	877,762	61,444	7.53%	939,206	50,717	42,400	93,117	16,248	23,436	39,685	132,801	14.14%
Longwen District	龙文区	134,690	167,463	32,773	24.33%	200,236	6,728	5,625	12,352	3,464	4,471	7,935	20,288	10.13%
Nanjing County	南靖县	342,165	333,969	-8,196	-2.40%	325,773	10,946	9,151	20,097	5,636	8,917	14,553	34,650	10.64%
Pinghe County	平和县	532,649	498,533	-34,116	-6.40%	464,417	15,604	13,045	28,650	8,034	13,311	21,345	49,995	10.77%
Xiangcheng District	芗城区	433,194	538,186	104,992	24.24%	643,178	21,611	18,067	39,677	11,127	14,370	25,497	65,174	10.13%
Yunxiao County	云霄县	403,617	415,835	12,218	3.03%	428,053	14,383	12,024	26,406	7,405	11,103	18,508	44,915	10.49%
Zhangpu County	漳浦县	795,347	802,971	7,624	0.96%	810,595	27,236	22,769	50,005	14,023	21,439	35,463	85,468	10.54%
Zhao'an County	诏安县	568,156	597,798	29,642	5.22%	627,440	21,082	17,625	38,707	10,855	15,961	26,816	65,522	10.44%
		4,581,675	4,809,983	228,308	4.98%	5,038,291	189,401	158,339	347,739	87,162	128,427	215,589	563,328	11.18%
Totals		34,398,913	36,894,217	2,495,304	7.25%	39,389,521	2,400,145	2,006,521	4,406,667	642,215	738,984	1,381,200	5,787,866	14.69%

© Asia Harvest - All Rights Reserved

Table 3. People Groups in Fujian

People Group	Official Nationality	Primary Language	Primary Religion	Population (all of China) 2020	All Christians		Evangelicals	
Ami	Gaoshan	Ami	Polytheism	2,000	0	0.0%	0	0.0%
Bunun	Gaoshan	Bunun	Polytheism	1,500	5	0.3%	5	0.3%
Han Chinese, Hui'an	Han	Chinese, Min Nan	Daoism	181,000	9,050	5.0%	7,602	4.2%
Han Chinese, Min Bei	Han	Chinese, Min Bei	Non-Religious	8,272,000	827,200	10.0%	727,936	8.8%
Han Chinese, Min Dong	Han	Chinese, Min Dong	Non-Religious	10,626,000	1,062,600	10.0%	966,966	9.1%
Han Chinese, Min Nan	Han	Chinese, Min Nan	Non-Religious	22,649,000	2,264,900	10.0%	1,993,112	8.8%
Han Chinese, Min Zhong	Han	Chinese, Min Zhong	Non-Religious	3,601,000	252,070	7.0%	208,858	5.8%
Han Chinese, Putian	Han	Chinese, Puxian	Non-Religious	3,063,000	245,040	8.0%	168,465	5.5%
Han Chinese, Shaojiang	Han	Chinese, Min Bei	Non-Religious	2,812,000	120,916	4.3%	104,044	3.7%
Paiwan	Gaoshan	Paiwan	Polytheism	700	0	0.0%	0	0.0%
She	She	She	Daoism	660,000	1,980	0.3%	792	0.1%
Totals				51,868,200	4,783,761	9.2%	4,177,780	8.1%

Groups primarily located in Fujian. Latest stats from www.joshuaproject.net

Researching Christians in China

For centuries, people have been curious to know how many Christians live in China. When Marco Polo made his famous journey to the Orient 750 years ago, he documented the existence of Nestorian churches and monasteries in various places, to the fascination of people in Europe.

Since I started traveling to China in the 1980s, I have met many believers around the world who are eager to know how many Christians there are in China. People are aware that God has done a remarkable work there, but little research has been done to put a figure on this phenomenon. In recent decades, wildly divergent estimates ranging from 20 million to 230 million have been published for the number of Christians in China.

Methodology

In the preceding table, I provide estimates of the number of Christians in Fujian. Full tables of the other provinces of China can be found at the Asia Harvest website (see "The Church in China" link under the "Resources" tab at www.asiaharvest.org). My survey provides figures for Christians of every description, arranged in four main categories: the Three-Self Patriotic Movement, the Evangelical house churches, the Catholic Patriotic Association, and the Catholic house churches. I have supplied statistics for all 2,800 cities and counties within every province, municipality, and autonomous region of China.

The information was gathered from a wide variety of sources. More than 2,000 published sources have been noted in the tables published online, including a multitude of books, journals, magazine articles, and reports that I spent years meticulously accumulating. I have also conducted hundreds of hours of interviews with key house church leaders from many different networks who are responsible for God's work throughout China.

It should be noted that none of the information provided in these tables is new to the Chinese government. Beijing has already thoroughly researched the spread of Christianity throughout the country, as shown by the director of the Religious Affairs Bureau, Ye Xiaowen, who in 2006 shocked the world by announcing that there were then 130 million Christians in China.[1]

The Chinese Church in Perspective

All discussion of how many Christians there are in China should be tempered by the realization that more than 90 percent of the country's present population face a Christless eternity. Hundreds of millions of individuals have yet to hear the gospel. House church leaders in China have told me how ashamed they feel that so many of their countrymen and women do not yet know Jesus Christ. This burden motivates them to do whatever it takes to preach the gospel among every ethnic group and in every city, town, and village—indeed, to every individual—in China, and to do whatever is necessary to see Christ exalted throughout the land.

Map of China's Christians

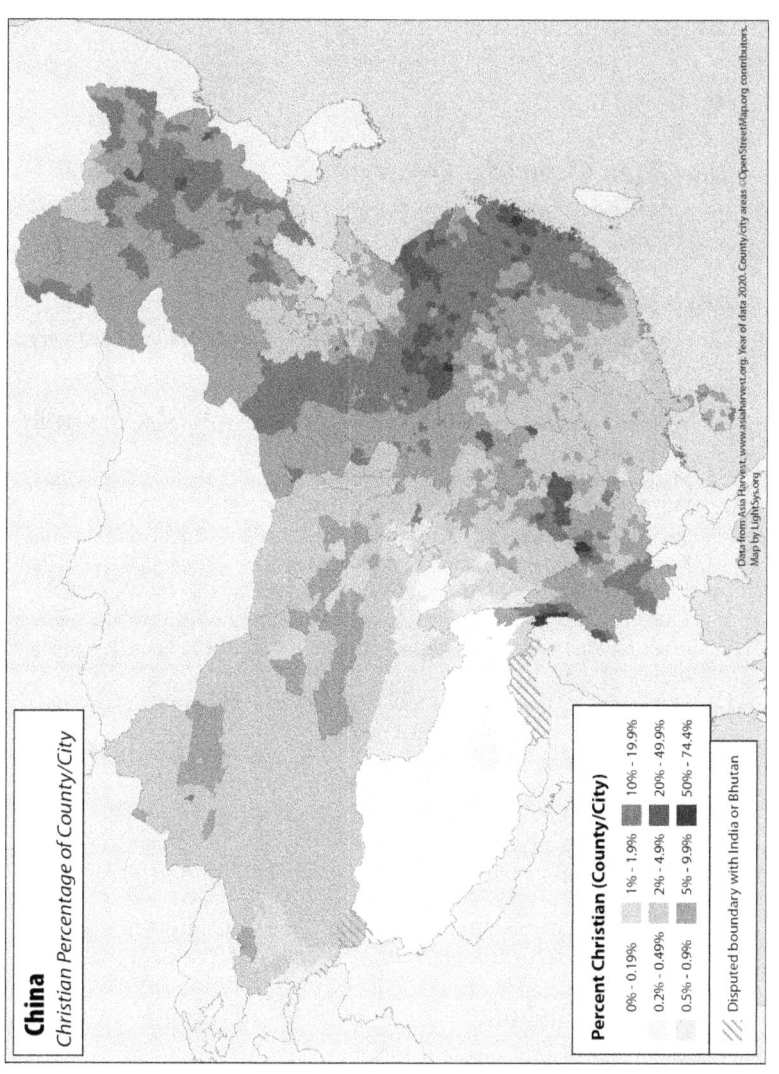

Notes

The China Chronicles Overview and Publisher's Note
1 R. Wardlaw Thompson, *Griffith John: The Story of Fifty Years in China* (London: The Religious Tract Society, 1908), p. 65.

Introduction
1 C. Campbell Brown, "Province of Fuh-kien," *China's Millions* (February 1904), p. 17.
2 Campbell Brown, "Province of Fuh-kien," p. 17.
3 William Marsden (trans.), *The Travels of Marco Polo* (New York: Dell, 1961), pp. 300–01.
4 Marco Polo, *The Travels of Marco Polo: The Complete Yule-Cordier Edition*, Vol. 2 (New York: Dover Publications, 1903), p. 231.
5 See Gavin Menzies, *1421: The Year China Discovered the World* (London: Bantam Press, 2002). In the United States the book was entitled, *1421: The Year China Discovered America* (New York: William Morrow Paperbacks, 2002). Some Western historians have strongly disputed many of the claims made by Menzies, but the Chinese have elevated Zheng He to legendary status.
6 Leo J. Moser, *The Chinese Mosaic: The Peoples and Provinces of China* (Boulder: Westview Press, 1985), p. 168.
7 Jonathan Fenby, *The Dragon Throne: Dynasties of Imperial China 1600 BC–AD 1912* (London: Quercus Publishing, 2008), p. 186.
8 Michael Buckley et al., *China: A Travel Survival Kit*, 4th edition (Hawthorn: Lonely Planet, 1994), p. 402.
9 Elaine Hui, "The Paiwan People of Taiwan," *China Tourism* (no. 82, n.d.), p. 71.
10 Charles Gutzlaff, *Journal of Three Voyages Along the Coast of China in 1831, 1832 and 1833* (London: Frederick Westley & A. H. Davies, 1834), p. 190.

A Linguistic Babble
1 Moser, *The Chinese Mosaic*, p. 166.
2 Moser, *The Chinese Mosaic*, p. 32.

Notes

3 J. E. Walker, "Shao-wu in Fuk-kien: A Country Station," *Chinese Recorder* (September–October 1878), p. 349.
4 Church Missionary Society, *For Christ in Fuh-kien: The Story of the Fuhkien Mission of the Church Missionary Society* (London: Church Missionary Society, 1904), pp. 168–69. Note: The translations mentioned here were only for language groups in central and northern Fujian, from Putian northward. Several other Bible translations also existed for languages and dialects in southern parts of the province, of which the Amoy (Xiamen) translation was the most widely used.
5 Gordon Hewitt, *The Problems of Success: A History of the Church Missionary Society, 1910–1942*, roman (London: SCM Press, 1971), pp. 241–42.
6 "Gaoshan" is an artificial construction by the Chinese Communist Party. The label consists of three distinct tribes—the Ami, Bunun, and Paiwan—which are found in much larger numbers across the strait in Taiwan.
7 Moser, *The Chinese Mosaic*, p. 174.
8 These statistics are the latest figures taken from the Joshua Project website (www.joshuaproject.net).
9 Moser, *The Chinese Mosaic*, p. 165.
10 Moser, *The Chinese Mosaic*, p. 163.
11 Moser, *The Chinese Mosaic*, p. 173.
12 J. Edwin Orr, *Evangelical Awakenings in Eastern Asia* (Minneapolis: Bethany House, 1975), p. 82.
13 Australian Academy of the Humanities and the Chinese Academy of Social Sciences, *Language Atlas of China* (Hong Kong: Longman Group, 1987), p. B-13.

Nestorians in Fujian

1 Cited in John M. L. Young, *By Foot to China: Mission of the Church of the East* (Tokyo: Radio Press, 1984).
2 A. C. Moule, *Christians in China Before the Year 1550* (London: SPCK, 1930), p. 82.
3 Moule, *Christians in China Before the Year 1550*, p. 142.
4 Arthur Moule and Paul Pelliot, *Marco Polo: The Description of the World*, Vol. 2 (London: Routledge & Sons, 1938), p. 350.

Early Catholics in Fujian

1 Polo, *The Travels of Marco Polo: The Complete Yule-Cordier Edition*, Vol. 2, p. 237.
2 L' Abbé Huc, *Christianity in China, Tartary, and Thibet* (London: Brown, Green, Longmans, & Roberts, 1857), p. 357.

Notes

3 For a thrilling account of the martyrdoms see Huc, *Christianity in China, Tartary, and Thibet*, p. 362.
4 See Henry Yule and Henri Cordier, *Cathay and the Way Thither: Being A Collection* (Delhi: Munshiram Manoharlal, 1998), pp. 191–94.
5 Huc, *Christianity in China, Tartary, and Thibet*, p. 277. For an account of the persecution of 1637–38 in Fujian Province, see Eugenio Menegon, *Jesuits, Franciscans and Dominicans in Fujian: The Anti-Christian Incidents of 1637–1638* (Aleni Conference, 1997).
6 From the Giulio Aleni profile at http://www.bdcconline.net.
7 See the "Table of Christians in Fujian" in the back of this book.
8 Chinese Regional Bishops' Conference, *The Newly Canonized Martyr-Saints of China* (Taiwan: Chinese Regional Bishops' Conference, September 8th Editorial Board, 2000), p. 70.
9 CRBC, *The Newly Canonized Martyr-Saints of China*, pp. 70–71.
10 Ji Li (ed.), *Missions Étranges de Paris (MEP) and China from the Seventeenth Century to the Present* (Studies in the History of Christianity in East Asia, Vol. 6) (Leiden: Brill, 2022), p. 247.
11 Standaert, *Handbook of Christianity in China, Volume One: 635–1800*, p. 386.
12 Standaert, *Handbook of Christianity in China, Volume One: 635–1800*, p. 325.
13 The Fujian Catholic community and its origins have been documented in an award-winning book by Eugenio Menegon, *Ancestors, Virgins and Friars: Christianity as a Local Religion in Late Imperial China* (Harvard-Yenching Institute Monograph Series) (Cambridge: Harvard University Asia Center, 2010).
14 James Carter, "The Yongzheng Emperor and Christianity in China: This Week in History," at: https://thechinaproject.com/2021/02/10/the-yongzheng-emperor-and-christianity-in-china/ (February 10, 2021).
15 CRBC, *The Newly Canonized Martyr-Saints of China*, p. 71.
16 CRBC, *The Newly Canonized Martyr-Saints of China*, p. 72.
17 CRBC, *The Newly Canonized Martyr-Saints of China*, p. 72.
18 CRBC, *The Newly Canonized Martyr-Saints of China*, p. 73.
19 CRBC, *The Newly Canonized Martyr-Saints of China*, p. 74.
20 CRBC, *The Newly Canonized Martyr-Saints of China*, p. 74.
21 Standaert, *Handbook of Christianity in China, Volume One: 635–1800*, p. 386.
22 Eugene Stock, *The Story of the Fuh-kien Mission of the Church Missionary Society* (London: Seeley, Jackson & Halliday, 1890), p. 252.

1830s and 1840s

1 *Chinese Around the World* (March 1995), pp. 9–10.

Notes

2 Our main profile on Karl Gutzlaff will appear in the Guangdong volume of *The China Chronicles*.
3 Jessie Gregory Lutz, *Opening China: Karl F. A. Gutzlaff and Sino-Western Relations, 1827–1852* (Grand Rapids: Eerdmans, 2008), pp. 78–79.
4 Lutz, *Opening China*, p. 80.
5 Jennifer Lin, *Shanghai Faithful: Betrayal and Forgiveness in a Chinese Christian Family* (Lanham: Rowman & Littlefield, 2017), p. 15.
6 Stock, *The Story of the Fuh-kien Mission*, p. 23.
7 Gutzlaff, *Journal of Three Voyages*, pp. 174–75.
8 Gutzlaff, *Journal of Three Voyages*, pp. 183–84.
9 Gutzlaff, *Journal of Three Voyages*, pp. 180–82, 191–94.
10 Arnold Foster, *Christian Progress in China: Gleanings from the Writings and Speeches of Many Workers* (London: The Religious Tract Society, 1889), p. 138.
11 *The Chinese Repository* (Vol. 4), p. 334.
12 A few sources say Abeel moved to Fujian in 1841, but his biography indicates 1842.
13 See G. R. Williamson, *Memoir of the Rev David Abeel, DD, Late Missionary to China* (New York: Robert Carter, 1848).
14 John Stronach, "Reminiscences of Forty Years Missionary Labour," *China's Millions* (October 1878), p. 135.

1850s

1 The first Evangelical martyr in China was Walter Lowrie, who drowned in remarkably similar circumstances in Zhejiang Province in 1847. His story was told in the Zhejiang volume of *The China Chronicles*. See Paul Hattaway, *Zhejiang: The Jerusalem of China* (London: SPCK, 2019), pp. 17–19.
2 I. W. Wiley (ed.), *The Missionary Cemetery and the Fallen Missionaries of Fuh Chau, China: With an Introductory Notice of Fuh Chau and Its Missions* (New York: Carlton & Porter, 1858), p. 43.
3 See the "Table of Christians in Fujian" in the back of this book.
4 Stock, *The Story of the Fuh-kien Mission*, p. 17.
5 See David Cheung, *Christianity in Modern China: The Making of the First Native Protestant Church* (Leiden: Brill, 2004), pp. 222–24.
6 Stock, *The Story of the Fuh-kien Mission*, pp. 49–51.
7 W. S. Pakenham-Walsh, *Some Typical Christians of South China* (London: Marshall Bros., 1905), pp. 6–7.
8 Pakenham-Walsh, *Some Typical Christians of South China*, p. 58.
9 Pakenham-Walsh, *Some Typical Christians of South China*, pp. 61–62.
10 Wiley, *The Missionary Cemetery and the Fallen Missionaries of Fuh Chau*, pp. 6–7, 45.

Notes

1860s

1. John Van Nest Talmage, *History and Ecclesiastical Relations of the Churches of the Presbyterial Order at Amoy, China* (New York: Wynkoop, Hallenbeck & Thomas, 1863), p. 37.
2. Talmage, *History and Ecclesiastical Relations of the Churches of the Presbyterial Order at Amoy*, p. 40.
3. Stock, *The Story of the Fuh-kien Mission*, p. 252.
4. Stock, *The Story of the Fuh-kien Mission*, p. 30.
5. *China's Millions* (July–August 1881), p. 93.
6. Stock, *The Story of the Fuh-kien Mission*, p. 32.
7. Pakenham-Walsh, *Some Typical Christians of South China*, p. 33.
8. Cited in Ryan Dunch, *Fuzhou Protestants and the Making of a Modern China, 1857–1927* (New Haven: Yale University Press, 2001), p. 9.
9. Dunch, *Fuzhou Protestants and the Making of a Modern China*, p. 204, note 1.
10. Dunch, *Fuzhou Protestants and the Making of a Modern China*, p. 2.
11. Sarah Sites, *Nathan Sites: An Epic of the East* (New York: Fleming H. Revell, 1912), pp. 189–91.
12. Sites, *Nathan Sites*, p. 233.
13. Sites, *Nathan Sites*, p. 236.

John Wolfe — "The Fujian Moses"

1. "Register of Missionaries and Native Clergy from 1804 to 1904" (London: Church Missionary Society, 1905). A paper printed for private circulation.
2. Stock, *The Story of the Fuh-kien Mission*, p. 34.
3. Stock, *The Story of the Fuh-kien Mission*, p. 55.
4. Stock, *The Story of the Fuh-kien Mission*, p. 110.
5. Stock, *The Story of the Fuh-kien Mission*, pp. 110–11.
6. Stock, *The Story of the Fuh-kien Mission*, pp. 118–19.
7. Stock, *The Story of the Fuh-kien Mission*, pp. 121–22, 135.
8. John Fitzgerald and Frances Slater, *JRW: Story of the Fuh-kien Mission* (self-published, 2007), p. 94.
9. See the "Table of Christians in Fujian" in the back of this book.
10. Fitzgerald and Slater, *JRW: Story of the Fuh-kien Mission*, p. 189.
11. Paul Hattaway, *Operation China: Introducing all the Peoples of China* (Carlisle: Piquant, 2000), p. 480.
12. Church Missionary Society, *For Christ in Fuh-kien*, p. 80.

1870s

1. *Chinese Recorder* (May 1880).

Notes

2 Dunch, *Fuzhou Protestants and the Making of a Modern China*, collated from tables on pp. 18-23.
3 Stock, *The Story of the Fuh-kien Mission*, pp. 56-57.
4 Stock, *The Story of the Fuh-kien Mission*, pp. 56-57.
5 Foster, *Christian Progress in China*, pp. 91-92.
6 Samuel and Maria Dyer served Christ in today's Malaysia and Singapore from 1827. They had five children, including two daughters also named Maria. The second one, Maria Jane, is remembered as the wife of the great missionary statesman Hudson Taylor.
7 "Chinese Fellow-Solder of Jesus Christ: Chitnio's Story," *India's Women* (March 1892), p. 99.
8 F. I. Codrington, *Hot-Hearted: Some Women Builders of the Chinese Church* (London: Church of England Zenana Missionary Society, 1934), pp. 29-30.
9 See the "Table of Christians in Fujian" in the back of this book.
10 Codrington, *Hot-Hearted*, pp. 31-32.
11 Stock, *The Story of the Fuh-kien Mission*, pp. 97-98.
12 Stock, *The Story of the Fuh-kien Mission*, p. 98.
13 Fitzgerald and Slater, *JRW: Story of the Fuh-kien Mission*, p. 60.
14 See the "Table of Christians in Fujian" in the back of this book.
15 *Tianfeng* (April 2009).
16 Stock, *The Story of the Fuh-kien Mission*, p. 100.
17 Stock, *The Story of the Fuh-kien Mission*, p. 101.
18 Stock, *The Story of the Fuh-kien Mission*, p. 101.
19 Church Missionary Society, *For Christ in Fuh-kien*, pp. 87-88.
20 Fitzgerald and Slater, *JRW: Story of the Fuh-kien Mission*, p. 144.
21 Fitzgerald and Slater, *JRW: Story of the Fuh-kien Mission*, p. 145.
22 Statistics from Church Missionary Society, *For Christ in Fuh-kien*, pp. 179-81.
23 A communicant was generally defined as a baptized church member qualified to receive Communion.

1880s

1 Dunch, *Fuzhou Protestants and the Making of a Modern China*, collated from tables on pp. 18-23.
2 Dunch, *Fuzhou Protestants and the Making of a Modern China*, pp. 18-23.
3 *Chinese Recorder* (March 1890).
4 Church Missionary Society, *For Christ in Fuh-kien*, pp. 145-46.
5 Church Missionary Society, *For Christ in Fuh-kien*, pp. 88-89.
6 Church Missionary Society, *For Christ in Fuh-kien*, p. 89.
7 See the "Table of Christians in Fujian" in the back of this book.
8 Cited in Donald MacInnis, *China Chronicles from a Lost Time: The Min River Journals* (Eastridge Books, 2009), p. 44.

9 Statistics from Fitzgerald and Slater, *JRW: Story of the Fuh-kien Mission*, p. 60.

1890s

1 Codrington, *Hot-Hearted*, p. 9.
2 Codrington, *Hot-Hearted*, p. 16.
3 Robert and Linda Banks, *Children of the Massacre: The Extra-Ordinary Story of the Stewart Family in Hong Kong and West China* (Studies in Chinese Christianity) (Eugene: Pickwick Publications, 2021), p. 20.
4 Dunch, *Fuzhou Protestants and the Making of a Modern China*, collated from tables on pp. 18–23.

The Gutian Massacre

1 Irene H. Barnes, *Behind the Great Wall: The Story of the CEZMS Work and Workers in China* (London: Marshall Brothers, 1896), p. 138.
2 A. J. Broomhall, *Hudson Taylor & China's Open Century: Book Seven – It is not Death to Die!* (London: Overseas Missionary Fellowship, 1989), p. 230.
3 Broomhall, *Hudson Taylor & China's Open Century: Book Seven*, p. 230.
4 Barnes, *Behind the Great Wall*, pp. 139–40.
5 See Banks, *Children of the Massacre*, pp. 30–31.
6 Barnes, *Behind the Great Wall*, p. 146.
7 Barnes, *Behind the Great Wall*, p. 141.
8 Marshall Broomhall, *The Chinese Empire: A General & Missionary Survey* (London: Morgan & Scott, 1907), p. 58.
9 A biography of the Saunders sisters was written by D. M. Berry, *The Sister Martyrs of Ku Cheng: Memoir and Letters of Eleanor and Elizabeth Saunders ("Nellie" and "Topsy") of Melbourne* (Melbourne: Melville, Mullen & Slade, 1895). Also see H. F. Turner, *His Witnesses: Ku-cheng, Aug. 1, 1895* (London, n.d.).
10 Broomhall, *Hudson Taylor & China's Open Century: Book Seven*, p. 230.
11 Broomhall, *Hudson Taylor & China's Open Century: Book Seven*, pp. 230–31.
12 Barnes, *Behind the Great Wall*, p. 143.
13 See The Religious Tract Society, *For His Sake: A Record of Life Consecrated to God and Devoted to China, Extracts from the Letters of Elsie Marshall Martyred at Hwa-Sang, August 1, 1895* (London; New York: The Religious Tract Society, 1896).
14 The Religious Tract Society, *For His Sake*, pp. 207–08.
15 Barnes, *Behind the Great Wall*, p. 143.
16 Barnes, *Behind the Great Wall*, pp. 150–51.

Notes

17 Broomhall, *Hudson Taylor & China's Open Century, Book Seven*, p. 230.
18 MacGillivray, *A Century of Protestant Missions in China*, p. 54.
19 Church Missionary Society, *For Christ in Fuh-kien*, p. 47.
20 Letter from R. C. Taylor, cited in Banks, *Children of the Massacre*, pp. 56–57.
21 Barnes, *Behind the Great Wall*, pp. 143–44.
22 Church Missionary Society, *For Christ in Fuh-kien*, p. 107.
23 See Codrington, *Hot-Hearted*. She also co-authored a book on the work of Christian Girls' schools in China (K. J. Macfee and F. I. Codrington, *Eastern Schools and Schoolgirls: An Account of the Educational Work of the Church of England Zenana Missionary Society* [London: Church of England Zenana Missionary Society, 1927]).

1900s — The Putian Revival

1 Campbell Brown, "Province of Fuh-kien," p. 17.
2 Dunch, *Fuzhou Protestants and the Making of a Modern China*, collated from tables on pp. 18–23.
3 Bertram Wolferstan, *The Catholic Church in China from 1860 to 1907* (London: Sands & Co., 1909), p. 450.
4 William Nesbitt Brewster, *A Modern Pentecost in South China* (Shanghai: Methodist Publishing House, 1909), p. 2.
5 Brewster, *A Modern Pentecost in South China*, p. 55.
6 Brewster, *A Modern Pentecost in South China*, pp. 12–13.
7 Brewster, *A Modern Pentecost in South China*, pp. 13–14.
8 Brewster, *A Modern Pentecost in South China*, pp. 32–33.
9 Brewster, *A Modern Pentecost in South China*, p. 22.
10 Brewster, *A Modern Pentecost in South China*, pp. 26–27.
11 Brewster, *A Modern Pentecost in South China*, p. 52.
12 See the "Table of Christians in Fujian" in the back of this book.

Amy Oxley-Wilkinson

1 *Sydney Morning Herald* (December 3, 1870).
2 *Church Missionary Gleaner* (November 1, 1898), p. 84.
3 Banks, *They Shall See His Face*, pp. 22–23.
4 Banks, *They Shall See His Face*, p. 23.
5 Banks, *They Shall See His Face*, pp. 42–43.
6 *Church Missionary Gleaner* (November 1, 1920), p. 245.
7 *Straits Times* (June 6, 1922).
8 Guage, "Remarkable Missionary Exhibition," *United Methodist* (May 1922), p. 248; cited in Banks, *They Shall See His Face*, p. 94.
9 Banks, *They Shall See His Face*, p. 109.
10 Banks, *They Shall See His Face*, pp. xix–xx.

11 For an up-to-date summary of the Fuzhou Blind School, see Lin Muli, "Century-old Fuzhou School for the Blind Founded by Missionaries," *China Christian Daily* (August 23, 2021).

1910s and 1920s

1 Hewitt, *The Problems of Success*, p. 249.
2 Dunch, *Fuzhou Protestants and the Making of a Modern China*, collated from tables on pp. 18–23.
3 "Margaret E. Barber, Letters" at http://mebarber.ccws.org.
4 Milton T. Stauffer (ed.), *The Christian Occupation of China* (Shanghai: China Continuation Committee, 1922), Appendix C, p. lvi.
5 Stauffer (ed.), *The Christian Occupation of China*, p. 74.
6 See Stauffer (ed.), *The Christian Occupation of China*, p. 167 (Guangdong) and p. 141 (Jiangsu). Today, Fujian has slipped back to seventh place on the list of most Evangelicals in China.
7 Dunch, *Fuzhou Protestants and the Making of a Modern China*, collated from tables on pp. 18–23.
8 J. Edwin Orr, *Twice Born, And Then? — The Life Story and Message of Andrew Gih* (London: Marshall, Morgan & Scott, 1939), pp. 44–45.

Margaret Barber

1 "Margaret E. Barber, The Story, Section 7" at http://mebarber.ccws.org.
2 Church Missionary Society, *For Christ in Fuh-kien*, pp. 85–86.
3 Church Missionary Society, *For Christ in Fuh-kien*, p. 86.
4 James Reetzke, *M. E. Barber: A Seed Sown in China* (Chicago: Chicago Bibles and Books, 2005), pp. 27–28.
5 "Margaret E. Barber, The Story, Section 3" at http://mebarber.ccws.org.
6 "Margaret E. Barber, The Story, Section 3" at http://mebarber.ccws.org.
7 "Margaret E. Barber, The Story, Section 1" at http://mebarber.ccws.org.
8 "Margaret E. Barber, The Story, Section 2" at http://mebarber.ccws.org.
9 "Margaret E. Barber, The Story, Section 2" at http://mebarber.ccws.org.
10 "Margaret E. Barber, The Story, Section 9" at http://mebarber.ccws.org.
11 "Margaret E. Barber, The Story, Section 2" at http://mebarber.ccws.org.
12 Orr, *Evangelical Awakenings in Eastern Asia*, p. 41.
13 "Margaret E. Barber, The Story, Section 10" at http://mebarber.ccws.org.
14 *The Present Testimony* (March 1930).

Leland Wang

1 Gustav Carlberg, *China in Revival* (Rock Island: Augustana Book Concern, 1936), p. 50.

Notes

2 *Decision Magazine* (August 1965).
3 *Decision Magazine* (August 1965).

1930s

1 Cited in Walter Lacey, *A Hundred Years of China Methodism* (Nashville: Abingdon-Cokesbury Press, 1948), p. 273.
2 Dunch, *Fuzhou Protestants and the Making of a Modern China*, collated from tables on pp. 18–23.
3 Hewitt, *The Problems of Success*, p. 250.
4 Hewitt, *The Problems of Success*, p. 251.
5 "Reds Executed 2,000 in Changsha Seizure," *New York Times* (August 6, 1930).
6 "Britain Dispatches Troops to Hankow," *New York Times* (August 7, 1930).
7 "Error Led to Chinese Kill," *New York Times* (October 7, 1930). A little-known book was written in honor of the two martyrs. See H. R., *Faithful unto Death: A Memorial of Eleanor J. Harrison and Edith Nettleton of Chungan, Fukien, China* (Birmingham: Church Missionary Society, 1930).
8 Orr, *Evangelical Awakenings in Eastern Asia*, p. 82.

John Sung — "China's John the Baptist"

1 Paul E. Kauffman, *Confucius, Mao and Christ* (Hong Kong: Asian Outreach, 1975), p. 99.
2 Leslie T. Lyall, *A Biography of John Sung: Flame for God in the Far East* (London: China Inland Mission, 1954), pp. 8–9.
3 Lyall, *A Biography of John Sung: Flame for God in the Far East*, pp. 10–11.
4 Stephen L. Sheng, *The Diaries of John Sung: An Autobiography* (Brighton: Luke H. Sheng & Stephen L. Sheng, 1995), p. 4.
5 From the John Sung profile at http://www.bdcconline.net.
6 Bertha Smith, *Go Home and Tell: How Answered Prayer Undergirded an Adventurous Witness in China* (Nashville: Broadman Press, 1965), p. 28.
7 John Woodbridge (ed.), *More than Conquerors: Portraits of Believers from all Walks of Life* (Chicago: Moody Press, 1992), p. 158.
8 Sheng, *The Diaries of John Sung*, p. 7.
9 Woodbridge, *More than Conquerors*, p. 158.
10 Carlberg, *China in Revival*, p. 61.
11 Timothy Tow, *John Sung My Teacher* (Singapore: Christian Life Publishers, 1985), p. 73.
12 Tow, *John Sung My Teacher*, p. 74.
13 Sheng, *The Diaries of John Sung*, p. 17.
14 Smith, *Go Home and Tell*, p. 30.

15 William E. Schubert, *I Remember John Sung* (Singapore: Far Eastern Bible College Press, 1976), p. 15.
16 Carlberg, *China in Revival*, p. 62. Sung later clarified, "The Bible comprises 1189 chapters. By the Lord's instruction I derived 40 methods of study, reading the Bible 40 times. Of course, I did not read the Bible crudely word by word." (Tow, *John Sung My Teacher*, p. 81).
17 Tow, *John Sung My Teacher*, p. 82.
18 Carlberg, *China in Revival*, pp. 62–63.
19 Tow, *John Sung My Teacher*, p. 207.
20 Orr, *Evangelical Awakenings in Eastern Asia*, p. 63.
21 From the John Sung profile at http://www.bdcconline.net.
22 Levi, *The Diary of John Sung: Extracts from His Journals and Notes* (Singapore: Genesis Books, 2012), pp. 166–67.
23 Timothy Tow said the Sungs later had a second son whom they named Moses.

John Sung — "China's Greatest Evangelist"

1 Sheng, *The Diaries of John Sung*, p. 43.
2 Sheng, *The Diaries of John Sung*, p. 88.
3 Sheng, *The Diaries of John Sung*, p. 38.
4 Sheng, *The Diaries of John Sung*, pp. 43–44, 54.
5 Levi, *The Diary of John Sung*, p. 227.
6 Levi, *The Diary of John Sung*, p. 230.
7 Schubert, *I Remember John Sung*, Appendix 3.
8 Tow, *John Sung My Teacher*, p. 153.
9 Lyall, *A Biography of John Sung: Flame for God in the Far East*, pp. 96–97.
10 Levi, *The Diary of John Sung*, p. xxviii.
11 Orr, *Evangelical Awakenings in Eastern Asia*, pp. 62–63.
12 Orr, *Evangelical Awakenings in Eastern Asia*, p. 62.
13 "The Footprints of an Evangelist," an article published on the website of the Chinese Christian Life Fellowship. See www.cclifefl.org/View/Article/2623. The story is also told in Levi, *The Diary of John Sung*, p. 313.
14 "The Footprints of an Evangelist," Chinese Christian Life Fellowship: www.cclifefl.org/View/Article/2623.
15 Sheng, *The Diaries of John Sung*, p. 109.
16 Lyall, *A Biography of John Sung: Flame for God in the Far East*, p. 122.
17 *Straits Times* (December 23, 1936).
18 Lyall, *A Biography of John Sung: Flame for God in the Far East*, p. xv.
19 Although he strongly resisted any attempts to label him as a Pentecostal or Charismatic, Sung later said he had received the gift of tongues, but he never used it publicly or taught it as a requirement for all believers to have.

Notes

He taught that the evidence of being baptized by the Holy Spirit was not speaking in tongues, but the God-given ability to live a holy life.
20 Tow, *John Sung My Teacher*, p. 37.
21 From the John Sung profile at http://www.bdcconline.net.
22 Sheng, *The Diaries of John Sung*, p. 40.
23 Sheng, *The Diaries of John Sung*, p. 112.
24 Sheng, *The Diaries of John Sung*, p. 111.
25 Serene Loland, *God in China* (Hong Kong: New Life Literature, 1985), p. 39.
26 Tow, *John Sung My Teacher*, p. 135.
27 Levi, *The Diary of John Sung*, p. 351.
28 Lyall, *A Biography of John Sung: Flame for God in the Far East*, p. 185.
29 Sheng, *The Diaries of John Sung*, p. 174.
30 Levi, *The Diary of John Sung*, p. 408.
31 Sheng, *The Diaries of John Sung*, p. 225.
32 Schubert, *I Remember John Sung*, p. 14.
33 Lydia Lee, *A Living Sacrifice: The Biography of Allen Yuan* (Tonbridge: Sovereign World Books, 2003), p. 162.
34 See Timothy Tow, *In John Sung's Steps: The Story of Lim Puay Hian* (Singapore: Far Eastern Bible College Press, 1976).
35 Lyall, *A Biography of John Sung: Flame for God in the Far East*, p. xv.
36 Levi, *The Diary of John Sung*, p. xxiii.
37 See Levi, *The Diary of John Sung*.

Watchman Nee — The Early Years

1 James Chen, *Meet Brother Nee* (Hong Kong: Christian Publishers, 1976), pp. 4–5.
2 Angus Kinnear, *Against the Tide: The Story of Watchman Nee* (Wheaton: Tyndale House Publishers, 1987), p. 110.
3 Graduating from school a year earlier than Watchman Nee, Lu went on to become one of Nee's closest co-workers, spending much of his later life ministering in Singapore, Malaysia, and other Southeast Asian nations.
4 Miao spent many years preaching in Manila, to such an extent that some sources say he was from the Philippines, but he was raised in the Fujian town of Lianjiang.
5 Chen, *Meet Brother Nee*, pp. 9–10.
6 Chen, *Meet Brother Nee*, p. 20.
7 Chen, *Meet Brother Nee*, pp. 26–29.
8 Lin, *Shanghai Faithful*, p. 133.
9 Tow, *John Sung My Teacher*, p. 179.
10 Kinnear, *Against the Tide*, pp. 126–27.
11 Cited in Chen, *Meet Brother Nee*, pp. 32–33.

Notes

12 "What about Watchman Nee's teaching on Soul and Spirit?" at www.gordonferguson.org.
13 Norman H. Cliff, *Fierce the Conflict: The Moving Stories of how Eight Chinese Christians Suffered for Jesus Christ and Remained Faithful* (Dundas: Joshua Press, 2001), p. 69.
14 Chen, *Meet Brother Nee*, pp. 43-44.
15 Chen, *Meet Brother Nee*, p. 49.

Watchman Nee — The Latter Years

1 Kauffman, *Confucius, Mao and Christ*, p. 101.
2 Chen, *Meet Brother Nee*, p. 60.
3 Cliff, *Fierce the Conflict*, p. 73.
4 Chen, *Meet Brother Nee*, p. 89.
5 Lily M. Hsu with Dana Roberts, *My Unforgettable Memories: Watchman Nee and Shanghai Local Church* (Longwood: Xulon Press, 2013), p. 67.
6 Chee Nan Pin, *The Search for the Identity of the Chinese Christian Church: Ecclesiological Responses of the Chinese Church in 1949-1958 to the Political Changes* (Hong Kong: WEC International, 2016), p. 132.
7 Chen, *Meet Brother Nee*, p. 80.
8 Witness Lee, *Watchman Nee: A Seer of the Divine Revelation in the Present Age* (Anaheim: Living Stream Ministry, 1991), p. 327.
9 Randy Alcorn, *Safely Home* (Wheaton: Tyndale House Publishers, 2001), p. 292.
10 Chee, *The Search for the Identity of the Chinese Christian Church*, p. 211.
11 Jonathan Chao, *Wise as Serpents, Harmless as Doves* (Pasadena: William Carey Library, 1988), p. 16.
12 Hsu with Roberts, *My Unforgettable Memories*, p. 86.
13 Hsu with Roberts, *My Unforgettable Memories*, p. 101.
14 Orr, *Evangelical Awakenings in Eastern Asia*, p. 127.
15 After meticulously studying every available document on Watchman Nee's life, including the accusations against him, and after consulting various Chinese church leaders who knew him either directly or indirectly, I believe that some (but, unfortunately, not all) of the charges of immorality against him were manufactured by the Communist authorities and are not true. Other charges that Nee admitted to doing have been confirmed by his former church members and victims. They do not appear to be people with an axe to grind, rather, they have reluctantly shared their experiences after many years of pain and confusion as they sought to reconcile what happened with the love and respect they held for their former leader.
16 Hsu with Roberts, *My Unforgettable Memories*, p. 111.
17 See Watchman Nee, *The Normal Christian Life* (Bombay: Christian Literature Service, 1957) and (Carol Stream: Tyndale House, 1977).

Notes

18 Watchman Nee, *Sit, Walk, Stand: The Process of Christian Maturity* (Fort Washington: CLC Publications, 1964).
19 John Foxe (updated by Harold J. Chadwick), *The New Foxe's Book of Martyrs* (North Brunswick: Bridge-Logos Publishers, 1997), p. 330.
20 Cliff, *Fierce the Conflict*, pp. 77–78.
21 Chen, *Meet Brother Nee*, p. 82.
22 Cliff, *Fierce the Conflict*, p. 80.
23 Cliff, *Fierce the Conflict*, p. 80.
24 "New Information Regarding Watchman Nee's Life and Testimony During His Imprisonment," *Assist News Service* (August 12, 2003).
25 Hsu with Roberts, *My Unforgettable Memories*, from the list of endorsements at the front of the book.

1940s to 1960s

1 Hewitt, *The Problems of Success*, p. 240.
2 Ralph Covell, *Pentecost of the Hills in Taiwan* (Pasadena: Hope Publishing House, 1998), pp. 215, 282.
3 Covell, *Pentecost of the Hills in Taiwan*, p. 282.
4 Compiled from diocese statistics at www.catholic-hierarchy.org.
5 See Daniel 3:19–28.
6 Brother David with Dan Wooding and Sara Bruce, *God's Smuggler to China: A Cry to the Chinese to Let us Love them* (London: Hodder & Stoughton, 1981), p. 143.
7 Leslie T. Lyall, *God Reigns in China* (London: Hodder & Stoughton, 1985), p. 148.
8 Brother David with Wooding and Bruce, *God's Smuggler to China*, pp. 133–34.

1970s

1 Lin, *Shanghai Faithful*, p. 213.
2 Lin, *Shanghai Faithful*, p. 214.
3 Lyall, *God Reigns in China*, p. 166.
4 Paul E. Kauffman, *China Today: Through China's Open Door* (Hong Kong: Asian Outreach, 1975), p. 119.
5 Brother David with Paul Hattaway, *Project Pearl: The 1 Million Smuggled Bibles that Changed China* (Oxford: Monarch, 2007), pp. 71–72.
6 Chao, *Wise as Serpents, Harmless as Doves*, pp. 32–33.
7 Brother David with Hattaway, *Project Pearl*, p. 72.
8 Brother David with Wooding and Bruce, *God's Smuggler to China*, p. 146.
9 Brother David with Hattaway, *Project Pearl*, pp. 72–73.
10 Lyall, *God Reigns in China*, p. 167.

Notes

11 Letter to Open Doors, cited in Brother David with Hattaway, *Project Pearl*, p. 74.
12 Letter to Open Doors, cited in Brother David with Hattaway, *Project Pearl*, p. 75.
13 Letter to Open Doors.

1980s

1 Lyall, *God Reigns in China*, p. 167.
2 Susan Pons, "A Most Unusual Story," *Asian Report* (March–April 1988), p. 9.
3 Tony Lambert, *The Resurrection of the Chinese Church* (Wheaton: Harold Shaw, 1994), p. 147.
4 Personal communication with a Taiwanese Christian, July 2017.
5 *Bridge* (January–February 1986).
6 Lambert, *The Resurrection of the Chinese Church*, p. 142.
7 Cited in Li Shixiong & Xiqiu (Bob) Fu (eds.), *Religion and National Security in China: Secret Documents from China's Security Sector* (Unpublished report, 2002), p. 18.
8 Chao, *Wise as Serpents*, pp. 145–46.
9 Personal interview with Peter Xu Yongze (October 2003).
10 Alex Buchan, "God's Nutcases," *Compass Direct* (January 1, 1998).
11 Letter to Open Doors.
12 *Pray for China* (September 1984).
13 *Pray for China* (September 1984).
14 *Pray for China* (September 1986).
15 *Pray for China* (March 1987).
16 *Pray for China* (April–May 1988).

The Local Church Today

1 Lin, *Shanghai Faithful*, p. 149.
2 Witness Lee, *The Four Major Steps of Christ* (Anaheim: Living Stream Ministry, 1969), chapter 1.
3 Witness Lee, *The Seven Spirits for the Local Churches* (Anaheim: Living Stream Ministry, 1989), chapter 5.
4 Chao, *Wise as Serpents*, pp. 153–54.
5 *Christianity Today* (March 11, 2002).
6 Neil T. Duddy and the Spiritual Counterfeits Project, *The God-Men: An Inquiry into Witness Lee and the Local Church* (Downers Grove: InterVarsity Press, 1981).
7 Jack N. Sparks, *The Mindbenders: A Look at Current Cults* (Nashville: Thomas Nelson, 1977).

Notes

8   In 2006, the Court of Appeals for the First District of Texas finally threw out the case against Harvest House and later rejected the Local Church's appeal. Although for years Harvest House Publishers appeared destined to fall into bankruptcy because of the lawsuit, they survived and continue to publish quality Christian books to this day.
9   "The Teachings of Witness Lee and the Local Church," Christian Research Institute (1996).
10 See www.open-letter.org.
11 Hank Hanegraaff, Eliot Miller, and Gretchen Passantino, "From the President: We Were Wrong!" *Christian Research Journal* (vol. 32, no. 6, 2009).
12 See David E. Lister, "Hank Hanegraaff Supports The 'Local Church'" at: https://blog.moriel.org/authors-1/david-lister/18935-hank-hanegraaff-supports-the-local-church.html.
13 Lister, "Hank Hanegraaff Supports The 'Local Church.'"

1990s

1   *Bridge* (January–February 1986).
2   Lambert, *The Resurrection of the Chinese Church*, p. 142.
3   *Amity News Service* (September–October 1997).
4   Compiled from diocese statistics at www.catholic-hierarchy.org.
5   *Bridge* (January–February 1986).
6   *China Study Journal* (December 1992).
7   Danyun, *Lilies Amongst Thorns: Chinese Christians Tell their Story through Blood and Tears* (Tonbridge: Sovereign World, 1991), p. 317.
8   Tetsunao Yamamori and Kim-Kwong Chan, *Witnesses to Power: Stories of God's Quiet Work in a Changing China* (Carlisle: Paternoster Press, 2000), pp. 43–44.
9   Yamamori and Chan, *Witnesses to Power*, p. 46.
10 This story was first told in Paul Hattaway, *Back to Jerusalem: God's Call to the Chinese Church to Complete the Great Commission* (Carlisle: Piquant, 2003), pp. 87–93.
11 The author was blessed to meet Enoch and his two daughters in 2002, more than five years after Sheng Ling was raised from the dead. She was a bright and energetic girl, and no one would ever guess she had died and come back to life except for the scar on her forehead.
12 Far East Broadcasting, January 1993.
13 *Pray for China* (November–December 1993).
14 *Pray for China* (May–June 1994).
15 *Pray for China* (July–August 1994).
16 *Pray for China* (July–August 1995).
17 Far East Broadcasting, February 1995.

18 *Pray for China* (July–August 1995).
19 Far East Broadcasting, July 1995.
20 *Pray for China* (January–February 1996).
21 *Pray for China* (March–April 1998).
22 Trans World Radio, April 1998.
23 Trans World Radio, May 1998.
24 Far East Broadcasting, January 1999.
25 Far East Broadcasting, January 1999.

2000s

1 "Lazarus is Raised," *The Challenge of China* (no. 5, date unknown).
2 "Lazarus is Raised," *The Challenge of China* (no. 5, date unknown).
3 See Zheng Huiduan, *A Masterpiece of God's Amazing Grace: An Autobiography of Grace Huiduan Zheng* (Alhambra: Chinese Christian Testimony Ministry, 2004).
4 David Wang with Georgina Sam, *Christian China and the Light of the World: Miraculous Stories from China's Great Awakening* (Ventura: Regal, 2013), p. 60.
5 Far East Broadcasting, February 2000.
6 Far East Broadcasting, October 2001.
7 *Lift up Our Holy Hands* (October 2001).
8 Trans World Radio, February 2002.
9 Far East Broadcasting, March 2002.
10 Trans World Radio, June 2002.
11 Trans World Radio, January 2003.

2010s and 2020s

1 "Yang Xinfei (1928–2011) — A Life Poured Out," *Global Chinese Ministries* (December 2011–January 2012).
2 Disturbing videos on how death vans operate can be viewed by searching "China's Death Vans" on YouTube.
3 "Authorities Break into Church, Harass Christians," *China Aid* (October 29, 2018).
4 "Fujian Church Experiences Multiple Raids," *China Aid* (November 8, 2018).
5 See www.chinaaid.org/2019/06/officials-attack-bible-study-harass.html for both an article and video of the raid.
6 "Xiamen Huoshi Church Insists on Requesting a Hearing," *China Aid* (July 24, 2019).
7 "Churches Ordered to Host Flag-Raising Ceremony," *China Aid* (September 20, 2019).

8 "Police Launch City-wide Raid on Churches," *Back to Jerusalem* (June 17, 2020).
9 "Two Anonymous Church Schools Raided One Right after Another," *China Aid* (December 21, 2021).
10 "Xiamen Christian School Raided and Fined over $15,000," *China Aid* (January 4, 2022).
11 "Annual Inspection: CCP Demands Total Loyalty from Government Churches," *China Aid* (May 10, 2023).
12 See Lin Muli, "Visit to Fujian Church in Shape of Noah's Ark," *China Christian Daily* (March 26, 2024).
13 "Final Notice: Pastor and His Wife Must Pay $55,000 Fine," *China Aid* (October 6, 2023).
14 "Fine Doubles for Xunsiding Church Couple," *China Aid* (June 30, 2023).

The Future of the Church in Fujian

1 In descending order, the provinces with the most Evangelical Christians (according to research conducted for *The China Chronicles*) are: Henan (17.6 million), Jiangsu (11.7 million), Zhejiang (10.5 million), Anhui (8.6 million), Guangdong (4.8 million), Shandong (4.41 million), and Fujian (4.4 million).

Researching Christians in China

1 Ye's figure was quoted in numerous publications at the time, including the *2007 Annual Report of the Congressional-Executive Commission on China: One Hundred Tenth Congress, First Session, October 10, 2007*. In December 2009 the national newspaper *China Daily* interviewed scholar Liu Peng who had spent years researching religion for the Chinese Academy of Social Sciences. Liu claimed the "house churches have at least 50 million followers nationwide." See Ku Ma, "Rule of Law Best Help to Freedom of Faith," *China Daily* (December 3, 2009).

Selected Bibliography

Attali, Marion Sutton, *Commitment to China: Family Letters from Fukien Christian University, 1923–1941* (Paris: Jets D'Encre Editions, 2009).

Banks, Robert, and Linda, *Children of the Massacre: The Extra-Ordinary Story of the Stewart Family in Hong Kong and West China* (Studies in Chinese Christianity) (Eugene: Pickwick Publications, 2021).

_____, *They Shall See His Face: The Story of Amy Oxley Wilkinson and Her Visionary Blind School in China* (Eugene: Pickwick Publications, 2021).

_____, *View from the Faraway Pagoda: A Pioneer Australian Missionary in China from the Boxer Rebellion to the Communist Insurgency* (Melbourne: Acorn, 2013).

Barnes, Irene H., *Behind the Great Wall: The Story of the CEZMS Work and Workers in China* (London: Marshall Brothers, 1896).

Berry, D. M., *The Sister Martyrs of Ku Cheng: Memoir and Letters of Eleanor and Elizabeth Saunders ("Nellie" and "Topsy") of Melbourne* (Melbourne: Melville, Mullen & Slade, 1895).

Bonar, Andrew A., *Memoir of the Rev. David Sandeman, Missionary to China* (London: J. Nisbet & Co., 1861).

Brewster, William Nesbitt, *A Modern Pentecost in South China* (Shanghai: Methodist Publishing House, 1909).

Brother David with Paul Hattaway, *Project Pearl: The 1 Million Smuggled Bibles that Changed China* (Oxford: Monarch, 2007).

Brown, C. Campbell, *A Chinese St. Francis, or The Life of Brother Mao* (London: Hodder & Stoughton, 1911).

Caldwell, John C., *China Coast Family* (Chicago: Henry Regnery, 1953).

Carlson, Ellsworth C., *The Foochow Missionaries, 1847–1880* (Cambridge: Harvard University Press, 1974).

Chao, Jonathan, *Wise as Serpents, Harmless as Doves* (Pasadena: William Carey Library, 1988).

Chen, James, *Meet Brother Nee* (Hong Kong: Christian Publishers, 1976).

Chinese Regional Bishops' Conference, *The Newly Canonized Martyr-Saints of China* (Taiwan: Chinese Regional Bishops' Conference, September 8th Editorial Board, 2000).

Church Missionary Society, *For Christ in Fuh-kien: The Story of the Fuh-kien*

Selected Bibliography

Mission of the Church Missionary Society (London: Church Missionary Society, 1904).

Church of England Zenana Missionary Society, *Through Deep Waters: The Story of the Years 1924-25 in the Work of the Church of England Zenana Missionary Society Abroad and at Home* (London: Church of England Zenana Missionary Society, 1926).

Clarke, Agnes, *China's Man of the Book: The Story of William Chalmers Burns 1815-1868* (London: Overseas Missionary Fellowship, 1968).

Cliff, Norman H., *Fierce the Conflict: The Moving Stories of How Eight Chinese Christians Suffered for Jesus Christ and Remained Faithful* (Dundas: Joshua Press, 2001).

_____, *The Life and Theology of Watchman Nee, Including a Study of the Little Flock Movement Which He Founded* (Ann Arbor: A. Bell & Howell, 1983).

Codrington, F. I., *Hot-Hearted: Some Women Builders of the Chinese Church* (London: Church of England Zenana Missionary Society, 1934).

Danyun, *Lilies Amongst Thorns: Chinese Christians Tell Their Story Through Blood and Tears* (Tonbridge: Sovereign World, 1991).

Darley, Mary E., *The Light of the Morning* (London: Church of England Zenana Missionary Society, 1903).

Davies, Evan, *Memoir of the Rev. Samuel Dyer, Sixteen Years Missionary to the Chinese* (London: J. Snow, 1846).

Davis, J. A., *Choh Lin: The Chinese Boy Who Became a Preacher* (Philadelphia: Presbyterian Board of Mission, 1884).

_____, *Leng Tso: The Chinese Bible-Woman: A Sequel to "The Chinese Slave Girl"* (Philadelphia: Presbyterian Board of Mission, 1886).

Dawson, Christopher, *Mission to Asia* (Toronto: University of Toronto Press, 1987).

Douglas, John M., *Memorials of Rev. Carstairs Douglas: Missionary of the Presbyterian Church of England at Amoy, China* (London: Waterlow and Sons, 1877).

Duncan, Annie N., *The City of Springs, or Mission Work in Chinchew* (Edinburgh: Oliphant, Anderson & Ferrier, 1902).

Dunch, Ryan, *Fuzhou Protestants and the Making of a Modern China, 1857-1927* (New Haven: Yale University Press, 2001).

Fitzgerald, John, and Frances Slater, *JRW: Story of the Fuh-kien Mission* (self-published, 2007).

Gutzlaff, Charles, *Journal of Three Voyages Along the Coast of China in 1831, 1832 and 1833* (London: Frederick Westley & A. H. Davies, 1834).

Gutzlaff, Karl, *The Journal of Two Voyages Along the Coast of China in 1831*

Selected Bibliography

and 1832 . . . with Notices of Siam, Corea, and the Loo-Choo Islands, and Remarks on the Policy, Religion, Etc. of China (New York: J. P. Haven, 1833).

Hattaway, Paul, *Back to Jerusalem: God's Call to the Chinese Church to Complete the Great Commission* (Carlisle: Piquant, 2003).

_____, *China's Book of Martyrs* (Carlisle: Piquant, 2007).

_____, *Operation China: Introducing all the Peoples of China* (Carlisle: Piquant, 2000).

Hewitt, Gordon, *The Problems of Success: A History of the Church Missionary Society, 1910–1942, Vol. 2* (London: SCM Press, 1971).

Hind, John, *Fukien Memories* (Belfast: James A. Nelson, 1951).

Holzmann, John (ed.), *The Church of the East: An Edited and Condensed Version of Nestorian Missionary Enterprise* (Littleton: Sonlight Curriculum, 2001).

Hook, Marion, *Save Some: CEZMS Work in Fuh-kien* (London: Church of England Zenana Missionary Society, 1900).

H. R., *Faithful Unto Death: A Memorial of Eleanor J. Harrison and Edith Nettleton of Chungan, Fukien, China* (Birmingham: Church Missionary Society, 1930).

Hsu, Lily M. with Dana Roberts, *My Unforgettable Memories: Watchman Nee and Shanghai Local Church* (Longwood: Xulon Press, 2013).

Huang, Y. Y., *Streams of Life: On the Anniversary of the Martyrdom of Rev. and Mrs. Stewart and their Colleagues, Fukien, China* (Singapore: Diocese of Singapore, 1972).

Huc, L'Abbé, *Christianity in China, Tartary, and Thibet* (2 vols) (London: Brown, Green, Longmans & Roberts, 1857).

Hunter, Alan, and Kim-Kwong Chan, *Protestantism in Contemporary China: Cambridge Studies in Ideology and Religion* (Cambridge: Cambridge University Press, 1993).

Ireland, Daryl R., *John Song: Modern Chinese Christianity and the Making of a New Man* (Waco: Baylor University Press, 2020).

Johnston, Meta, and Lena, *Jin Ko-Niu: A Brief Sketch of the Life of Jessie M. Johnston for Eighteen Years WMA Missionary in Amoy, China* (London: T. F. Downey, 1907).

Kauffman, Paul E., *Through China's Open Door* (Hong Kong: Asian Outreach, 1979).

Kinnear, Angus, *Against the Tide: The Story of Watchman Nee* (Wheaton: Tyndale House Publishers, 1987).

Lambert, A. P. B. (trans.), *A Short History of the Little Flock: Written by a Mainland Chinese Christian in January 1982 for the Benefit of New Believers* (Hong Kong: Christian Communications, Ltd., 1984).

Lambert, Tony, *China's Christian Millions* (Oxford: Monarch, 2006).

Selected Bibliography

_____, *The Resurrection of the Chinese Church* (Wheaton: Harold Shaw, 1994).

Levi, *The Diary of John Sung: Extracts from His Journals and Notes* (Singapore: Genesis Books, 2012).

Lin, Jennifer, *Shanghai Faithful: Betrayal and Forgiveness in a Chinese Christian Family* (Lanham: Rowman & Littlefield, 2017).

Loland, Serene, *God in China* (Hong Kong: New Life Literature, 1985).

Lutz, Jessie Gregory, *Opening China: Karl F. A. Gutzlaff and Sino-Western Relations, 1827–1852* (Grand Rapids: Eerdmans, 2008).

Lyall, Leslie T., *A Biography of John Sung: Flame for God in the Far East* (London: China Inland Mission, 1954).

_____, *God Reigns in China* (London: Hodder & Stoughton, 1985).

_____, *Three of China's Mighty Men* (London: Hodder & Stoughton, 1973).

MacGowan, John, *Christ or Confucius, Which? Or, The Story of the Amoy Mission* (London: London Missionary Society, 1889).

MacInnis, Donald, *China Chronicles from a Lost Time: The Min River Journals* (Eastridge Books, 2009).

Matthewman, Phyllis, *William Chalmers Burns* (London: Oliphants, 1953).

Menegon, Eugenio, *Ancestors, Virgins and Friars: Christianity as a Local Religion in Late Imperial China* (Harvard-Yenching Institute Monograph Series) (Cambridge: Harvard University Asia Center, 2010).

_____, *Jesuits, Franciscans and Dominicans in Fujian: The Anti-Christian Incidents of 1637–1638* (Aleni Conference, 1997).

Moffett, Samuel Hugh, *A History of Christianity in Asia, Volume 1: Beginnings to 1500* (Maryknoll: Orbus, 1998).

_____, *A History of Christianity in Asia, Volume II: 1500 to 1900* (Maryknoll: Orbus, 2005).

Moule, A. C., *Christians in China Before the Year 1550* (London: SPCK, 1930).

Moule, A. C., and Paul Pelliot, *Marco Polo: The Description of the World* (2 vols) (London: Routledge, 1938).

Orr, J. Edwin, *Evangelical Awakenings in Eastern Asia* (Minneapolis: Bethany House, 1975).

_____, *Twice Born, And Then? — The Life Story and Message of Andrew Gih* (London: Marshall, Morgan & Scott, 1939).

Oxley Wilkinson, Amy, *Soul-Lighted School* (London: Church Missionary Society, n.d.).

_____, *They Shall See His Face* (Sydney: Bible Society of Australia, 2018).

Pakenham-Walsh, W. S., *Some Typical Christians of South China* (London: Marshall Bros., 1905).

Park, Polly, *To Save their Heathen Souls: Voyage to and Life in Fouchow, China.*

Selected Bibliography

Based on Wentworth Diaries and Letters, 1854–1858 (Eugene: Pickwick Publications, 1984).

Pitcher, P. W., *Fifty Years in Amoy, or A History of the Amoy Mission, China* (New York: Reformed Church in America, 1893).

Project Canterbury, *A History of the Dublin University Fuh-kien Mission, 1887–1911* (Dublin: Hodges, Figgis, 1911).

Reetzke, James, *M. E. Barber: A Seed Sown in China* (Chicago: Chicago Bibles and Books, 2005).

Roberts, Dana, *Understanding Watchman Nee: The Newest Book on Watchman Nee* (Plainfield: Logos Associates, 1980).

Schubert, William E., *I Remember John Sung* (Singapore: Far Eastern Bible College Press, 1976).

Sheng, Stephen L., *The Diaries of John Sung: An Autobiography* (Brighton: Luke H. Sheng & Stephen L. Sheng, 1995).

Sites, Sarah, *Nathan Sites: An Epic of the East* (New York: Fleming H. Revell, 1912).

Slater, Frances, *The Wolfe Sisters* (self-published: Lulu.com, 2007).

Smith, Bertha, *Go Home and Tell: How Answered Prayer Undergirded an Adventurous Witness in China* (Nashville: Broadman Press, 1965).

Song Siong Chat [Song Shangjie], *My Testimony: Being the Autobiography of Dr. John Song (Song Siong Chat), the Chinese Evangelist* (Kuala Lumpur: Caxton Press, 1936).

Stewart, John, *Nestorian Missionary Enterprise: The Story of a Church on Fire* (Edinburgh: T. & T. Clark, 1928).

Stewart, Louisa, *Women's Work in Fuh-kien Province* (London: Church Missionary Society, n.d.).

Stock, Eugene, *For Christ and Fukien: The Story of the Fuh-kien Mission of the Church Missionary Society* (London: Church Missionary Society, 1904).

_____, *The Story of the Fuh-kien Mission of the Church Missionary Society* (London: Seeley, Jackson & Halliday, 1890).

Sze, Newman, *The Martyrdom of Watchman Nee* (Culver City: Testimony, 1997).

Talmage, John Van Nest, *History and Ecclesiastical Relations of the Churches of the Presbyterial Order at Amoy, China* (New York: Wynkoop, Hallenbeck & Thomas, 1863).

The Religious Tract Society, *For His Sake: A Record of Life Consecrated to God and Devoted to China, Extracts from the Letters of Elsie Marshall Martyred at Hwa-Sang, August 1, 1895* (London and New York: The Religious Tract Society, 1896).

Selected Bibliography

Thompson Brown, G., *Earthen Vessels and Transcendent Power: American Presbyterians in China, 1837–1952* (Maryknoll: Orbus, 1997).

Tow, Timothy, *In John Sung's Steps: The Story of Lim Puay Hian* (Singapore: Far Eastern Bible College Press, 1976).

_____, *John Sung My Teacher* (Singapore: Christian Life Publishers, 1985).

Turner, H. F., *His Witnesses: Ku-cheng, Aug 1, 1895* (London: n.d.).

Wang, David, with Georgina Sam, *Christian China and the Light of the World: Miraculous Stories from China's Great Awakening* (Ventura: Regal, 2013).

Wang, Leland, *The Arrows of the Lord* (New York: Fleming H. Revell, 1948).

Watson, Mary, *Robert and Louisa Stewart In Life and Death* (London: Marshall, 1895).

Weigh, K. H., *Watchman Nee's Testimony* (Anaheim: Living Stream Ministry, 1981).

White, Chris, *Protestantism in Xiamen: Then and Now* (Global Diversities) (Cham: Palgrave Macmillan, 2018).

White, William C., *Without the Gate, or Leper Work in Longuong, China* (Toronto: Literature Committee of the Missionary Society of the Church of England in Canada, 1903).

Wiley, I. W., *The Missionary Cemetery and the Fallen Missionaries of Fuh Chau, China: With an Introductory Notice of Fuh Chau and Its Missions* (New York: Carlton & Porter, 1858).

Williamson, G. R., *Memoir of the Rev. David Abeel, DD, Late Missionary to China* (New York: Robert Carter, 1848).

Wu, Silas H., *Dora Yu and Christian Revival in 20th-Century China* (Boston: Pishon River Communications, 2002).

_____, *Shell Breaking and Soaring: The Imprisonment and Transformation of Watchman Nee* (Boston: Pishon River Communications, 2004).

Yamamori, Tetsunao, and Kim-Kwong Chan, *Witnesses to Power: Stories of God's Quiet Work in a Changing China* (Carlisle: Paternoster Press, 2000).

Zheng Huiduan, *A Masterpiece of God's Amazing Grace: An Autobiography of Grace Huiduan Zheng* (Alhambra: Chinese Christian Testimony Ministry, 2004).

About Asia Harvest

Paul Hattaway is the founder and director of Asia Harvest, a non-denominational ministry that serves the church in Asia through various strategic initiatives, including Bible printing and supporting Asian missionaries sharing the gospel among unreached peoples.

The author can be reached by email at **office@asiaharvest.org** or by writing to him via any of the addresses listed below.

For more than 35 years Asia Harvest has served the church in Asia through strategic projects that equip the local churches. At the time of this printing, Asia Harvest has successfully printed and delivered more than 430,000 Bibles to house church Christians in Fujian, in addition to supporting many evangelists and providing aid to hundreds of persecuted church leaders and their families.

Opportunities exist for interested Christians to support native evangelists working among many of Asia's unreached people groups through the Asian Workers' Fund.

If you would like to receive the free Asia Harvest newsletter or to order other volumes in *The China Chronicles* series or Paul's other books, please visit **www.asiaharvest.org** or write to the address below nearest you:

Asia Harvest USA & Canada
PO Box 621150
Charlotte NC 28262
USA

About Asia Harvest

Asia Harvest Australia
Ground Floor, Suite 80
97-99 Bathurst Street
Sydney NSW 2000
AUSTRALIA

Asia Harvest New Zealand
PO Box 1757
Queenstown, 9348
NEW ZEALAND

Asia Harvest U.K.
c/o AsiaLink
31A Main Street
Ballyclare
Co. Antrim BT39 9AA
UNITED KINGDOM

Asia Harvest Europe
c/o Stiftung SALZ
Moehringer Landstr. 98
70563 Stuttgart
GERMANY

www.ingramcontent.com/pod-product-compliance
Lightning Source LLC
Chambersburg PA
CBHW050850160426
43194CB00011B/2102